LUCK OF THE DEVIL

My Life as a Drug Smuggler

JACK H. W. COLLINS

Dedicated to: Jonathon Chance White

ISBN-100692750509

ISBN-13: 978-0692750506

Contents

Chapter 1:

I thought I was Going to Die

It all started when I thought I was going to die. I looked at my son Johnny. He fumbled for the phone, and then the receiver slipped from his sweaty palms. He struggled to swallow as he frantically punched in the short number that we all memorize but hope to never use.

Time crawled as he waited for an answer. After an eternity, he shouted in frustration, "What's taking so long? Why aren't they answering?!"

I sat slumped down in an overstuffed chair, holding my chest, and struggling to breathe. For the first time in my life I felt old and weak.

After what seemed like another eternity someone answered, and Johnny nearly yelled, "My dad is having a heart attack! We need an ambulance!"

Yes, I was having a heart attack – the second one in three months. Sweat was pouring down my face as I clung to my chest. My breath came in short, labored gasps as Johnny answered the many questions the 9-1-1 Operator asked him.

Johnny had been rattled the first time, but now he looked frightened. And I didn't blame him – I was all he had left.

It was so strange to sit in a chair and struggle for breath. I considered myself a tough SOB; I never backed down from anyone or anything. But this was different from three months ago. Back then I refused to sit down. I wasn't going to let anyone tell me what to do. I just walked out to the patio and smoked a cigarette while I waited for the ambulance, and then I flicked the butt on the ground when the ambulance pulled up.

As I thought about that heart attack, I looked at Johnny. I knew he was nervous when he hung up the phone and then yelled "Shit!" He frantically dialed 9-1-1 again. "Yes. I just called. My dad is having a heart attack. I accidently hung up."

He looked at me and said, "Don't worry, Dad. The ambulance will be here in a few minutes."

I tried to relax a little and reassure him by nodding my head, but I still clung to my chest, and my breaths were getting heavier. Johnny continued to answer more questions as the room started to spin. Was I moving? I blinked a few times as my eyes tried to focus.

"I'll be alright son," I said. But Johnny's face made it clear that he wasn't so sure. I don't think it occurred to him that his dad was getting older. Hell, I don't think it even occurred *to me*. I had always been invincible in his eyes – a man always on the go. Even after I got out of prison I traveled to Colombia when I could afford it.

I wasn't sure why, but at that very moment I suddenly remembered the first time my son had any indication that I was involved in something illegal. He was seven years old. My partner Luco (Uncle Luco to Johnny) had come to visit, and he was carrying two very large gym bags. We shook hands and then went upstairs.

Johnny walked in on us as we were counting our take. His eyes nearly popped out of his head when he saw the $2 million piled on the bed. The money was wrapped together in small stacks about an inch thick – just like in the movies. Luco and I stopped talking and watched as Johnny walked over to the edge of the bed and just stared at all the money.

After a few minutes Johnny looked up at me with wonder in his eyes. He still couldn't believe how much money there was. I nodded towards the corner at the back of the room where my 12-gauge shotgun and my AR-15 assault rifle were leaning against the wall.

"You know those guns are loaded, and you are not to touch them unless we take you out shoot'n." It was a statement more than it was a question.

"Yes, sir," Johnny replied as he looked at the guns.

I pointed to the pile of money on the bed. "You know the rules. If you tell anyone you'll get taken to the orphanage."

Johnny nodded as he looked back at the pile of money. After a few seconds he asked, "Do I get any of this money?"

Luco laughed quietly. "Smart kid," he said.

I didn't answer. I wanted to see what he would do, but all he did was look at me and wait.

Finally I reached for a stack of bills. As I handed it to him I said, "Yes, you get $5,000."

I still remember how excited he was. He ran out of the room and down the stairs. When he reached the bottom, he turned and ran into the kitchen shouting at the top of his lungs, "Mom! Mom! I got $5,000!"

Instead of being excited like I expected, his mother instructed him to go back upstairs. As he started back up the stairs she hollered behind him, "Jack, you send that boy back down with $10,000 ... and not a dollar less!"

When he returned to the bedroom, I gave him two stacks of bills and said, "Give this to your mother".

Johnny did as he was told and took the money down to his mother.

From that day forward Johnny never had to ask for money. He just waited, and I gave it to him when I had it.

"What are you smiling about?" Johnny asked as he covered the phone piece so the 9-1-1 operator wouldn't hear him.

This brought me back to the immediate situation. I didn't realize I was smiling. I looked at Johnny and said, "Remember that $5,000 I gave you when you were a boy?"

Johnny thought for a moment and then smiled, "Yes, why?"

His smile faded when we both heard the sirens of the fire department as they arrived outside.

"I can hear the sirens. I think they're here," Johnny said into the phone as he went and opened the door just as the EMT's were about to knock.

He let them in, and they immediately went to work in a flurry of activity.

Johnny hung up the phone as the EMT's lifted me onto the gurney. They placed an oxygen mask on my face and then strapped me down. As they started to wheel me out I reached out and grabbed Johnny's arm and then pulled the oxygen mask down with the other hand.

I still struggled to breathe, but I was able to get out, "I gave that money to you ... and your mother ... to make you both happy. And to keep you both ... quiet."

Johnny smiled, but his smile faded as they wheeled me out the door. Johnny closed then locked the door and followed us out.

As they loaded me into the back of the ambulance, I looked at Johnny and said, "I'll be alright son ... I've always been lucky."

He tried to smile when they closed the back doors. As the ambulance pulled away from the curb, I just hoped that my luck held out a little longer.

Chapter 2:

Fuck Them Yankees

As I rode in the back of that ambulance I realized that for the first time in my life, I was worried. I felt like shit. My chest felt like I had an elephant standing on me, and I could hardly breathe. I didn't let the Emergency Team know how I felt as they watched the monitors and worked to keep me alive. I had spent my life molding a tough, 'I'll-kick-your-ass' attitude in everything I did, and I wasn't about to let that go – especially in this situation. But I knew it was different this time ... luckily, we lived only a short distance from the VA hospital, and that thought cheered me up a little.

It had only been a little while ago that my friend, The Good Cuban also known as The Rock, gave us a house to live in just outside New Orleans, otherwise we would be in Maine where I grew up and a good hour from the nearest hospital.

I looked around. There were two EMTs – one on each side of me. I felt my chest grow heavier and found it even more difficult to breathe.

One of the technicians broke into my thoughts, "You're going to be ok, sir."

"Shit, Son ..." I coughed out between breaths as I tried to keep my head up. "I'm from a military family ... and I'm from Maine ... We don't back down ... to anything ... or anyone." I was fighting for each breath, but I wasn't going to just lie down and die.

"Lie back, sir. We'll be to the hospital soon."

Reluctantly, I laid my head back and closed my eyes. Maybe because I was going to die, I'm not sure, but I suddenly thought about my family. I hadn't gotten my tough attitude from them, but they sure as shit were great examples for me growing up.

My father and his brothers were all World War II veterans. My father actually didn't think there'd be any more wars after World War II, so he stayed in the reserves and was called back for Korea. One of my uncles was mean and bad-as-a-mother-fucker to everyone except children.

As bad as he was, he was also the coach of the little league team I played on when I was a boy. One season my Uncle promised the team that if we could get out there, get ahead, and start winning games, the coaches would give us a big treat and take the team down to Fenway Park to see the Red Sox play. Oh, how I loved the Boston Red Sox! As I thought back to when I played on that team, the pain in my chest seemed to lessen just a little.

It was 1954.

Playing little league in those days was real baseball. Not everyone got a trophy like today. Quite frankly, I think that idea is turning the kids of today into pussies. How can you learn anything if you never know what it's like to lose? Shit, the world today is training kids so that even when they do suck, they still get rewarded. And businesses wonder why their having such problems with their employees under 25 today? It's because society is rewarding mediocrity.

No ... Back then it was in and out, up and down, high and tight, stealing bases, and sacrifice bunts. If the other team hit one of ours, my Uncle would have the pitcher throw right at the kid's head the next time he was at bat. He was a baseball aficionado who taught the game to us boys and taught us to love and respect the baseball, but still, mostly we thought about Fenway Park. Fuck the trophies. The chance to go see the Sox play; THAT was motivation! We worked hard, and we won ... so we got to go to Fenway Park.

There was only one player all the boys on the team wanted to see – Ted Williams. We worshipped that man. We wore our little league uniforms to the game because we were called the Red Sox. There was no I-95 back then, so we had to caravan down Route 1 ... all the way past Brunswick, through Bath, down to Boston, and then to the beloved Fenway.

I don't remember who was playing. I'd need Bob Costas sitting with me for that one. But I remember watching the field for the team to run out, and sure as shit, number nine – Ted Williams – ran onto the field. It was thrilling! I don't remember much of the game after that point. I don't remember shit about the game itself, but I will always remember what happened on the way home.

We had taken off and were going back up Route 1. It was in the afternoon around 5:00 or 6:00 pm. We had stopped at a gas station up in Lynn – one of those little towns north of Boston. Everyone got out of the car. I was riding with my three cousins; all of whom I was very close to. As we were walking from the ice cream machine to the car my youngest cousin threw his wrapper on the ground. All of a sudden this big guy came out of the store ... he was an Italian guy.

He looked at my Uncle and said, "You ought to take these god-damn kids off into the woods and shoot 'em. Little fuckin'-"

Before he got anything else out of his mouth, my Uncle (the coach) rocked him. With a quick left and a right he knocked him flat. Then he jumped on the guy and started pounding the piss out of him at the gas pump. He was giving him a fucking "Maine-boy-beating" – as we liked to say back home.

In those days my cousins and I could openly swear around my father and uncles just as long as we didn't swear in front of the women. So my cousins and I gathered around and started yelling, "Kill him, Uncle! Kill that cocksucker! Beat that motherfucker! Kill that piece of shit! That cocksucker, kill him! Kill him! Beat that motherfucker!"

I remember looking at my father who just stood there calmly and said, "Hey, Brother, stop beating on this fucking man. Police are gonna come ... gonna fuck things up. We'll be in jail. Stop beating him."

But my Uncle ... he didn't let up.

He started choking the guy. My father spoke up, but still remained calm. He was kind of the sensible one of his brothers, and he said, "Hey! I said stop beating on that man. Now give him a couple more shots, and it's over."

So my Uncle rocked the guy a couple more times in the mouth.

And then we took off.

My cousins and I were thrilled. We got to see Ted Williams play ball, AND we saw my Uncle beat the piss out that big guy ... all in the same day.

Even though I was only seven at the time, that was not the first time I'd seen my Uncle fight someone. He was always beating up either umpires or other coaches – anyone that gave him any fucking shit.

The ambulance slowed and made a quick, but smooth turn, and I opened my eyes to look out the back window. I recognized the parking lot from my trip here three months ago; we were approaching the VA hospital.

It's funny that at that moment I had remembered that story about growing up in those back woods of Maine. But boy, how I loved them Boston Red Sox! Still do today. I've stuck by 'em from '54 to 2004

– which was especially unbelievable ... beating those fucking Yankees. I have hated the Yankees since I was a little boy. My father, uncles, grandfathers, and even my grandmothers, hated the Yankees. Everyone I knew growing up hated the fucking Yankees.

But I digress.

At this point, they pulled me out of the ambulance and wheeled me into the emergency room. As I was wheeled past the Nurse's Station I saw a TV on the wall behind her, and I couldn't help but look at the screen.

ESPN was on, and scrolling across the bottom of the screen were the MLB scores for the day. I was only partially paying attention because it was only pre-season, but as they rolled me across the room and through the doors into the hallway beyond, one score caught my attention: Boston Red Sox 8, New York Yankees 2. Even though I felt worse than I had ever felt in my life, I was able to produce a small smile.

Good, I thought to myself ... fuck those Yankees!

Chapter 3: The Military

My smile quickly vanished as the intense pain pounded in my chest. I was taken into a small room about halfway down the hallway. As I was wheeled in, two older nurses – a female in her mid-forties and an older man probably in his mid-sixties – placed sensors on my chest. A man about 45 years old stepped to the side of the bed and spoke to me.

"I'm Doctor Johansson. I'm going to have a couple of tests run and will return in a couple of minutes, ok?"

I just nodded. I was in too much pain to do much else.

Doctor Johansson gave some orders to the female nurse and left. She went to work and replaced my oxygen facemask with an oxygen tube right under my nose. Then she hooked me up to a new IV filled with blood and checked the IV lines. After she drew a couple of vials of blood, she left too.

The male nurse checked the data on the monitors to make sure that everything was recording correctly and then typed in some notes.

"You're a lot older ... than the other ... nurses" I struggled to say.

The nurse turned around and smiled faintly. "Yeah, I could have retired a couple of years ago, but I love what I do here. It's about the only place that I feel I can really give back to the guys and gals in the armed services."

I don't know if it was the drugs or what, but I finally started to breathe easier. I still felt like shit though.

"You ex-military?" I asked.

"Yep, I joined up during Vietnam."

"Vietnam?"

"Yeah, I was a medic for my unit, but got tired of tramping through the rice fields, so I requested a transfer to a M.A.S.H. unit. They trained me to be a nurse. It made it easy to get a job when I got out. But I found that the men and woman still serving deserved better. I've been with the V.A. for a long time."

I nodded as the nurse turned back to the computer.

"What about yourself?" the nurse asked as he began typing notes. "When and where did you serve?"

"I was on the USS Intrepid," I responded. "CVS 11."

"Navy boy, huh?" "Yes," I replied. "My father was in World War II and Korea. Both of his brothers were in World War II. My whole family is military – all Navy. So of course I ended up in the friggin' Navy."

I watched as the nurse continued to type his notes for a few seconds.

"Unless you were in the military, you really don't have a clue what a person goes through."

The nurse finished his notes and turned around, "I have to agree with you on that one. People who have never been in the armed services just can't understand how much someone sacrifices to protect their country."

I thought for a moment, "It's kinda funny", I said. "Once you're out and you look back ... you know, what sticks with me most is the camaraderie. Did I bitch when I was in there? Yes, I did – I bitched and whined. But as I look back, I should've stayed. Part of me misses that friendship with the guys."

The nurse smiled, "I think that is why I joined the V.A. I just wanted that camaraderie again."

I could feel the pain in my chest increase a little, but the conversation was helping me ignore it so I continued. "It's too bad, but we're having so many boys coming home – men and women – that are in terrible shape. I'm sure you'd agree that it's a little different now than when we came home."

The nurse nodded, "Indeed it is. Did anyone say anything bad to you when you got home?"

"Did anyone say anything bad to me?" ... I thought for a moment. "No ... No, I never heard any of that. I did see them throwing rocks and bottles and burning their draft cards. But you know? I was fine with all that. The guys that went to Canada ... I was fine with that; the deferments for marriage, college ... that was good. That was good. I didn't have any problem with it because although I only went to Vietnam one time, I volunteered to go three times."

"Three times?!" The nurse sounded surprised.

I nodded and continued, "Today some would say, 'Well ... what a fucking idiot!' But really ... I *really* wanted to go to Vietnam just as much as I wanted to get out of those back woods of Maine up in the mountains on the Canadian border. I just didn't know how to get out of paradise. It was the most beautiful spot in the world. I grew up just like Tom and Huck, but I had to get out. I had to get away. And the military ... it was the way to go. Luckily, the Vietnam War was going on, and I could not fucking wait to get into it."

"Well, at least in the Navy you weren't in any real combat", the nurse said.

That comment really pissed me off ... I tried to sit up, but it was too painful, and I collapsed back into the pillow.

"Did I get into combat?" I asked myself more than the nurse. "Oh, Jesus ... like with the Marines and getting to kill the enemy? Well ... no. But do I know people that were up there? Yes – I was on the USS Intrepid, and I lost my brother. I lost my good, good brother Billy Justin. I lost him up on the flight deck of the USS Forestall in '67, so I don't think it makes much difference if you get killed up on the flight deck or you get killed up on Hill 881."

"I guess you're right," the nurse said. "I apologize. I spent so much time in that M.A.S.H. unit patching up guys that were all blown apart that I still forget that if you're in the military; you're in the war ... wherever that war is." I nodded. "You know, a lot of trouble with the boys coming home today. Civilians just don't get it. They sit on the outside, no clue. 'These guys, oh, Jesus, what's the matter with them. They're killing themselves.' Well, a lot of the boys get fucked up because they didn't get a chance to do enough killing. You know, and that fucks a lot of Marines and Army boys up. It fucks 'em up. I know a few personally, and it really destroys them because they wanna be in the action, they wanna get into the shit."

The nurse nodded in agreement and then asked, "What did you do on the Intrepid?"

"Me? I had a great job in Vietnam. In fact, it was probably the best time of my goddamn life. I ran a little slush fund – loan sharking if you will – and maybe sold a little bit of hash. I had a little thing going there, but cards were mainly the game. As I look back, I loved it ... I loved it. Of course in 1968, I was a fucking old man. I was 21 years old.

And the best part about the whole goddamn thing of the Vietnam experience – the best time of my life

– is when I came home, the fucking government kinda turned their back on us. You know ... they didn't back us up. And some of the people actually said terrible things like the boys did this and that, and they killed women and children ... Ah, fuck. And the government kinda said, 'Who are these fucking guys with long hair, and who the fuck are these guys? We don't care if they're Vietnam Veterans or not. They're like a disgrace.' And the government turned their backs on the Vietnam veteran. Barack just said it this Memorial Day, 'It was a fucking disgrace then, and it's a disgrace now'."

"I know how you feel," the nurse commented. "A lot of guys who served during that time say the same thing. It is a disgrace how we were all treated."

"You know as well as I do," I continued, "that there are some out there today saying, 'Well who the fuck is this shit-bag? Is he a republican or a democrat?' You know what I say to them?"

I didn't give the nurse a chance for a response.

"'Fuck you. I'm an American ... period. President Obama is the first president that ever said anything like this about Vietnam. On Memorial Day he said it was a disgrace in '62. It's a disgrace in 2012 the way we were treated."

My vision was suddenly seared with blinding light, and I stopped breathing as a sharp pain hit my chest. It felt like someone had just run a hot poker right through me. My vision blurred, and sounds became muffled. It was only a second or two, but it seemed like ten minutes before the pain subsided and my vision cleared. When I opened my eyes, the nurse was standing at the computer station looking at some monitors.

"Take it easy, Jack," he said, "I know how you feel. It's easy to get angry, but we need you to keep calm until the Doctor gets back."

He was right ... me getting angry was making the pain worse. I needed to change gears and think about something else.

"I think things are getting better," I said. "VAs are a lot of better, and everything's coming around the clock. I remember a story back in 1970 when I had taken way too much acid, and Jesus! The mirror blew off the wall and knocked me in the head.

I had long hair, and I went up to the VA with an Army guy. I mean this guy had seen some terrible shit.
He was an Army medic like you, and he had seen bad, bad shit. A Marine that was in Khe Sanh was with us, and we all had long hair. We went up to the VA in Miami. I had cut my head, and I could barely see because of the amount of blood running down my face. As we pulled up, the nurses came out. They gave us one look and then one of them said, 'What are you guys doing here?' I said, 'Well ... we're all Vietnam veterans, and I got hurt. Mirror flew off of the wall and hit me in the head'. And the nurse said, 'We don't want your kind here. We don't like the way you guys look.'"

"We went, 'What are you talking about? We're fucking Vietnam veterans. Put some stitches in my head, and we'll go home'. He said, 'Get the fuck outta here, or we'll call the police.' So my Marine friend goes, 'Fuck you!'

Now he had a little bit of damage from 'Nam, and he did get a chance to do some killing. I mean he loved to fucking kill. He said, 'Fuck you, cocksuckers.' They called the police. Can you believe it? They actually called the Miami Police, and they came.

Well ... the Miami police showed up, and this is the first time I really got a good feeling about our police in the United States. Even though we were kinda on the other side of the line, you know? We were just selling Mickey Mouse acid and a little bit of weed.

So the police pull up and get out of their cars, and they apologized. They said, 'Boys, we're sorry. These fucking clowns wanna arrest you, and we can't help you. We're gonna have to take you down to Jackson Memorial. You know ... basically down in the fucking ghetto, but they've got a really great trauma unit because they're used to stabbing and shooting. We'll take you down there.'

We all looked at each other, and the lead officer said, 'Boys, just bear with us. Don't cause any trouble ... don't flip out. Hey, we're all Vietnam veterans as well!'

These were the police, and in those days, we called them 'pigs' and 'you mother fuckers' because there was all kinds of trouble when the police showed up." But this time the police were kind and said, 'Hey, hey! We're here to help you!'"

"I felt the same way about the police when I got home," the nurse said. "I did some acid and weed myself, and it wasn't until they helped me out of a sticky situation that my opinion changed. A lot of the police were veterans as well. You said Miami ... Is that where you went when you got out?"

"Yeah, I got out in October 1969, and went right to Miami. The best move I ever made. We ran into all the hippie shit. You know ... dropping acid which was incredible. I was seeing some of the top bands in the world, and I actually saw Jimi Hendrix."

"Jimi?"

"Yes! I mean ... c'mon! We saw Frosty, the Allman Brothers ... I mean, I could go on and on and on. But Jimi? Jimi was incredible! I just never thought those days would end. I love those guys and the ones that are fighting now. I mean ... a couple years ago I was driving up through Massachusetts, and I stopped at a little picnic area. As I got out of my truck I saw National Guard boys there that were part of a little convoy. They saw my Vietnam tags on my pickup, and they said, "Hey! How are you, sir?" And when I walked into the middle of those guys – maybe 30-40 of them – I never felt so comfortable in my whole life. They were all a little bit older than the Vietnam guys 'cause the ones I was around were a lot of 18-, 19-, and 20-year olds. But these guys were like 22 to 27 years old; I never felt so good. The last time I felt like that was when I was on the Intrepid.

As far as I'm concerned everyone of the people that have served, are serving, or will serve in the military, men and women, are to be honored. I can't wait to give back to those people.

I can't wait to see more of them because every time I'm around military guys, I feel good and warm inside. Because, you know ... they'll give their fucking blood. They'll give their blood, their lives for America, and that's a big fucking deal."

As I was finishing the story my son Johnny walked through the door.

"Hi, Dad," he said as he walked to the side of the bed. "How are you feeling?"

"Like shit," I replied. "But ... hey! What is your name?" I asked the nurse I had been talking to.

"Bob."

"Bob, here, has been keeping me alive while we wait for the Doctor to get his report back."

"Sounded like you were telling some of your stories," Johnny commented.

"I guess I was. Keeps my mind off the pain and how bad I feel."

"Dad, I've been thinking we should get some of these stories recorded."

I tried to smile and nodded. It was a good idea, but I wasn't sure how to go about it.

Johnny had another good idea, "Why don't I bring in my video camera tomorrow? You can just start talking, and I'll record it?"

Just then Doctor Johansson burst into the room with three more nurses. Johnny was pushed aside by one of the nurses who pulled the monitors off of my chest.

"What's going on?" Johnny asked.

"We've got to do an emergency operation and insert a stent if we want your father to live," Doctor Johansson replied. He stepped to the computer and looked at some information.

"What?" Johnny was stunned.

"Bob," the doctor ordered, "You go with them to the O.R. Make sure that they get him prepped as soon as possible."

"Yes, Doctor." Bob turned to another nurse and said, "Smith."

"Yes, Bob?"

"Take Jack's son to the waiting room."

"Ok." And he turned to Johnny and gestured towards the door, "This way please."

Johnny looked at me lying on the gurney, and I could tell he was concerned. "Make sure you bring the camera back tomorrow, and we'll talk about my stories then."

Johnny nodded as they wheeled me out of the room and down the hallway. I lost sight of him when they turned me down another hallway, but I'll never forget the look of complete helplessness on his face. It really got me worried. And as I thought about my situation, I realized that I was really scared I was going to die.

Chapter 4:

My Best Friend, That Piece of Shit

As they moved me to the operating room I felt like I was being wheeled to the death chamber. Two heart attacks in 90 days? That's not good.

Blood Transfusion – The young nurse tried to inject freshly frozen plasma too quickly using two bags. Jack's reaction made his whole body feel like it was on fire.

"Fuck, I'm going to die", I thought to myself. I felt that my luck had finally run out, and I was going to die. As I thought about this, I started to get sick to my stomach. The nurse from the O.R. came up and slowed it down. It was too fast so he fixed it and asked, "How you doing?" "Ok – except for this", pointing to bags. "Oh, we'll get it fixed." After he fixed it, I felt better. "Let it drip that way; it will still get you ready."

I decided I wanted to sit up. As I tried to sit up, my phone rang. I had forgotten that it was in my pocket, so I pulled it out of my pocket and answered.

"Hello?"

"Hey, Jack," came a deep, Sicilian voice from the other end. "How are you?"

"Luco?"

"Yeah, Jack. It's Luco. So how are you?"

I couldn't believe it. Luco was one of my oldest friends. He had been in the smuggling business with me since the beginning, but he had finally gotten caught by the Feds and had been in a federal prison for the last three years.

We talked over the phone a couple of dozen times while he was there.

“I’m good.” I replied. “But ...-“

“Glad to hear it.”

One of the nurses swabbed my free arm with alcohol preparing it for an IV line.

“Luco, hold on. They’re giving me a blood transfusion.”

“Blood transfusion?”

“Yes, and they’re wheeling me to the operating room for a stent.”

“Jack, don’t you fucking die on me! Let me tell you something, Jack – you piece of shit. If you die on me I’ll dig up your fucking bones and shit on them!”

I couldn’t help but chuckle, “Wow, no one has ever said anything that sweet and kind to me before.”

Luco was quiet for a few seconds, “Well ... I love you. Oh, shit! My phone card minutes are running out. I’ve got to go, but don’t you die on me!” The phone went dead.

I laughed as I put the phone on my chest. “Well that piece of shit ...” I chuckled again to myself. For the first time since my heart attack started I knew that everything was going to be alright.

Chapter 5:

Time to Tell My Story

That night seems like a distant dream and a nightmare all wrapped into one. I can only imagine what it was like for my son. He told me later that he had sat in the waiting room with nothing to do, and that time had crept at a snail's pace. Eventually the Doctor told him that the surgery was a success and that he should go home to get some sleep, so that's what he did.

The next morning I woke up in a typical hospital room with a large window in the far wall, a TV hanging from the ceiling across from the bed, a few small chairs scattered around the room, and too cramped to be comfortable.

I was conscious, but I didn't feel very good. And they also didn't give me a chance to rest. Anyone who says that you should get some rest in a hospital is full of shit. Nurses and Doctors came in and out like I was at some whorehouse. I don't know why they put a door on my room.

I started to get frustrated with it all when a fairly attractive nurse in her mid-fifties came in to check my vitals. She was about 5'8" and rather slender. She had brown hair that was done up in a bun and brown eyes. In the cramped room it wasn't hard to notice how curvy she was. That helped me to focus on something other than how I felt. She was taking my blood pressure when I heard a knock on the door.

Johnny took two steps into the room and then stopped. The look on his face said it all. I had always been a giant of a man in Johnny's eyes, and yet here I was in a hospital bed, IVs in my arms, and monitors attached to my chest. I'm pretty sure he thought I was going to die.

When I asked him later what his first impression was when he came into the room, he told me he was surprised because for the first time in his life I looked old. My skin was much more pale than usual, and my eyes had bags under them. My hair seemed a lot whiter and thinner than usual. I looked frail.

"Don't just stand there," I said, "come in and sit down."

Johnny did the best he could to hide his fear. He walked over to the nearest chair and sat down.

"This is my nurse Charlene," I said pointing to the female nurse and winking.

"Hi, Johnny," she said as she undid the cuff around my arm. "Your dad was just telling me about you. Very nice to meet you."

Johnny looked at Charlene. "Nice to meet you as well", he said.

Charlene walked around the bed and checked the IVs to make sure they were dripping correctly. "Ok, John, I'll be back in about an hour."

"Thanks, Charlene. I look forward to it." Charlene laughed as she walked out of the room.

"How are you feeling, Dad?"

"Like shit. They've been in and out of here so much I haven't had a chance to even try to rest."

Johnny didn't know what to say, so he didn't say anything.

"At least they let me eat something a little earlier," I continued. "But, hospital food isn't that great. They told me to watch some TV to get my mind off of everything, but all that's on is crappy soap operas. You'd think they'd upgrade to cable or satellite."

Johnny chuckled. "I'm glad you're feeling better," he said. He knew that if I was well enough to complain about things then I would be ok.

"If you want something to take your mind off of things, I brought the camera from home." He reached into his bag and pulled out his small digital video camera.

I sat quietly for a few minutes with my eyes closed thinking about where to start, but nothing came to my mind.

Johnny thought that I had fallen to sleep, and he started to put the camera back into his bag.

"Don't put the camera away," I said as I tried to sit up a little.

"Oh, sorry. I thought that you had fallen asleep."

"No, I think this is a good idea. I need the distraction, and it would be good to reminisce a little. I was just trying to figure out where to start. There is so much to tell. You know a little bit about my life, my involvement with drugs, and what not, but you don't know hardly anything. I used to worry about what you might think of me if you knew the truth. But I'm at that age where I don't give a fuck anymore. It's who I am, and you deserve to know who your father really is ... or was."

Johnny reached into his bag and pulled out the tri-pod, attached the camera to it, and set it up straight ahead of the bed so that I could talk directly into the camera. He pushed the button and said, "OK, go ahead".

I hate to admit it, but my mind just went blank. I was uncomfortable and a bit embarrassed to talk to a camera. I wasn't like these young kids today who record their whole lives, and then post them on the web for everyone to see.

Johnny could sense my uneasiness, "Maybe you should start by talking about one of your friends? You told me that Uncle Bobby was one of your oldest friends. Why don't you just start by telling me about him? How did you meet him?"

"Bobby?" I said as I looked at the ceiling and thought back. "I met him when I was 18 years old in the Navy. We instantly got along from day one because we were both put into sort of a shit situation."

"Sorry to interrupt, Dad," Johnny said, "but can you look at the camera when you are talking?"

"Oh, sure," I said and then continued. "As I said, we got along from day one. We had been assigned mess duty. Mess duty was kind of a pain in the ass because both of us were plane captains. We had to taxi in airplanes, take them out, and learn how to pre-flight them. We were glorified gas-station attendants, if you will. It was kind of fun, but you worked your balls off. But everybody had to do mess duty. Even though the Packer was from another squadron he had mess duty at the same time as me.

We both got 90 days. I was mad as hell when I showed up because 90 days is a pain in the ass. You work 12 days on from 6:00 in the morning to 6:00 at night and two days off. You even had to change barracks. You had to move into the mess barracks.

Well, I went to my new barracks, and I put my gear down then headed into the shower. As I enter the shower area there's this guy standing there shaving. Now this guy looks like a movie star – blond curly hair, blue eyes, and really fit. So I put my shaving kit next to him, and I went, "What a pain in the fucking ass!" He continued to shave and said, "Oh, man, you know? I'm going to shave, and I'm going to go down and get a drink."

I said, "I was thinking of doing the same thing."

"Well, let's go down and get a beer together."

"That sounds good."

So I shit, showered, and shaved, and we went down to the club.

In 1966 we wore tight, tight dress pants, slit pockets, no belt loops, black socks, Puerto Rican shoes, and dress shirts. We smothered ourselves in English Leather and Old Spice, and we thought we were just something.

He told me his name was Bobby, and we just hit it off. After that we started doing stuff together. We would drink and chase girls at the clubs, and even do some recreational drugs from time to time. But the best part was that we had a car. When I say "we," I mean HE had a car – a Volkswagen.

On base were 5,000 guys and only 48 girls – WAVES as we called them. And boy, did I really luck out with my first job! I was the guy in charge of checking in the WAVES, and the NAVCADs – which were guys – training to be officers. In those days you couldn't have any women eating with enlisted men. You couldn't have NAVCADs eating with enlisted men either and certainly no officers. We enlisted men were shit, so we had to eat in a separate part of the chow hall. Anyway, my job was to check in the wanna-be officers and the WAVES.

Well, one day these two girls come through the line. Jesus, were they good looking! Oh, man ... one of them was from South Dakota, and she looked at me and goes, "Hey! Where are you from, sailor?"

"I'm from Maine."

She points to the girl next to her and says, "Well, I'm Betty, and this is my girlfriend, Susie".

"Wow! How are you, honey?"

They both smiled that wicked smile and knew I would do anything for them. Then Betty went in for the kill, "Nice to meet you. You wouldn't have a car, would you?"

"I do."

Susie got excited and said, "You've got a car!"

"Yeah."

Then she said, "How'd you like to go out sometime? Do you have a friend?"

"Well, my friend owns the car. Can I go get him?"

Man, those girls got so excited, and they both said at the same time, "Yeah, go get your friend."

So I went behind the line and found Bobby. He had a kind of a shit job ... he had to serve the food to the men and help clean up afterwards. All I had to do was check in the girls and the wanna-bes. So I get Bobby and introduce him to the two girls. Later that night we met the girls at the club. It was a great night to remember.

Meeting these two girls at the club became a regular routine. We'd go to the club, and we would drink. These girls would dance with the other sailors and grind and kiss, and we'd shoot pool. Of course, Bobby and me, we were the ones who took 'em home and fucked 'em, so we didn't care what they did on the dance floor.

There ended up being a crew of us. There were 11 of us, and we were all Yankee boys. The South was a little different in those days back in '66. It was segregated, and none of us really knew anything about that.

In fact, me ... I'd never even seen a black person. I'd never seen a black person in my life up in the middle of Maine, so we were a little different. The Southern boys didn't really like us, and we really didn't like them. Now ... I'm generalizing because that' wasn't the case with all of them. But with the majority of them, they didn't talk to us. We dressed different; We talked different. I think they thought we were a little snobby, and looking back ... we were.

But anyway ... Bobby and I had the girls. And oh – my – god! What a time! It was a wonderful couple of years. That was how my friendship with Bobby started, and our friendship goes along until today."

I finished talking and looked at Johnny who sat in the small chair enthralled.

Johnny stood up and turned off the camera, "I think that's a good start. Why don't we take a break? You look like you could use some rest."

I didn't want to stop because talking about the good 'ole days was making me feel better, but I realized he was right. I nodded, laid my head back on the pillow, and closed my eyes.

"This could be something special," I thought to myself as I drifted off to sleep.

Chapter 6:

The Drive Home and the Hitchhiker

I woke up to a sound next to my bed. I opened my eyes to see Charlene putting up the last of the new IV bags.

“Oh, I’m sorry I woke you”, she said.

“That’s ok. I don’t mind if you wake me up.”

Charlene chuckled as she turned to the monitors and wrote some notes on a clipboard.

I looked around the room to see it was nighttime. I had slept through most of the day.

“Where’s Johnny?”

“He went to get some dinner. He said he’d be back in an hour or so.”

I nodded. Even though I had slept all afternoon, I was still groggy because of all the drugs they had me on.

Charlene finished her notes and then we chatted for a few minutes before she left. She had overheard part of my story yesterday and was curious.

I lay back in bed and began to think about how it all began. I thought back to my childhood in Maine. I thought about my home and my family. I thought about my time in the Navy followed by my move to Miami when I got out. I thought about the 30+ years I had been a smuggler.

I was 65 years old ... 65 years. Doesn’t it go by in a blink?

When Johnny returned he wanted me to tell more stories for him to record, but I wanted a few days to think about it. Having a camera staring me in the face made it hard to focus. It was good to talk about Bobby, but I would be more comfortable at home. I didn't want to tell my stories while I was lying in a damn hospital. I could just imagine all those guys that thought I was a tough son-of-a-bitch seeing these videos on the web. No, it was better to start when we got home.

I could see the disappointment on his face as he put the camera and tripod away, but he didn't have to wait long.

Medical technology today is amazing. Here I had suffered my second heart attack in less than three months, had a fairly major surgery, and I was still released within one week.

Fittingly, rain poured from the sky as they wheeled me out to the car. I could hardly see across the street, it fell so heavily. It was going to be a slow drive home.

As we drove down the highway towards home and turned onto the freeway, we passed a hitchhiker who was standing on the side of the road with his thumb up in the air.

"That sucks for him," Johnny said as he started to pull over.

"What the fuck, Johnny? What are you doing?" I said.

"Dad, it's pouring out. Give the guy a break."

I could see in the side mirror that the guy was gathering up his gear.

"Get back on the goddamn road – now!"

Johnny looked at me and knew not to argue.

"Shit," he said as he put the car in gear and drove away.

Johnny looked in the rearview mirror at the guy standing in the rain, “Don’t you even feel a little bit bad that you got that guys hopes up like that?”

“No, one bad experience is all that it takes. I once picked up this guy ... I thought I was picking up just another freak.

“I was living in Miami at the time. It was in the early 70’s, and I had started flipping pills. I had a connection out of Galloway Road which was on 87th Avenue Southwest. I went over to his house and sold him – oh, I don’t know – 3,000 or 4,000 hits of those pills for $1.00 apiece. He paid me in fives, tens, and twenties so I had what we called ‘a wad’.

So I was bareback driving my ’60 Thunderbird feeling like I was right on top of the world because I had a wad of $3,000.00 - $4,000.00 on me in my shorts. I still remember I was wearing a white, washed-out piece of cloth tied around my head with a blue bandana. It was one of those hot, hot Miami days. I was heading east, down 8th Street, and as I passed the Palmetto, there was a guy hitchhiking.

He had the long hair like I was wearing. In those days we called one another ‘freaks’, so like a fool, I stopped and picked him up. I have no idea why I picked him up. I guess it was just the times.

So he gets in, and I started to drive down the road.

I looked over at him and said, ’Hey, buddy. How you doing, bro?’

He looks back at me, and he says, ‘N-n-n-not good.’

I suddenly realized that he seemed a bit nervous or agitated because he wasn’t sitting still. He was very jittery so I asked him, ‘What’s the matter?’

‘I-I’ve taken too much acid.’

'Hey, man, don't worry – I'll get you home. Don't worry – wherever you're going in the city, I'll take you. It doesn't make any difference where you're going.'

'I-I live on Miami Beach.'

'Ok ... Hey, listen, bro! Don't worry. I'll take you over to the beach, no problem whatsoever. Just kick back. I've been right where you are.'

So I'm headed down 8th Street, and everything seems good. But he's fidgety, and he starts acting weird.

I wasn't sure what to do so I said to him, 'It's just you've taken a little too much acid. No problem.'

'But – but I'm feeling weird.'

It was at that moment I thought, 'Oh, shit! I might have to shoot this fuck.'

Then I realized that it might be a little more than difficult because all I had was a .22 Derringer with one single shot, and I had the fucking thing in the goddamn left pocket of my shorts.

Then I started to feel nervous because I didn't want to kill this guy, but I realized I might not have any choice. I started to fuck around with my left hand as I tried to get the gun out of my pocket and put it underneath my leg.

While I was fidgeting, he kept glancing back at me, but he's doing it in real herky-jerky movements.

Then all of a sudden he goes, 'M-man, I'm-, I–I'm not feeling comfortable with you.'

I decided I'd try to play doctor with the guy and said, 'Hey, hey, hey, bro – listen – listen. Take it easy, will you? C'mon! Everything's all right. I'll take you right to your doorstep.'

All the time, I'm fidgeting with the wad, and I'm thinking, 'Oh, my god! I've got $3,000 - $4,000 on me. If I shoot this fucker... the fucking police ... holy shit! What's this guy gonna do? If he makes a move towards me I'm gonna shoot this piece of shit. And all I've got is a .22 with one single shot. Shit!'

I was still trying to get the gun out of my pocket, and finally I was able to get the gun out. I went, 'Aha!', and I slid the gun underneath my left leg between my ass cheek and the crook of my leg. I cocked the hammer back and said to myself, 'I'm gonna shoot this motherfucker.' I couldn't believe it, but I was going to have to shoot him. Jesus! I didn't wanna do it, but I had to do something. He was tripping the shit out.

I had my left hand on the gun, and I looked over at him and said, 'Okay, bro – listen. Listen – just take it easy.'

He looked at me and screamed, 'You-you're the fucking devil!'

I was ready for the guy to attack me, but I didn't pull out the gun. I figured I could still calm him down.

'C'mon, man! I'm not the devil – I'm not the devil, bro. I just wanna give you a ride over to where you're going – where you live. Let me take you over to Miami Beach. Everything's fine.'

He looked at me, grabbed the door handle, and the motherfucker jerked open the door right as I crossed Ponce de Leon and jumped out of the fucking car!

Now we were traveling about 40 miles an hour, and right on the corner was a hardware store. He hit the road, rolled several times, and smacked right into the hardware store.

'You piece of shit!' I screamed as I slammed on the brakes. 'You fucking mother fucker!'

Once the car was stopped I snapped the hammer back down on the gun and got the gun tucked away in a hole in the seat. I was so fucking mad I wasn't even thinking clearly.

I jumped out of the car. I figured he was dead, and I thought, 'Oh, fucking, no – Coral Gables Police ... a dead fucking shit-bag fucking out in front of the hardware store ... me ... money ... gun ... dope – shit! I'm fucked!'

As I went around the end of the car the mother fucker gets up and takes off running down the street screaming, 'Fuck you! You're the devil!' And he ran down the street just as fast as he could go.

I was so angry that all I could do was yell, 'Fuck you, you mother fucker!'

He ran to the end of the hardware store and turned down an alley. I looked around and expected to see a group of people ready to pounce on me while they called the cops, but there were no people, no cops, no one.

I got back in the car and drove off. I've never picked up a hitch-hiker again."

Johnny was laughing so hard by the time I finished that it took him a couple of minutes before he could speak.

"Why the hell didn't you just pull over and kick him out of the car? Really? Your first thought was 'I'm going to have to shoot him'?"

"Jesus, Johnny, I don't know why I didn't think to pull over. I just didn't. But it doesn't matter because he just leaped out – just like that ... 40 miles an hour. The son-of-a-bitch was lucky he wasn't killed."

"That's a great story, Dad. We have to record that one."

"Yeah, that would be a good one to record."

Chapter 7:

Let's Talk About the Numbers

The story about the hitchhiker really got Johnny excited about recording my story, and he was anxious to get to it as soon as we got home. The next morning he asked me if I wanted to record more, but I needed a few days to figure out how I should tell it.

I wanted to think about where it all started. And really, it goes all the way back to Maine and the lessons I learned while I was young. While they didn't lead directly to me getting involved in the drug world, they did help me develop an attitude that would allow me to step into it without any regrets.

My grandpa was what the world would call an "outlaw", and he was the one who first impressed upon my mind the need to take care of your family. He taught us to be grateful for what we had, and that family always comes first. He taught us to work hard, and if you needed something to go out and get it. I want you to understand that he wasn't a thief; he didn't go stealing from his neighbor. He just took care of his family the best way he knew how.

Even back then people would stand there with their judgments and say that shooting a deer out of season was wrong. All I know is this – we needed food, and he got it. So what if a few deer are shot out of season if an entire family was saved from starvation?

That's how I feel about smuggling narcotics as well. Too many uneducated people stake out a falsely created moral high ground about the entire drug industry without having a clue as to what the truth really is.

I can equate it to when people asked Hemmingway why he hunted. Why did he like to shoot springbok, lion, and hippopotamus? Hemingway would always answer the same way, "Either you get it, or you don't". Well, it's true in this game as well. Did I plan on being an international drug smuggler? A gangster working with various Mafioso families? No – I did not have a clue. It just happened; it was just business. I feel ... I consider myself lucky to have survived it.

But let's look at drugs, narcotics, and straight America strictly by the numbers:

- 500,000 die a year from tobacco-related diseases like cancer.
- 75,000 die a year from alcohol related accidents like, crashing into trees, rolling cars over, etc., because they are fucked-up drunk.
- Nearly 100,000 Americans die every year from adverse reactions to FDA-approved prescription drugs, yet you don't see the CDC, FDA, WHO, or the mainstream media running around screaming about the extreme dangers of aspirin, do you?
- *Drugs and narcotics of all kinds only kill about 10,000 people a year.*

So what about the guy that runs the liquor store? While he's kicking out liquor, does he think about how many people he's hurting a day? No.

Do you even care that he is selling alcohol to a known drunk driver? No.

How about the guy that runs the 7-11 down the street? When he is selling cigarettes is he worried about the person getting cancer? No.

Do you even care that he is selling cancer to someone else? No.

But the guy flipping crack on the corner or selling a few rocks is considered an evil, evil man, and this country spends *billions* of dollars to make sure he gets thrown in prison for life for it.

Come on, people! Do you see the picture? This is strictly about the numbers, and what is actual reality. It's all a pile of shit.

We should legalize it all.

Do I have the answers for any of this? No.

Do I really care who does what – snorting, drugs? No.

I'd be a hypocrite if I said I cared.

Do I wish I could change? That's just stupid. It happened – I was in the game for 23 years. It was a job; that's all. People were paying me money to smuggle cocaine, marijuana, and heroin. People paid me money to smuggle guns. People paid me money to smuggle people. People paid me money to smuggle money.

That's what I did. Very few people – especially us white boys, "gringos" – are put into a position where they work with the Colombian Mafioso families. I consider myself lucky because I have friends today that I worked with over 30 years ago. They survived, and I survived.

And it was pure stupid luck that we did.

I'm always taken a little aback when someone asks, "Oh, how many people did you hurt?" You just don't have a clue what it was like to be in the dope game. You just don't know; you believe all the government sponsored propaganda. I don't want to be rude to the millions of Americans, to the millions and millions of people who believe the propaganda worldwide, but you just don't know unless you've worked in the game.

And by the time you've finished this book – my story – you'll have a much deeper view of how the game *really* worked ... unlike anything else you may have seen or heard.

Until now, I haven't gotten into long conversations about my past because most people just don't get it. All they do is sit in their supposed-white towers and judge.

The ones out there who have been in the game, who are in the game, who are gangsters ... you automatically get it. You automatically know the deal. You know you're put into a situation where you can turn a buck and make some quick money, so you do what you have to do.

I was in the dope game from 1970 to 1993. I'm just reaching out and trying to grab a few of you. Hopefully ... now you'll understand.

Those of you who don't ... *go fuck yourselves.* I'm not writing this for you.

Chapter 8:

USS *Intrepid*

1969

It was the first week in February 1969, and we were returning from Vietnam. I was onboard the USS *Intrepid*. We arrived at the port in Norfolk, Virginia, around February 5th or 6th. After about a week, the ship had to go into dry dock so we moved to the Philadelphia Naval Shipyards. That shipyard is quite a place. I was excited because my friend Bobby had gotten out of the Navy a year before me and lived not too far away off the New Jersey Turnpike.

On the weekends I would hitchhike from Philadelphia to New Jersey. In those days you could wear your uniform and you wouldn't be out there two minutes, and you'd have a ride. I went to see him the first weekend I was free.

After I put my stuff away and changed clothes, he suggested that we go over to Greenwich Village because he had this connection that could get us some hash.

As we were traveling to the Village I asked him, "What are we gonna get?"

And he said, "Let's get a half ounce".

"What's that gonna cost us?" I asked.

"Well, it's like twenty-five bucks."

When we got to Greenwich and met his contact, I decided I might want more than a half ounce. So I asked him, "What's an ounce go?"

"Forty dollars".

"Forty, that's good."

So we got our ounce of hash, and we smoked it while we were listening to Dylan and others. You know? It just felt great.

I saved some of the hash and took it back to the *Intrepid* with me because I had two Italian friends that really loved the stuff.

Just as soon as I got back to the ship I found them, and asked if they wanted to find a place to take a hit.

They nodded and followed me back to where I slept. It was on the fantail about six decks down. We made sure no one else was around, and then we smoked a bowl of hash. Holy shit, it was really good! So good that Jimmy asked me how much it cost.

"Forty dollars an ounce," I said.

Jimmy thought for a moment and then said, "Well, there's 28 grams in an ounce. Let's make it 30 grams, chop it up, and sell 'em for 10 bucks a pop. We get $300.00 an ounce. If we each buy an ounce, we can flip it in a day. We'll each make $260.00 in one day."

"Jesus Christ," I said. "$260.00?! That's a lot of money!"

Up to this point in my life I hadn't thought about selling drugs; I was just happy to be smoking them. But the thought of making $260 in one day got my attention. You have to remember it was 1969, and that was a lot of money – especially if you could do it once a week, and Jimmy was talking about doing it in one day. In 2013 that would be the equivalent of making just under $1300 ... in one day!

I looked at Ralphie who looked as surprised and as excited as I was, and he simply nodded.

"Ok, Jimmy", I said. "What's your plan?"

Jimmy looked around to make sure that there were no other servicemen around. He smiled and in a quiet voice said, "It's easy. You go out and see your friend up in Jersey, and go to the Village. When you come back, bring three ounces, and we'll chop it all up."

Jimmy stopped and thought for a moment before he continued, "No, it might be better if you have it chopped up before you get back to the *Intrepid*, then everything will be good. You bring us the chopped up hash, and we will flip it for you. You don't have to see anyone – do anything. You know ... $260.00 clean."

It sounded so easy. Here was a way to make $260 in one day, and all I had to do was buy the stuff, cut it up, and sneak it onboard. They'd do all the rest. I couldn't believe how easy it all sounded.

We decided to launch "Operation Cut n' Run" the following weekend. I bought three ounces of hash, and we took it back to the house, and I chopped it up into 90 grams. When the weekend was over, I took it back to the ship.

I had to hitchhike back and forth from Jersey to Philadelphia. And even though I had hidden the hash in my bags, I was really nervous about getting caught. I mean, I was still in the Navy, and I didn't need something like this on my record.

But the trip back went smoothly. When I got onboard and showed Ralphie and Jimmy, they just flipped out. They started to flip it, and just like Jimmy said, we each had $260 in two days. It was the easiest money I had ever made.

So ... we did it again the next weekend.

And the next.

I was making over $1,000 a month, and all I was doing was buying the hash, cutting it up, and sneaking it onboard. This went on for better part of three months.

Then one day this E5 from Rock Island, Illinois, comes up to me and says, "Hey, what are you guys doing every day at noon?"

"What?"

"I see you, Jimmy, and Ralphie out in the parking lot every day at noon."

Now we were smoking hash, but I didn't want this piece of shit knowing about it. So I just blurted out, "We're eating our lunch".

"You eat your lunch out in the parking lot?"

I didn't answer because I didn't want anyone knowing what we were doing. He had done a tour in Vietnam with us, and he was an E5 so he outranked us. As a rule, guys who held rank tended to be real cocksuckers, and this guy was one of them. E5 in the Navy is a second-class petty officer. In the Marines, Air Force, or Army, he's a sergeant.

When I didn't answer he said, "You mind if I have a sandwich with you out in the parking lot?"

I was surprised by his request, but I didn't want any trouble so I said, "Yes".

He smiled and said, "Great – I'll see you guys tomorrow for lunch."

When I told Jimmy and Ralphie, they couldn't believe it either. As we discussed it we all agreed that we'd done a tour with him in Vietnam, and we didn't think anything of it. So we all agreed to go ahead with it.

To this day I don't know if it was a setup or exactly what the deal was, but when he came out in the parking lot, we made a decision that would make things real scary for us.

Ralphie had a car so we all sat in his car. We all sat there – eating our hoagies and talking about this and that. When we got done eating he says, "Well, shit – we might as well get straight before we get back on the ship".

"What do you mean?" the E5 asked.

I turned to him and said, "Do you wanna smoke a bowl of hash?"

I was surprised when this Rock Island, Illinois, boy said, "Sure".

Ralphie loaded up the pipe and lit it. He took a long hit and then passed the pipe to Jimmy who did the same and passed the pipe to me. I took a quick hit, and then passed the pipe to the E5. He didn't even hesitate – put the pipe to his lips and took a hit. Then he passed the pipe back to Ralphie. We just passed the pipe around and around and around until the hash was gone.

When we finished the Rock Island, Illinois, boy says, "Holy shit!"

I looked around for security officers, but I didn't see any, so I turned to him and asked, "What's the matter?"

He smiled and said, "Oh, man – that shit is fucking groovy, man!"

I think you could hear the rest of us sigh in relief.

Then Jimmy spoke up, "Yeah, you like that shit? Wait 'til you hear Donovan sing, and you smoke some of this hash." Ralphie and I laughed.

We didn't think much of it, and all of us went back on the ship. That weekend I went back to New Jersey, and just by luck, I didn't go to the Village. I didn't re-up. I had a girlfriend there and for some reason, I decided to go see her instead and ended up spending the whole weekend with her. Late Sunday afternoon I hitchhiked back down to Philly and boarded the ship.

At 0700 Monday morning the chief calls me in and says, "Hey, there's some guys looking for you. You report over to ONI." That's Naval Intelligence.

"Naval Intelligence?" I asked, surprised. "What the fuck do they want?"

"I don't know, but anytime those mother fuckers are after you, you got a problem."

The Philadelphia Naval Shipyard was such a big place that I didn't even know where ONI was. When I walked through the door and looked down the hallway, I saw Ralphie and Jimmy sitting in two Samsonite chairs. The third chair was empty. I walked down the hall and sat down next to Ralphie and Jimmy. And we sat there all day ... no one came for us until nearly 4:00 in the afternoon. I can only guess that they were making us wait so that we'd get nervous and say something we shouldn't.

The first thing they did was to split us up. They took me into a small empty room that was painted white and had a small table and two chairs.

Sitting on the other side of the table was an officer looking through a small file. He looked up at me and said, "Sit down".

I sat down and waited. After a few minutes of reviewing the file he nearly shouted at me, "Sound off, mother fucker."

That meant he wanted my last name, rank, and wanted to know who the hell I was. So I sounded off.

When I finished he looked at me and said, "You ... you've been selling hash. What do you have to say for yourself?"

"I don't have anything to say."

He eyed me for a few seconds and said, "I'm gonna make this real simple. Either tell us what the fuck you are doing, who you're selling the hash to, and who you're getting the hash from, or we're going to get you dishonorably discharged, fuck face."

"Well, listen," I said. "I don't know what you're talking about. I never have sold any hash. I've never smoked any hash. What in the fuck is going on? I don't know a goddamn thing."

"Nice try, but Ralphie and Jimmy just gave you up. They said that you go buy hash somewhere here in town."

Right then I knew I was in trouble. But I also knew that my boys hadn't given me up because they knew full well I didn't buy the hash in town. I figured I might be able to bluff my way out.

"Those fucking lying cunts," I said. "I don't know a thing."

The officer put the file on the desk and looked at me, "Well, you're entitled to an attorney under the Uniform Code of Military Justice, so you get an attorney. His name is Lt. J. G. Dombrink from Berkley, California, and he's right down the hall. Go knock on his fucking door."

Now I didn't know that I was entitled to an attorney at the time, so I went down the hall, knocked on the door, went in, and sat down.

The attorney looked across the table at me and said, "Hey, what's going on?"

"Hey, listen. I'm an E3 over 3."

Now an E3 over 3 means I've been in the United States Navy over three years. It means I know what the fuck's going on in the United States Navy. I'm salty at that time. At this point in my Naval career I did not trust officers; I did not like officers. Officers do not like enlisted men; they play a little game. They're different – they have their own country where they sleep, they have their own food where they eat, they eat like kings, and we eat like shit. The majority of them treat the enlisted men like low-class citizens. I do not like or trust fucking officers. Period. Of course that was 1969 – I feel a little differently today.

When I didn't say anything else, he sat back in his chair and said, "Listen, buddy. My name's Lt. J. G. Dombrink. Anything you say you have attorney-client privilege. I'm here to help you. Now just tell me the fucking truth ... what is the truth?"

"Well, excuse me, lieutenant", I said, "I'm just not used to being helped by any officers."

"I'm not just an officer; I'm your fucking lawyer."

"Okay, but I'm a little nervous to tell you what's going on."

"Just tell me the fucking truth so we can get out of this."

"Okay, well, here's the truth", I said. "I've been going up to New York City, and I've been buying ounces of hash and bringing them back to the ship, chopping them up, and selling them."

"Are you selling them to those two guys in the hallway?"

"I can't say."

"Okay, let me make sure I understand. You're going to New York City – to the Village more than likely."

He paused and waited for a response before he continued.

"I go there as well," he said. "You're buying ounces of hash for a really, really cheap price. You're bringing them back, chopping them up into grams, and you're flipping them, correct?"

"Correct."

"How much are you making?"

"Three hundred an ounce."

"Damn, that's not a bad little business. That's good. You're making more money than I do."

“Yeah, everything’s good.”

“No, everything *was* good”, he said sitting up straighter in his chair.

“Listen, this is how we beat this. These guys do not know shit from Shinola. They don’t have a fucking clue.”

Of course in those days there was no standard drug testing. They didn’t know a fucking thing about dope. If you were a spy, hopefully they’d catch you and hang you by the nuts. But I was selling hash just trying to supplement my Mickey Mouse income.

Lt. Dombrick continued ...

“This is real easy to beat. All you have to do is sign the paperwork and subject yourself to a search.”

“Search?” I said with alarm.

“Relax,” he said. “If you subject yourself to a search, first they’ll search you. Then they’ll bring in the Marines, and they’ll search you and your locker ... by the way, you don’t have a thing in your locker, do you? Do you have any fucking hash in your locker?”

“No.”

“So you’re clean?”

“Well ... not exactly.”

“Oh, Jesus Christ,” he said frustrated. “What are you talking about?”

“I had one of those great big horse capsules of mescaline, and I had four or five of them.”

“You took fucking mescaline on the *Intrepid*?”

“Yeah, but one of the capsules broke open in my shit kit (toilet bag), and I got a great big yellow smear in it.

The Lieutenant smiled and said, “Oh, these stupid fucks won’t know. Let’s sign you over to search. I’ll be right there with you. Let’s go down, and we’ll see what happens.”

“Are you sure? You’re not gonna give me up?”

“I’m your fucking lawyer; I’m from Berkley.”

Well, goddamn it, in 1969 I didn’t even know what “I’m from Berkley” meant. I didn’t know what that meant, and I didn’t know this guy was cool as shit. I just didn’t know. And of course I didn’t trust him
– he was a fucking officer.

I was scared. Fucking scared. I was terrified that after 3½ years I might be dishonorably discharged. I was almost out the Navy; I only had five months to go, and I thought an honorable discharge was a big deal. And it turned out it *was* a big fucking deal to be honorably discharged out of the United States military!

So my lawyer and I walked into the hallway, and there’s Jimmy and Ralphie. We’re out in the passageway, and all three of us are taken by ONI suits. Of course they bought their suits at Robert Hall, and none of their suits cost more than $8.00. I can still remember how shitty they were dressed.

There were about 12 of them. They led us back to the ship and up the officer’s gangway, and the Officer on Duty wanted to know what was going on.

The lead ONI suit pulls out some papers and hands them to him and says, “Naval Intelligence – We caught these three shitheads, and we’ve got papers to search them”.

The lieutenant reviewed the papers and said, “Hold it right there. Nobody just walks onto the USS *Intrepid*.” He got on his radio and talked to someone, and within five minutes I’m looking at the XO – the full commander.

“What the fuck is this!?” he demanded.

"These men are being accused. We have really good information that they're selling dope on this ship ... hash." The commander got really fucking mad and said, "These are my fucking boys. My boys don't sell dope."

Then he turned and looked at all three of us and said, "Atten-hut! Sound off, mother fuckers."

After we had sounded off he said, "If you three pieces of shit are selling dope on my fucking boat, I'll hang you from the fucking yardarm. You understand, you cocksuckers?"

After we all nodded he turned and pointed to the ONI Suits and said, "But if they're not, then you mother fuckers can get off my ship. So what do you need?"

"We need a detail of Marines for a security perimeter. We want to cordon them off, and we want to search their lockers. They've all agreed to the search, and they've signed the proper paperwork."

Once the Marines arrived we walked the length of the hangar deck and worked our way down below to my locker. The Marines then put a yellow tape around it like it was a goddamn crime scene.

Then the ONI boys opened my locker, and the first thing they pulled out is my shit kit. They opened it, and there's that great big yellow smear of mescaline in the middle of it.

They looked at it and then put it on the rack. I glanced at it and then at Lt. Dombrick – he was as cold as ice, so I did my best to be cold as ice too. They pulled out everything – all the pieces, all my skivvies, all my clothes, and all my uniforms ... all my shit.

When they had emptied my locker they looked at me and said, "Where the fuck is your sea bag, sailor?"

I pointed to a bag on the deck under the bunk and said, "Right there, sir."

He pulled my sea bag out, dumped it, and went through it all. It was clean as a whistle. Once they had finished, the ONI in charge nodded to the Marines who took down the yellow tape. When that was done, the Marines and ONI suits all walked away leaving me and Lt. Dombrick below.

I let out a sigh of relief and nodded his direction. "Lieutenant," I said.

"You don't have to say anything. I told you they're a bunch of shit bag motherfuckers. Let's go to the head now and get that shit kit cleaned out. And I suggest that you not sell any more hash on the USS *Intrepid*. You understand that, sailor?"

"Yes, sir," I replied as I grabbed my shit kit. As we walked into the head and I washed out the kit, I thought about how lucky I had been not to go to the Village that weekend.

"Just by the luck of the devil," I thought to myself.

Chapter 9:

Orange Sunshine Acid

I left the military in October of '69 and moved to Miami shortly after that. I was 22 years old at the time. Miami was probably one of the most beautiful places I had ever visited, and that's saying something because I had already been halfway around the world.

I met up with Bobby as soon as I got there. He had gotten out a year earlier than me and was in the throes of the Miami drug scene. It wasn't long before we were into the LSD scene and were tripping virtually every day.

We had an ambulance – a white metro ambulance – with a red cross painted on the side. It had an eight-track tape player, beads, and Day-Glo paint. Every Sunday we went to Greynold's Park which was up off Biscayne Boulevard and absolutely incredible. It certainly was no Woodstock or big pop festival, but there were a few thousand people gathered at the park every Sunday.

On one particular Sunday that I will never forget, we had taken three girls to the park with us. The girls were probably 17 or 18 years old. Just before noon each of us took a hit off a barrel of sunshine or "orange barrels" as we called them. After 15 to 20 minutes we realized that we weren't feeling the effects of the first hit. We looked at each other and said, "What the hell? We've got some beat acid. Let's take another hit." So we did, and as soon as we took the second hit, the first hit kicked in. In other words, we had taken a little bit too much acid.

While we were enjoying the trip the band came out and started playing *Sympathy for the Devil.* It was pretty groovy – as we said in those days. All of a sudden, right in the middle of the song, the music stopped, and all we heard was a bunch of static. One of the band members started to tinker with something on stage. After a few minutes the lead singer stood up and asked the crowd, "Does anyone have a pair of bolt cutters?"

I looked at the rest of my group and said, "Why does he need a pair of bolt cutters?"

I stood up and looked across there park. There was a crowd of probably 30 or 40 people in the parking lot at the far side of the park. They were screaming and yelling as they rocked a Metro Dade Sheriff's Department car up onto its side.

As I looked at the stage, I saw a black guy with his hands handcuffed behind his back. The lead singer

– who had somehow found a pair of bolt cutters – cut the cuffs off the black guy and tossed them into the crowd. Then he and the rest of the band ran off the stage and were gone.

We were so fucked up that all we did was stand there and watch what was happening. It wasn't long before we heard sirens in the background. Police swarmed the park trying to arrest people who were screaming and fighting to get away. It was like a mini riot.

Then it hit me what was happening. I turned to Bobby and the girls and said, "Shit! We better get out of here!"

We turned and ran toward a bunch of mangrove trees about 100 yards behind the main stage. Now to give you an idea of what mangroves are ... they grow all along the ocean, and basically they're a swamp. These are trees that grow like a jungle in shallow water where it's muddy, and the stench is terrible.

We bolted into those mangroves and just kept going. The grove wasn't very big – probably 200 or 300 yards deep –

but the effects of the drugs finally caught up to us, and it didn't take long for us to get lost in there.

As we were trying to find our way out one of the girls mentioned the Amazon. We were so fucked up that in our minds, we were instantly transported to the Amazon. That's where we thought we were ... we were discombobulated to say the least.

We wandered around that goddamn mangrove forest all afternoon until we finally stumbled out and onto a highway about 5:30 or 6:00 that night. Fortunately we were coming down from the high, but we were all filthy dirty, and covered in mud and sweat. So there were five of us going southbound on what turned out to be Dixie Highway, but we did not having a clue where we were. We were lost, and we were just filthy. For some reason, we all started laughing ... it was just an innocent time.

We finally made our way back down to the entrance to the park. It was getting dark when we stumbled through the entrance and saw our ambulance. But by that time, no one was there. We got in and drove off, and I guess we were lucky that no one got injured in the mangrove forest. I don't know what we would have done. As high as we all were I'm sure we would have come up with some crazy idea.

That was the first time I took too much acid, but things in my life were just getting started.

Chapter 10:

Meeting the FBI

My first experience actually selling dope started off with pushing pills. We sold it as THC, but it was not. It was actually a PCP hog tranquilizer since this was in 1970 – the hippie days.

We had a little one-bedroom apartment that we rented, and there were six of us – three guys and three girls – so obviously it was a little tight. We had it painted up with day-glow paint and some real hippie-looking shit. None of us had a job so we'd virtually do anything to make money. I started the pill business to supplement income from selling a little acid and some weed.

We knew a couple of junkies who stole bicycles. They stole the high-end Raleigh Internationals and Schwinns. They would steal them and sell them to us then we would flip them for a profit.

One day the junkies came to our place and start banging on the door. As soon as we opened it, they ran into our place with two bikes they had stolen – a Raleigh and a Schwinn. We soon discovered that the police were sweeping the neighborhood looking for the Raleigh.

When we asked them whose bike they had stolen, they told us they thought it belonged to Mike Gordon's son. The fucking morons had stolen Mike Gordon's son's Raleigh International. Any of you familiar with Miami know that Mike Gordon's was a very nice restaurant. It's right before you cross over the 79th Street causeway and just around the corner from where we lived.

We had them take the bikes to the back bedroom and close the door. No sooner had they closed the door then the police knocked.

I opened the door and asked, "What can I do for you officer?"

"We're looking for a stolen bike," he said as he handed me a picture of the bike and then looked over my shoulder into our apartment. "Have you seen this bike?"

"Can't say that I have," I said as I looked at the picture.

My two roommates came to the door and looked at the picture.

"Have either of you seen this bike?" I asked them.

"Nope."

"Me neither."

"I guess we can't help you," I said as I handed the picture back to the officer.

"If you do see this bike, give us a call – ok?"

"Ok, officer. We'll let you know if we see it," I said as I closed the door.

We waited about 20 minutes before we went to the bedroom and spoke to the junkies. They wanted $20 for both bikes, but I offered them $10.

"$10?" one of the junkies said, "they're worth $30 or $40 each."

"Yes," I replied, "but we just saved your sorry asses from going to jail."

After I paid them with a $10 bill, we helped them sneak out the back window.

That night we met up with a little redheaded girl who had stopped by a few times and bought some acid. We met her at Greynold's Park, and she brought this guy with her. He was probably 35 years old with long, brown hair, and he was dressed in nice clothes. He kind of carried himself like a gangster, but we weren't overly impressed with him. We just wanted to off a bicycle to him.

We negotiated for the bike, and he bought the Raleigh from us for $40.00. I felt pretty good about that deal because we still had the other bike to sell.

One of the guys living in the house with us was a good friend named Richie, but unbeknownst to us, he was a federal fugitive. In 1968 he came across the Mexican border near McAllen, Texas, carrying 40 pounds of pot. After getting caught, he jumped bail and fled to Miami. I spent about four to five months of 1970 hanging out with him.

We also lived with this guy who opened the first adult book store in Miami. It caused quite the controversy when it opened due in no small part to the fact that he had topless shoeshine girls out front that would give blowjobs.

Now I had no problem getting laid because I was right in the mix with the whores, the drugs, and the gangsters. We were flipping everything – dope, counterfeit money, and even the stolen bicycles, but it was all nickel and dime shit.

In January 1971, Richie and I took a trip to New York looking for hash, and when we returned to Miami, we drove straight through. When we got home, we went to the kitchen and were unloading the dope, weed, and pills onto the table. I had the cash in my pocket when all of a sudden seven or eight guys crashed through the door screaming "FBI"!

That's not a good sound.

I was 22 years old, and that was kind of like a twitch. I was already a Vietnam veteran, and I'd been halfway around the world. I had done a tour in Vietnam and spent just under four years in the Navy. I had seen quite a bit, but I wasn't ready for "FBI".

As they rushed across the living room I noticed their suits and jackets. They were cheap, J.C. Penney $12 suits, and they all wore the stereotypical J. Edgar Hoover fedora-style hats. One of them stuck a shotgun right at the back of my head while another one stuck a .38 right at my neck then another guy went around me and stuck a .38 with the hammer cocked at my temple.

As all of this was taking place one of the agents yells, "Freeze, you motherfucking piece of shit – Jack!" I was surprised they knew my name. I hadn't met any of these guys before.

They frisked me and found my ID and the money I had in my pockets. They put the money and my ID out on the table with the marijuana and pills, and then one of the agents turned to me and said, "Listen, Jack – we're here for your buddy. He's a federal fugitive that jumped bond."

Richie was down on the floor with his hands cuffed behind his back.

As they are getting him up the agent said, "Jack, here's the deal, motherfucker ... You can take this money. You can take this dope. You can take this weed. You can take these pills, and you can get the fuck out of this apartment right now. We have wind that you're banging the local girls in the neighborhood, and you're giving LSD to some of them. Word is a few of them may even be under age. You're a piece of shit. You're a slimy fuck. The only reason you're not going down with fuck-face here is because you're a Vietnam veteran. Get your fucking shit."

He stepped in front of me and paused for a couple of seconds and then asked, "Are you ready to go?"

"Yes, Sir!" I replied.

"Ok, get your fucking ass into the wind."

I had a cheap-ass suitcase that I used to pile the weed, pills, and cash into, and when everything was in I turned to leave. As I walked passed Richie we didn't speak – I just nodded at him as I passed by. I left the apartment, grabbed the second bike, and then walked across the street to a Burger King. I called one of my buddies, and he came and got me.

He had rented an old house in Coconut Grove for $220/month, and it was perfect. He took me to that house and I moved in.

Once I got settled I realized how lucky I had been. If those agents had not been so cool about my service in Vietnam, I would have spent several years in jail. But instead, that move made it possible for me to meet the guy who really got me started in the drug game.

Chapter 11: Selling Illegal Hog Tranquilizer

After I moved to Coconut Grove, I started to ride to Peacock Park in the mornings. That Schwinn those junkies had lifted turned out to be a really nice bike. One morning I rode down to the park, and the guy who bought the Raleigh pulls into the parking lot. He was driving a brand new Buick Riviera. It was dark brown ... just a beautiful car.

He saw me sitting on my bike, walked over, and asked me how I'm doing.

"Good."

He smiled and said, "Well, I checked out your living arrangements up there with the girl. Are you ready to make some real money?"

"I'd love to make some money."

He looked at me sternly and said, "You know you fucked me on that bike you sold me."

I laughed. "You got a hell of a deal on that bike. You got a Raleigh International for $40.00."

He started laughing and said, "Listen, why don't you put the bike in the back seat of the car. I'd like to show you something."

I loaded the bike into his backseat then climbed in, and he drove me to his house. He didn't live a block away from my new place.

He took me inside and opened up a couple of American Tourister suitcases completely full of those blue PCP tablets.

"Oh, man," I said, "those are nice."

"What do those go for?" he asked.

"I could flip those all day long for a buck a hit. It'd be pretty easy to sell on quantity – a hundred at a time."

"Really?" he said, "ok ... good. They're 50 cents to you."

"Oh, man," I said, "well ... I don't have very much money."

"You don't need any money – they're on the arm. Get the fuck out there and get hustling."

And that's how it started.

I got out in the street, and I started flipping those pills for him. It was pretty easy – he supplied the pills, and I flipped them. He never once asked for money up front. He just expected me to pay him once I sold the lot.

After about 30 days of this he comes to me and says, "Hey, you're doing a very good job. I want you to meet a couple of friends of mine."

He introduced me to a couple of guys that I'd seen in the park, and they were doing the same thing. With this group we started flipping pills all over the place.

And then, just like that, he tells me he has a problem and has to move.

Away he went leaving me thinking, "Holy shit! I just lost my connection."

Fortunately in the interim I had met this guy named Luco. He was a huge motherfucker so we all called him "The Big Guy". Luco and I had been selling cocaine and flipping weed during the time I was also selling the pills.

We made enough money to buy a house with cash. The house was off of Quail Roost, and it came with two guard dogs and five acres all fenced off.

One day I said, "You know what? I could sell the shit out of that PCP if we had a connection."

Luco surprised me when he said, "I got a connection. I got a connection in Oakland for that."

"No kidding?"

"Yeah, I think it's 6,000 a pound," he said. "We could go buy the raw merchandise, tab it out ourselves, and make maximum money."

"Cut out the middle man, huh? I like that idea."

And just like that ... we were in business for ourselves.

But we soon ran into a problem. And to solve the problem, we needed to find a guy that I knew from selling pills earlier. Unfortunately only a few people knew this guy.

The guy we were looking for was a strange man. He was never happy and always had a scowl, but for some reason, he always had beautiful girls hanging around him.

We started by visiting my old stomping grounds looking for him. It took us a couple of days of working the streets real hard, but eventually we got his name – "Fingers". And the only person who knew who he was happened to be a good friend of mine.

So we go over to my friend's house, and I said, "We're looking for this guy that never smiles. His name is Fingers. Do you know where Fingers is?"

My friend replied, "Yeah, I know where he is, but he'd be really pissed if I told".

"There's no way I'm going to mention you giving him up, but I need to talk to him. I'll cut you into a piece of the action if you tell me where he is."

He just smiled and said, "I'm making so much fucking money selling weed in New York that I'll just tell you where he lives. He lives between Red Road and Dixie Highway on the right-hand side just before you get to Ludlum. There's a little house all the way down. It's a hundred yards down the driveway, and if he's there, that's where you'll find him."

"Hey, I think I know somebody who used to live in that house."

"No shit – it's an old stash house. They've been in and out of there. He just moved in, and they're new tenants."

"Thanks, man. Let me know if I can do anything for you in the future."

So Luco and I drove to the house. As we pull up to the gate, I see him out in the driveway so I blow the horn. I scream down from the fence, "It's Jack!"

He waved and walked up to the gate, "Hey, Jack. Come on in."

He opened the gate, and I drove down.

As we were getting out of the car he asked, "I haven't seen you in awhile. What can I do for you?"

"I've got some hits. I've got some pills. Can you flip them?"

He looked surprised. "Goddamn ... since that guy went to New York City, I have been struggling to meet the demand. I can sell as many as you can get your hands on."

So we made an arrangement.

We would get the powder, and Fingers would guarantee that he could sell a couple *hundred thousand* at a time and work his way up. We would turn them to him in quantity at 12 cents apiece. It took us 6 cents apiece to make so we would double our money.

We set up the operation in our house on Quail Roost. And when we started, we only had a single punch pill machine that could make only 50 pills per minute.

That's all it took to start a career in the pill business – 50 pills at a time!

At first it was trial and error trying to get the mix right. I knew absolutely nothing about chemistry, but the Big Guy had been to college. He'd had a few years of chemistry so at least he knew the basics.

When you're making pills you have to add some cornstarch to hold it together. You also have to add some non-toxic paint – yes, paint. What the fuck do you think makes your candy so colorful? Regardless of how the food industry spins it, it's fucking paint. Anyway ... I digress.

With pills you have to get the formula just right because you want them to dissolve right after the client swallows them. If you get the formula wrong it can take four or five hours to break down, and people won't get off. And people want to get off quick - like within 15 minutes.

So we set up the pill machine and were ready to start making some pills. Now I'm not the most mechanically inclined guy, and right off the bat, I turned the machine on by accident. It had a big pulley on it, and the Big Guy got his hand caught in the thing. He was mad as a motherfucker.

As he pulled his hand out he turns to me and said, "Hey! Your job is to sell this shit. I never want to talk to those hippie cocksuckers. You sell the shit, and you handle the money. I'll handle the making of the pills ... We got a deal?"

"Yes, we do", I said as I tried to hold in my laughter.

That machine was our initiation into the pill business, and we slowly worked our way up. Eventually we got a new machine that had a 32-head punch. Oh, my god ... could she ever click it out! It made a hell of a nice noise, and every time she cranked and we heard that click, we knew we had just made 6 cents profit.

Within a year we were selling a million hits a month.

Chapter 12: Jack's First Bust

1971

In 1971 I really started selling cocaine. I had a connection that lived right next door to me on Whitehead Street in Coconut Grove – I'll call him "Carlos". I bought a lot of cocaine from him, and he was also one of my connections for LSD, PCP, and marijuana – the whole thing. He was married, and they were the typical Hippies of that time period.

One day Carlos came over to my house and said, "I need a half a pound of blow."

Now I never thought anything of it really. I'd been buying cocaine from him for three or four months, so for him to say he was out was common.
Sometimes guys had it, and sometimes they didn't.

So I said, "Ok – let me get it."

"Great." He said, "Come on down to the new house tomorrow for the wedding." I was a bit surprised by this but figured that if he wanted it for his wedding, I might be able to sell some more to the other guests. So I got half a pound of blow together and went to his wedding the following day.

I arrived at the address and went into the house. It was a small wedding – only about eight or nine people had been invited. I found Carlos and told him that I had half a pound of blow for him. He smiled and called one of his guests over to inspect the merchandise.

The guy looked at the blow and said, "I need to go out to the car and get the money."

When he said that I got a weird vibe. As he walked out of the house the feeling got stronger ... something was just not right. I looked out the window and watched him walk to his car. When he got to his car, he pulled out a cigar box and put it on top of the car, and then he looked down the street to the right. I followed his gaze and saw eight or nine guys coming down the street carrying shotguns and screaming, "BNDD". BNDD stands for the Bureau of Narcotics and Dangerous Drugs (predecessor of the DEA).

"Shit!" I yelled.

Everyone in the party looked at me and then out to the street. One of the guests was a little Cuban girl. Christ, she couldn't have been any more than 5'3" or 5'4", and she didn't hesitate. She slammed the door shut, locked it, and then braced herself against the door. The agents slammed into the door, but it didn't give in so they started kicking the door trying to knock it down. As they were kicking at the door, I took the half of pound of blow into the bathroom and flushed it down the toilet. I had just returned to the living room when the agents finally kicked the door in. The poor Cuban girl went flying to the floor as the agents entered the room with their guns drawn.
They kicked us around and beat on us a little bit. One of the guests tried to stand up to one of the agents and got a couple of shotgun butts to the head in return. They put us all on the floor, handcuffed us, and then got us up on our knees with our legs crossed. Then one of the agents said, "Ok – where's the blow?"

Nobody said a fucking word. The agent went around the room demanding that same thing from each of us personally. When no one answered, they took us outside one at a time. Carlos was on the end, and I was second to the end. They dragged us to our feet and took us outside where they stuck me in one car, and then put Carlos in another with his friend the informant. The informant turned out to be the rat. A few minutes after Carlos was put into the car with him, the agents pulled the informant out of the car. The window was down and I heard him say, “Hey, they flushed it down the toilet.”

“That dirty cocksucker,” I thought to myself, “selling his friend out on his wedding day. What a piece of shit.”

The BNDD Agents told the informant to leave, and he got into his car and drove off. I wasn’t sure what was going to happen, but I was confident that the agents couldn’t get the blow because I had flushed it down the drain. But as I was sitting in the BNDD car thinking this, an agent opened the trunk of the other car and pulled out a couple of sledgehammers. He and another agent went back into the house, and a few minutes later they emerged with eight, one ounce bags of blow.

Someone said, “How in the hell did you get that?”

One of the agents laughed as he put his sledgehammer back into the car. He turned around and said, “We just knocked the toilet right off and pulled it out of the pipes.”

I was shocked – I couldn’t believe it. I learned more about plumbing at that moment than at any other time in my life, and I knew I wouldn’t make that mistake again.

They took us downtown and threw us in Dade County jail where we spent the night. The next morning they transferred us to another jail. In those days, there was a city jail in Miami that was half state, half federal. They put me on the federal side, and I felt lucky because on the state side it was just a pack of wild animals. There must have been 100 guys over there screaming and yelling, but there were only two guys in the cell I was in. One of them was a black guy who had robbed a meat truck out of Tampa. The other guy was a Costa Rican guy who had a couple of kilos of blow. They had charged me with possession with intent to distribute half a pound of blow.

By now it wasn't uncommon for me to have several thousand dollars on me all the time. At the time I was arrested, I had about $7,000 on me. Of course they confiscated the money, but they let me keep about $100 because there was a canteen wagon that came down for the federal prisoners only. When it came down I asked the other guys if they wanted something to eat, and they did. So we got some chicken salad, egg salad, tuna fish salad, iced tea, and a bag of chips. There we were ... just the three of us quietly enjoying our meal while 100 other guys sat in the other cells across the aisle screaming and fighting with each other.

It didn't take long for the boys to send an attorney for me. I won't give his name right now, but it's easy to figure it out. So this attorney gets me in front of the judge by the name of Peter Pelermo. In those days, they only had one federal magistrate, and I was expecting to get a pretty bad sentence. But at the arraignment the judge said there was insufficient evidence, and he walked me.

It wasn't until after I was set free at the arraignment that I found out what a piece of shit my mother- fucking attorney was. He took me back into Judge Palermo's office and put four $100 bills underneath a picture of Judge Palermo's family. I jerked my head around because even though I saw it, I didn't want to see it. I walked away, but I did not like that fucking move. That was horrible. If he was going to do that, he should never have done it in front of me – plus the case was already dismissed. The motherfucker should have never done that in the first place. I found out later that Judge Palermo didn't take any chances. He reported him to the bar and to the federal authorities.

In August, I was re-indicted and had to go to back to court. I was facing 35 years in the can, so this time I hired the attorney myself. He only charged me $1,000, but his plan was for me to give up my connection. Well ... I wasn't going to give up my connection. The attorney begged me to, but I wouldn't do it because I felt that it wasn't my connection's fault – I bought the merchandise. And if I was going down, I was going to go down alone. I wasn't going to become a rat.

So I had to go to trial. At that time I had real long hair, and on the day of the trial my wife pinned it up to look like I had short hair. And even though I swore I would never do it, I shaved my beard and mustache.

I went to trial in downtown Miami federal court where the U.S. attorney was a guy by the name of Sullivan. He had worked his way up the ladder to become a big guy.

As I was standing in front of the Judge, I looked over at the jury and went, "Oh my fucking god." There were like five school teachers, two plumbers, three FBI agents, a couple of house wives and a substitute. It was just terrible – I knew they were going to hang me out to dry.

Well, the trial got underway, and at noon my attorney whispers to me, "When we dismiss for lunch we've got to go out in the hall and talk."

Once we were in the hall and by ourselves my attorney says, "If you plead guilty, you'll only get three years of probation. You'll walk out of here today."

I said, "Yeah, but I've got this beat."

"Yeah, but take a look at the jury. What do they look like to you? They're a bunch of straight motherfuckers, and they don't know shit. They're going hang you."

I thought about the jury and had to agree. "Oh, god damn it! I'll take plea and the probation."

So I took the plea, and Judge King sentenced me to three years of probation. It was sickening ... just sickening. I was a convicted felon by 1971, and that sticks with you for quite a while. At the time I thought I had that case beat, but I didn't dare to take a chance.

As I look back now I see that I got off easy. I could have been locked up for 35 years. Instead, I walked away with only three years of probation. It wasn't long after this that things really began to pick up for me in the dope game.

Chapter 13:

Cocaine 101

1971 - 1972

1971 was a most interesting year. Not only did I meet the guy that got me into the pill business, but that's also the year I met this Cuban family over in Hialeah, a suburb of Miami. They were my cocaine connections, and I had been introduced by one of the hippie boys in the street.

It was a whole family of Cubans, and the old man taught me about the importance of cutting the merchandise. He said, "This merchandise is so good, make sure you never sell it straight up. Always cut it."

When I asked him why he said, "Because you can't guarantee merchandise like this all the time, and they will all be expecting it. So always put a little step on it, and that way you'll be able to maintain the quality."

Well, the year went on, and things were going good right up until I got busted at my friend's wedding. That was in May, and as I mentioned, the attorney got me three years of probation instead of being thrown into prison.

And just so you understand how this business works ... even though I was now on probation, within a month I was right back to selling cocaine. You know ... just doing my normal shit.

One day my wife and I were over at a friend's house – well, more of a buyer/seller "friendship". I used to go over there and sell three or four ounces of blow daily – and I do mean on a daily basis. This couple was good business for me. Luco was there as well, and we are all doing cocaine.

In those days, Quaaludes were big. Quaalude was a brand name sedative/hypnotic drug. It became popular in the late 1960s and early 1970s. It had many names such as "*ludes" and "sopers", and "soapers"* were common in the U.S. In Great Britain they called it "*mandrakes*" and "*mandie*". When it was used at clubs or discos, it was called "*disco biscuits*".

My friend, the one who owned the house, had taken too many Quaaludes one time, and he went to sit on the couch. When he sat down his head fell backwards, and he hit the wall so hard that he knocked himself out. So there he is ... knocked out in his own house. But we didn't think anything of it – it was just part of the dope game.

His old lady, who was a little blonde from Australia, my wife, and Luco start talking about artichokes

– artichoke bottoms with Hollandaise sauce.

They might as well have been speaking Greek because I didn't even know what that meant. So I asked, "What the fuck is an artichoke?"

They all stopped talking and looked at me for a moment. I think they would have all started laughing, but my wife knew better so she described them for me. Suddenly they are all talking about how they're going to make them for me, and I was going to love them – especially in Hollandaise sauce. And the entire time they are talking I was thinking, "What the shit? I have never even heard of Hollandaise sauce. These people all have trained palates."

As our conversation went from one topic to the next, I quickly discovered that Luco and I had some things in common. Turns out the Big Guy had been in the Merchant Marines for three years. While serving in the Merchant Marines he actually got his draft notice while up the Saigon River. He spent time up the Saigon River with 16 tons of bombs, but instead of making some nickel and dime shit money like I made in the Navy, he was making $1,600 to $1,700 a month.

We started talking about the places we had both seen, and Olongapo comes up. For those of you who don't know, Olongapo is a city in the Philippines, and it was one of the wildest cities in the world at the time. It was a little town right off the base at Subic Bay where there were just bars, hotels, money exchanges, and monkey meat. The merchants sold chicken, but man – those were some really, really long-legged chickens! It looked like monkey meat, so that's what we called it. They sold that with french fries wrapped in a newspaper for $1.00. But what really made Olongapo such a great place was the 17,500 girls that lived there.

Luco and I talked for hours and found out that we had something in common. And over the course of the next three or four months, he was always there – mainly because he was a friend of the guy that had just knocked himself out from taking too many Quaaludes.

This relationship between Luco, my friend, and I went on until around Christmas time.

Then one day Luco says, "You know, I can't take this guy any longer. This guy's a fucking whack job. He snorts cocaine, he eats pills, and he treats his wife like shit. I got a little something coming up ... how about you and I forming a partnership?"

I really liked Luco so it was easy to say, "Ok, let's talk."

Well a few days after New Year's there was a knock on my door at 8:00 in the morning. Now in 1972 I stayed up late so 8:00 in the morning was early for me, and I wasn't too happy to have to get up that early.

I got up and answered the door, and there he was. He had an ammunition box in his hand. I just looked at the box and said, "What? You got some bullets?"

"No, I don't," he said, "but I'd like to come in and talk a few minutes. Is that alright with you?"

I opened the door and said, "Well ... come on in."

My old lady heard our conversation, got up, and started making coffee for all of us. We walked into the kitchen, and he put the box up on the counter. He opened it and pointed to the $7,000 in ten-dollar bills that were in the box.

I looked at the money and said, "Jesus! What do you have there?"

"I've got seven grand in ten-dollar bills. I just sold a guy's boat, and I want to use the money. I want to pay him for the boat, but I want to make a little money before he gets it. He's in California so we have a little bit of time. Can you make any money with $7,000 in cash?"

"Yes, I can."

"Alright."

"Let me take a quick shower and then let's get on the road."

So I took a quick shower and got ready. We went out to my car and drove over to Rocky's house. He was a friend of mine who had a connection.

When we got there it was all business. I walked in and said, "Hey, man, call your connection. I need a pound of blow."

In those days, it was $7,200 for a pure pound of blow.

"It's $7,500." Rocky said.

I reached into my pocket and pulled out another $500.

Well, sure as shit, the connection comes. When he walked in I'd never seen anyone quite like him – he was dressed to the nines. He had a brand new Grand Prix, and wore a beeper on his belt. We called him 'Walkie Talk.'

I pointed to the beeper and said, "Hey! What's that?"

"That's a beeper," he said. "This is a new technology ... you call this, and you leave a number for a payphone that you want me to call you at. Then I call you back from a payphone."

I couldn't believe it, "Oh, shit! I'm going to need one of those right away."

"Yeah, you probably are."

Then he told me where to get one.

As we were talking I noticed that when Walkie Talk spoke to Rocky, he treated him disrespectfully. He talked to him curt – without manners. I never liked that, but as far as me and the Big Guy, he was talking to us like we were his brothers.

So we got down to business, and he said, "What do you need bro?"

"I need a pound of blow." I said.

"No Problem." He replied.

We had Luco's $7,000, and I kicked up another $500. After he saw the money he brought in a big pear can. It was the same size as a coffee can, but it had a label for pears on the outside.

"Let's go in the kitchen," Walkie Talk said.

We all went into the kitchen, and Rocky got a can opener. We opened it up, and inside the pear can – wrapped in plastic – was a pound of cocaine.

"Wow!"

I thought that was the highest tech shit in the world. I'd never seen anything like that.

We opened the can, took out the pound of blow and checked the merchandise. It was beautiful. I handed him the cash.

When we were done I said, "Ok, bro ... if this all works out, we'll be doing business on a regular basis."

He just nodded and then walked out the door with his cash, got into his Grand Prix and drove off.

As soon as he was gone I went to my friend's bedroom and took the mirror down off the wall. I dumped out the one pound of pure cocaine onto the mirror. I took an ounce and hit it 100% with dextrose hydrous 6740. (Dextrose hydrous 6740 cost about $1 a pound). I did the ounce.

"Jesus! This shit is good," I said.

I hit the rest of the pound with one pound of dextrose hydrous 6740 (also known as baby laxative) that I purchased at one of the Cuban pharmacies. Bang! I made two pounds right there on the spot.

The Big Guy said he had a connection that would buy pounds of cocaine at $6,500 a pop, so we flipped the two pounds for $6,500 a piece – $13,000 total. The guy fronted the money which was unheard of at the time. The big guy goes and gets the $13,000, and we leave a car at a prearranged spot with the two pounds of cocaine in it. After that we started doing the same thing two or three times a week, and it went on for about six or eight months. It seemed like years, but we started making a killing.

That's how I met Luco, The Big Guy, and how I got started in the cocaine business. The Big Guy was with me for the entire 30 years I was in the drug business.

He's still my closest friend today.

Chapter 14: Toilet Blow

When I arrived in Miami the cocaine business was just starting. I was right there in the beginning of the game. And even though I knew four or five guys who sold cocaine, and four or five guys who bought cocaine, cocaine was a funny, strange business. Sometimes you wouldn't be able to find it even though you knew everybody and their brother. There was one time when there was no blow – none whatsoever. I was going out of my mind, and people were screaming for it. I was calling everyone I knew trying to buy it, but I couldn't get any no matter how hard I looked.

I kept beeping one particular guy over and over, but he wouldn't return the beep. Finally, around 10:00 or 11:00 pm, I get a beep on his number so I rushed out and called him. But I sure was surprised when his old lady answered the phone.

She was a bit hysterical and said, "Jesus, Jack, please come to the house right away. The old man has lost his mind – he's flipped out. He's been doing blow for a couple of days, and he's all paranoid, tweaked, and looking out the window. He thinks the cops are coming. He's saying crazy, weird shit, and he's threatening to flush the blow down the toilet."

I realized that this might be the only blow I could get so I said, "Wait a minute ... Where is he, and how much blow does he have?"

"He's got a pound of blow, and he won't come out of the bathroom."

"He's got a pound of blow, and he's threatening to flush it down the toilet?"

"I'll buy the pound. I'll buy the fucking thing. Has he got his hands all over it? Is it moist? Is it wet? Condensation? What's the merchandise look like?"

"No, no, no, no, the merchandise is good, but he's in the bathroom and he won't come out. The only person he'll talk to is you."

"I'll be right over."

Now I lived in the southwest section of the town – most of the time in Coconut Grove – and this guy was living up off Northwest 81st Street between Biscayne Boulevard and Mike Gordon's. I drove as fast as I could, but it still took over 30 minutes. The entire time drive I'm thinking, "*Please don't flush the blow – please don't flush the blow*".

I pulled up, parked on the street, ran to the door, and knocked.

"Shit!" I said as I knocked on the door. Finally his old lady came to the door. She was a girl from Connecticut, and she was always nice as pie and a sweetheart of a woman. But when she answered the door she was crying and distraught.

"Where is he?" I asked.

"He's in the bathroom, and he won't come out."

I wasn't sure what to do because I knew he was tripped out so I just spoke through the door, "Hey, bro! It's me."

After a couple of seconds he responded, "Is anyone with you?"

"No, no – I'm alone. Open the door."

He didn't open the door.

"I know the police are coming, and I know they're gonna arrest me. I've been fucked up ... I've been doing blow for a little bit."

I knew I had to get in there and save the blow.

"Hey, listen ... just settle down, and open the door. Please – open the door, and let me in."

After this conversation repeated itself a couple of times, he finally opened the door, and I stepped in the bathroom. He shut the bathroom door and locked it immediately. As I looked around the room I saw that up on the sink he had a pound of cocaine. He had it double-bagged in clear plastic bags.

Before I could do anything he took the bag and held it right over the toilet and said, "I'm gonna flush it."

I put my hands up in front of me in a sign of peaceful intent. "No, no, no, no, man. Don't do that. I'll buy it – I'll buy it right now."

He looked at me with a weird look on his face, but he didn't do anything.

I had to act fast, "Have you cut it? Have you whacked it? Have you gotten it wet? You're sweating and dripping. You're all wringing wet."

I slowly reached out for the bag, "C'mon! You're gonna ruin the fucking merchandise."

He just shook his head, stared down the drain, and said, "I'm worried about the cops ... I'm worried about her. I don't trust her ... I don't trust anyone. You're the only guy in the world I trust."

"Listen, bro! Listen," I said, "please just look at me ... just settle down. C'mon! Let's take the blow ... let me have it. Just step away from the toilet, and hand me the blow."

He stared at the toilet a few seconds, and then just like a child, he stepped away from the toilet. But he was still holding the bag ready to drop it down the drain.

"Just hand me the bag – let me have the merchandise." He waited a few seconds and then turned and handed me the bag. I immediately inspected the merchandise and could see that it wasn't coagulated – it wasn't fucked up.

He had sweat all over the bag, but it hadn't gotten into the merchandise. It was good, and I could see the big rocks in the bag.

There was some kind of a grocery bag in the garbage can, so I grabbed the bag and put the merchandise in it.

"See?" I said, "Here ... put the toilet seat down and sit on the toilet. Just take it easy ... I'm with you, bro. You got any more merchandise in the house?"

"No," He said as he sat down on the toilet.

"You got any pills?"

"Yes, I got some tuinals and some seconals."

"What strength are those tuinals?" I asked.

"They're three grain."

"I'm here, and everything's good," I tried to reassure him. "Take a couple of tuinals, take a seconal, have a shot of whiskey, get into bed, tell the old lady you love her, and c'mon! Don't worry about the police."

He looked up at me like he was trying to comprehend what I was saying, and then he looked at the bag in my hand.

"Don't do any blow for a while," I said. "I'll save you some out of this bag. Tomorrow ... I'll bring you some blow. Right now ... we're all good."

"Here's the cash," I said as I reached into my pocket and pulled out the wad. "Let me give it to your old lady. I'll count it all out for you first, but I'm not gonna fuck ya. Just remember what you were doin' ... you were gonna flush it down the toilet. Now that's not gonna happen."

After I counted out the money I said, "You've got your money, and I'll call you tomorrow when you wake up. Ok, bro?"

"Ok."

I went out, hugged and kissed his old lady, got in my car, and drove off.

Now I can't tell you I know exactly what I paid for it, but I gave him the going rate. He had taken probably an ounce or so because he had his nose in the bag all day and the day before. That left me about 15 ounces I could sell, and because of the demand and quality of the merchandise, I was able to flip all of it immediately at a huge profit. I walked away with about $7,000 profit.

Chapter 15:

Jack's First Shootout

Early 1972

Luco and I were moving cocaine – pounds, half pounds, quarter pounds ... you name it. We were selling cocaine 24 hours a day. As I mentioned earlier, we were buying it for $7,200 a pound from the Jew, and whacking it 100% with dextrose hydrous 6740 – baby laxative. We even had guys who would actually front the money. It was in the early stages of the cocaine business in the United States, and we were right flat in the middle of it. It was exciting, and of course we were high all the time. We were taking pills and snorting blow day and night – just a couple of yahoos.

Things were going so well that looking back, I should have seen that something bad was going to happen. There was this one particular guy who was weak, and he lived in Coconut Grove. He didn't have a beeper – just his home phone which was never a problem for us because he never left his house. He was always fucked up, and he had his old lady with him all the time. No matter where he went – home or in the street – his old lady was with him. She was a junkie herself – a skanky bitch. I remember her hair it was wet, close to her face, and not very attractive. She was just a skanky broad, but we never thought they were a threat. They were just a couple of junkies who were good customers.

Over a few weeks of time, he had gotten into us a little bit. He owed us nearly $9,000, and one night around midnight I called him.

The phone rang for several minutes before he finally answered.

I like to take the respectful approach in my dealings ... you know, use your manners. So I said, "Hey, buddy. How are you doing?"

"Hey, quit calling me." He said.

"What?" I said. This piece of shit was trying to get out of paying us, so it was time to be a hard ass, "What the fuck are you talking about? I haven't called you in two days. You owe us nine grand."

"I'm sick and tired of you on my back."

"Hey, motherfucker listen! You owe me fucking money."

"Well, I'm just sick of you two pushing me."

"Listen, man. I'm gonna come over and talk to you about it. I'll be over there in 20 minutes."

"Don't come to my house."

"Hey, fuck you!" I barked out. "I'll be over there in 20 minutes."

I hung up the phone, looked over at Luco, and said, "Hey, fuck face is giving me a bunch of shit – telling us not to come over."

He just looked at me and said, "Well, fuck him and that skank ass bitch of his! Let's just over to the house."

The little prick lived right down the road on Mary. If you're coming down Tigertail, and you make a right headed up to Bird Road, it was an apartment building on the left-hand side of the street. There were about three or four of them that had these second story balconies. He lived in one that was close to the end.

At the time I had a 1970 Pontiac Catalina, so Luco and I got into my car and drove to his place.

Now a few months earlier Luco and I had talked about what we would do if someone started shooting at us. All you want to do is get behind cover. We both agreed that if that is how we felt, then that is how the other guy would feel if we were shooting back at him. So we decided that if someone started to shoot at us, we would start shooting back at him. We wouldn't even have to aim. The fact that we were shooting back should cause the motherfucker to stop shooting at us and dive for cover.

I was glad that we had that conversation because as I pulled up to the apartment building, I see fuck face and his old lady standing on the balcony. He waited until I pulled into the parking spot, and then he pulled out a pistol and opens up on us. He put four bullet holes right through the windshield of my car. One hit the dash, two hit the seat, and one hit The Big Guy.

"You motherfucker!" I screamed. I reached under the seat and grabbed my 9mm with my left hand. I opened the window and gave him ten rounds with my Browning. I just snapped them off ... I wasn't even pointing at him; I wasn't even aiming. I just cracked them off to see if I could get him down before he ended up killing us; that piece of shit.

It worked just like we hoped it would. They jumped out of sight into their house. I was thinking about going up there and fucking the two up, but I looked around and realized that the police were going to be there any minute. I pulled my hand back into the car and took off.

As we were leaving the scene I dropped the gun between my legs and looked over and saw that Luco had been shot. That piece of shit had shot hit him in the extreme right-hand side of his chest. Luco was grunting and groaning a little bit so I drove down Mary as fast as I could go and then crossed over to Bird.

I took The Big Guy down to my house. It was about 1:00 in the morning, and I knew we couldn't take him to the hospital because they would call the cops. Luckily we had been hooked up with numerous Vietnam veterans, and one of them was an army medic. But he was crazier than a loon and usually wasted on heroin. He shot dope day and night because the war really fucked him up although not to the point where he was weak or – oh, my god – whining and bitching all the time. He just got fucked up because he saw so much bad shit.

Of course his nickname was Doc. Doc lived all the way down in Homestead so I called him. I said, "Doc – listen. The Big Guy's been shot."

"Oh, Christ," he said. "Well, I don't ...", and he just starts stuttering.

"Listen, Doc – let me come down and get you. Can you put your black bag together, and I'll bring you back up to the house? We've got to take care of The Big Guy. He's in a world of hurt."

"Where was he shot?"

"Well, the best I can tell he was hit in the right-hand side of his chest. It looks like a bullet hit a rib or something and bounced out and went into the fat underneath his right arm."

We learned later that it was a .357 Magnum. This is a big caliber weapon. Luco was in a world of hurt, and the bullet was lodged in the fat underneath his right arm.

I drove down and got the doc. When we got back to my house, Doc said, "I don't have any pain killers. Can you find something?"

"I've got a junkie I know. I can get some smack."

"Wait a minute," he said, "I've got some smack. We can use that."

Now there's another reason we call Luco "The Big Guy". Not only is he a huge man, but he is also a tough motherfucker. He didn't whine – he didn't piss – he didn't moan. We shot him up with some smack, and then doc went to work on him.

Doc shot some smack as well. It was kind of a Cheech and Chong surgery – he got in there and started probing. He started digging on The Big Guy who didn't whine too bad, but he did some grunting and groaning. There was blood everywhere. After a few minutes, Doc pulled out his tools and held up the bullet that he had just pulled out. He dropped it on the glass coffee table, and it sounded like dropping a rock on glass. It sounded just like in does in the movies ... the clink and ting as they drop a bullet in a cup.

As he was sewing up The Big Guy, Doc said, "We can't get him to the hospital because there are gonna be all kinds of questions. The police are gonna want to know about a gunshot wound. We can't be having any of that shit. Just let me take care of him."

We all nodded in agreement.

"And in return," he continued, "you guys are gonna take care of me."

I just smiled and said, "Yeah, yeah, yeah – we got a few thousand dollars. Let's get some smack." I knew that Doc was a junkie, so we took care of the junk habit, and we took care of the cash. After about four or five days of convalescence, The Big Guy was up and raring to go.

I'll tell you what happened to that piece of shit and his skank-ass fucking ho that shot The Big Guy later.

Chapter 16:

Jack's First Bet on a Major Sporting Event

January 14, 1973

1972 was an unbelievable year for me. Just a few years before that I was in the Navy with nothing, and in 1972, I probably sold close to 100 pounds of cocaine. I already had two smuggling trips under my belt from Jamaica with probably upwards of 7,000 or 8,000 pounds. I had sold close to a couple million hits of THC/PCP. Living in Miami meant that we were die-hard Miami Dolphin fans.

We worshipped the team, and lucky for us, that year the team went undefeated. They were the first and only team in the NFL to never lose a game, and they would be facing the Washington Redskins in the Super Bowl.

In those days they had two newspapers, the *Miami Herald* and the *Miami News*. In the *Miami News* two weeks before the game, the line came out – "Miami was the underdog by seven-and-a-half points". When I read it I couldn't believe it ... it had to be a mistake. What's the matter? Did Csonka, Kick, or Griese get injured? What about Paul Warfield – did he break his leg? What's the deal? So we studied the news.

We looked at the paper – the Brooklyn Boy, The Big Guy, and me. We all came to the same conclusion ... this doesn't make any sense. We also knew that the bookies weren't often wrong.

"What the fuck is this?" I said. "They're going to play against the old boy Billy Kilmer? There's no way. There's something wrong."

Well ... we let it go for a couple of days. We had been making small bets all year, you know, $400 or $500, but nothing serious.

Then one day we got to talking about it.

"This is a big fucking deal," I said to the Brooklyn Boy and Luco. "Miami has not lost a game. There's no way ... there's just no way. They're hot, and they're going to win this game."

The Brooklyn Boy looked at both Luco and I and said, "Let's bet $20,000 each. We've got another load coming. We're getting all ready to get another trip underway, and we all have a few hundred thousand dollars. You boys are cooking with that pill business, and the blow business has been hot. I say, 'Fuck it!' Let's bet $60,000."

"Jesus Christ, that's a lot of fucking money," I said. "I'd hate to lose $60,000. I'd hate to give the money to those motherfuckers. I hate those fucking bookies."

But the Brooklyn Boy was persistent.

"No, it will be easy. We'll go over to Coconut Grove, and we'll go to the Laughing Loggerhead.

We'll go, and we'll deal with those fucking bookies in there. There's one team – the guy's Sicilian and his partner's Cuban. We always get along with them. We're always paying those motherfuckers so they're always smiling. Let's see if we can get into their pocket and bet $60,000."

I still wasn't convinced, but Luco thought for a moment and said, "You know, I think the Brooklyn Boy's right on the money. Fuck it. Let's go down there and bet $60,000."

"Ok," I said. "If we're all in agreement we'll have to see if they'll take the goddamn bet first, and then we'll have to go and see them face-to-face."

So I called Frankie at the Laughing Loggerhead and said, "We'd like to meet you."

"Sure – What's up?" Frankie asked.

"We'd like to get down on Miami."

"Ok, how much?"

"Sixty dollars."

"You'd better come over and see the boss."

So we went over to the bar. When we strolled in, Frankie was already there. He asked us to wait while he got the boss, and after a few minutes he came out with a short, slender Cuban. He had a mustache and was smoking a cigar.

He walked over to the bar, looked at us, and said, "I understand you'd like to get down."

"Yeah, we would – 60 dollars."

He didn't even blink an eye.

"No problem, boys, none whatsoever. I think it's a good bet."

Well ... I was on the edge of my seat for the next 10 days. Finally, Super Bowl Sunday came. The Big Guy and the Brooklyn Boy came over to my house. We had two of the old ladies there, and we started snorting cocaine and drinking.

The game went well, and Csonka and Kick were moving on them. Warfield and Griese were on the same page – it was just beautiful. Right up until the goddamn field goal kicker, Garo Yepremian, screwed up. He kicked the ball into the line, and I think it was Bass who intercepted it and ran it back.

Fortunately, Miami won the game 14 to 7. That was my first major bet, and oh, god ... when we picked up the winnings, it felt *really* good. The best part is that every year when the Super Bowl comes around, I think back to January 14, 1973, and all that money we won, and I get a nice warm feeling.

I still love the Miami Dolphins, but they haven't won another Super Bowl since.

However, since I'm a Boston Red Sox fan I have learned to stay loyal to my team – both in the good times as well as the bad.

Chapter 17: The Pillow

1972

In the last chapter I mentioned the Brooklyn Boy. He was born and raised in Brooklyn, but when he was seventeen years old, he moved to North Miami Beach in the mid-1950s. He was about 5'9" and had long, black hair.

But it was his face that really got your attention. He had a bad acne problem when he was a young boy, and his face was pockmarked. Then when he was fourteen he was working with his uncle in a machine shop and caught a piece of steel in his right eye. Unfortunately he didn't get it fixed because they didn't have the right doctors in those days, and his eye was a little cockeyed. So he was pockmarked and cockeyed which really made an impression when you first met him.

He carried himself just exactly like George Clooney – I mean he fancied himself as a movie star. When I met him in 1972, I was twenty-six, and he was thirty-four or thirty-five.

I loved this man.

We lost him in 1989, but this guy was cool as shit and just a nice, nice man. He was the only Italian that I ever met that didn't know anything about food. He liked Howard Johnson clam strips, and that's kind of ridiculous. I'm from the backwoods of Maine – they tasted like shit then, and I'm sure they still do now.

One day Brooklyn Boy comes to me and says, "I got a guy who's got a guy, and he's got a German. He lives down on the Miami River, but he's an old man. He's like 50."

"Yeah, what's the deal?" I asked.

"This guy built a boat by himself in Holland."

"Wow! That's impressive. Did he sail it all the way over here to Miami?"

"Not only did he sail it all the way over here to Miami, but he's got 20 kilos of hash that he brought over from Holland."

"Wow! No shit? No one's got any hash – that's all up in Canada."

At the time New York City and Boston had some hash, but Miami had no hash.

"The guy that knows this German ... he wants a brokerage fee. And the German, he's gonna sail this boat alone."

"Gonna sail it alone?" I said. "I thought you said he was here?"

"No, no, no – he's here, but he wants to go down to Colombia for us, load it up, and sail it back alone."

"Goddamn! Isn't that a little dangerous?"

"No – he's sailed across the pond all alone. Going across the Caribbean will be easy for him."

Now I was really interested, "Well ... how big is the boat?"

"It's not that big ... about 35 feet long," Brooklyn Boy said, "but if he could load it full, we could get a ton of that Santa Marta Gold. That's 2,000 pounds of Santa Marta Gold."

I couldn't believe what I was hearing. We could get 2,000 pounds of top grade weed. That would be easy to flip.

"How much does he want?" I asked.

"He'll do the whole job alone for $70,000."

"Well ... that's not out of the question. Let's work this thing out."

So we started to make the arrangements – which were really easy, but we ran into a little hook. We found out that the Governor of Magdalena Province had a bastard son that he wanted brought to the United States.

I figured the best thing we could do was offer to bring the boy back on the boat. We could bring the kid into the country and then work out all the papers. This would really hook the connection up and make the connection more solid. The connection would then also owe us a favor. The biggest question was whether the German would go for it.

"There's another problem," I said to the Brooklyn Boy. "My whole family hates Germans and Japanese. That's all I've ever heard my whole life – the Germans, World War II, trouble ... and the Japanese in the Pacific? Oh, Jesus! I've heard terrible, terrible war stories. In fact, my grandmother once told me to never bring home any Asian girls. 'Don't bring an Asian girl back home to the back woods of Maine,' She said, 'she will not be welcome.' Ever since I was little I was told what they did to our boys in World War II. This sailor is German, and he's about 50 years old. Shit, he may have fought in the Hitler Youth or World War II on the side of the Germans."

"Well, what do you suggest we do?" he asked.

I thought about it a moment and said, "Maybe if I meet the guy I can get over all this stuff."

"Ok, let's set up a meeting with him."

We contacted the connection and set up a meeting.

When we talked to him he said he was going to give us a real good deal on the hash. He'd front all the hash to us, and then we would nickel and dime it out – whatever we wanted to do. He just wanted to sail to Colombia, load the boat, and sail back home.

Now I mentioned earlier that this wasn't about the dope, it was a business. And just like any business, people get into it for different reasons. I got started so that I could get free dope, and eventually it lead to a great living. As we talked about it, I realized that this guy just wanted to pay for his sailing adventures. That's why he was doing it, and that was all I needed to know. If he did fight for the Germans in WWII, it really didn't matter. He wanted to make a deal that was good for all of us so that's all it was – just business.

The conversation went really smooth. He agreed to pick up the boy and bring him back along with the hash.

"Ok, let's make the arrangements," I said. "How much money do you need to get down to Colombia?"

"I don't need any money," he said. "Just pay me a down stroke on some of that hash."

Honestly, I don't remember exactly what that shit was going for, but it was pretty good merchandise.

So we sent him down to Riohacho, Colombia.

In those days we didn't need to use the police or the army. The Indians just brought the merchandise down out of the mountains and loaded it right there on the beach. And of course, the Governor brought his bastard son and put him on board. Once the boat was loaded he brought the boat up to the lower keys.

Once the boat arrived we started to unload. There were three of us – Luco, the Brooklyn Boy, and me. Smuggling is very, very exciting. Here it was the middle of the night, and we're unloading a ton of weed from our boat. Oh, god! It just felt good – especially in the Florida Keys at night in October ... just beautiful weather ... beautiful.

It had gone off without a hitch so far. We got the merchandise loaded into the truck, and we got it to a house that we'd rented off Calle Ocho. So we unloaded the merchandise into the house.

I called Rocky and said, "Let's meet."

I met Rocky, and he followed me over to the house.

After he checked out the weed I said, "We have 2,000 pounds of weed, and we want you to move it all".

"Holy shit!" he said. "I can't sell all 2,000 pounds. I'm probably good for 500 pounds. You give me a couple of weeks, and I can move 20 here, 20 there, maybe 30. But you need to break it up so you can maximize your dollars."

"We need the money," I said. "We need to take care of our people and take care of our expenses. We'll give you 200 pounds to get you started. Get it into the street and dump it. We need you to get the first thousand pounds under your belt. On the backside, we can get you the other thousand at a lower the price on the back."

He looked at Luco and the Brooklyn boy and said, "Ok," so we loaded up his car, and he took it to Miami. It was noon before he finally left.

Now we did need the money right away, and I wanted to start the grease rolling as soon as possible. But by 6:30 pm that night, he still hadn't called.

Now Brooklyn Boy was getting impatient and finally said, "Well, what the fuck? I thought you said this guy's always on the money?"

"He usually is," I replied. "He must have got tied up. I'll get another 200 pounds, take to his house, and find out what's going on."

I picked up 200 more pounds and took it over to his house. He lived in one of those little Miami houses where the concrete driveway had room enough for each tire on each side of the car, and there's grass in the middle. The house had Jalousie windows on the front door, and when you went in the back of the house, there was a little Jalousie door that was back in a small Florida room that had a washer and dryer.

At this time I was still a bit naive when it came to smuggling weed. I just backed in my Pontiac and put the weed in the back of his little Florida room. I didn't even think about him not being home. I just set it next to the washer and dryer. When I was done, I got into my car and drove home.

We waited until near midnight, but he still hadn't called us. And this time I was the one who said, "Well, what the fuck? Where is this guy?"

I had just said it, and the phone rang. It was him.

"Well, where have you been, man?!" I asked.

"I've been in jail."

"What? What do you mean you've been in jail?"

"Don't worry," he said, "I've got your money. The fucking police popped me. I was selling merchandise when it happened. Luckily I had already sold most of it. I got your money. Don't worry about it."

"What do you mean?" I asked.

"Well, I got most of your money," he said. "I'm only missing a few thousand dollars ... really! Don't flip out – I didn't rat! I sold most of the merchandise, but I went down for 20 pounds. A friend of mine I'd known since I was a kid ... he set me up."

"So you went to jail ... what was the bond?"

"Oh, my mother came down and bonded me out. The bond was $10,000, She put up 10%. But they fucked me around, kept me down there, and tried to get me to give up who owned the merchandise."

"Really? Do me a favor. Go on out back, and before you do, let's just make sure I understand this correctly ... the police have been to your house and tore your house all to pieces?"

"Oh, they just tore my house apart, but I sold most of the 200 pounds." he said. "I sold it, and I got the money. My mother's got all the money over at her house. Don't worry – I didn't rat you guys out."

"Ok," I said. "We'll see right now. Go in the back and check out your Florida room."

All I could hear was, "Oh, my god."

"That's another 200 I just dropped off," I said.

"Holy shit! Ok – ok, come get what money I have now."

"All right, you've got the 200 pounds, and everything's good. I'll meet you in the same place I met you three days ago where the water is." That was a call signal for going down to Dinner Key Marina in Coconut Grove, so I went down and picked up the money.

When I got back I told Brooklyn Boy and The Big Guy.

"Hey, this motherfucker got popped. I took another 200 over after they popped him. It's in his Florida room, but he's paying. And he didn't flip anymore."

"Fuck this," The Big Guy said. "Let's get this merchandise out of the house right now and take it to New York City. And we don't trust no one going forward!"

I knew this guy from Montreal that had overstayed his visa and was in the country illegally, and he was looking for work. Nice boy, but a total hippie. I offered him $10,000 to drive the merchandise up to Exit 10 on the New Jersey Turnpike to Brunswick, New Jersey. I told him that we'd be up there to pick it up in two days.

But as I was talking to him, I notice that he didn't have a shirt on, and he was bare foot ... it was October. I said, "Where the fuck are your clothes?"

"I live in Key West. I don't have any clothes."

The next morning we got the truck, and we loaded the merchandise. We didn't even pack it up. We just threw the merchandise in the back of the truck, put a padlock on it, and took it over to my house.

After we loaded it all up, I took the guy from Montreal to Kmart and got him some warm clothes, some boots, and some shirts. Then I told him what to do.

"Drive the shit to the Howard Johnson's up on Exit 10 in New Brunswick, New Jersey, and we'll be up there in two days to pick that merchandise up from you. You get ten grand."

"Ok," he said.

As he jumped into the truck I handed him $500 for expenses.

Two days later we flew to New Jersey. We picked up the truck, paid the driver a downstroke, and took the merchandise down to some guys in Princeton. They gave us $4000 and started working it. But after four or five days, they'd only sold like 80 or 90 pounds.

I was more than pissed off, "What the fuck is this? You guys said you could flip some merchandise."

"We're doing the best we can!"

"Well ... that's not good enough!"

The Big Guy said that he had a friend from Key West that ran a candle shop that might be able to help us out.

"Well, where the hell does he live?" I asked.

"He lives in Bedford Stuyvesant."

The Brooklyn Boy looked a bit disturbed and said, “Wait a minute, Bedford Stuyvesant? Hey! No disrespect, but that’s a bad part of town. I don’t know about this. Is he a white boy?”

“Yeah, yeah,” Luco said, “but he grew up in Queens, and he’s a nice guy. Let’s go over and at least check it out. He knows how to flip weed. I met him in Key West so I know this guy real well.”

So we went over to his house. He had an apartment, but he lived right on the edge of the hood. Well, we go upstairs to his apartment, and it was all tripped out. I felt like I was in India.

He had beads hanging everywhere, and you could smell the incense. I was a bit shocked by his appearance because he didn’t have a shirt on, and you could see he was burned all the way down from his neck to his waist. I asked Luco about it later, and he said that he was all fucked up because the candle shop had caught on fire and burned him from his neck down to his nuts.

Even though he was all fucked up, he was a real nice guy. He had another guy with him, but it didn’t look like either one of them were a threat. They looked like just another couple of hippies. We were in cowboy boots, jeans, and leather jackets, and oh, god! The three of us together were a terrible looking bunch of men. We looked mean, and we meant business.

He invited us into the living room and offered us some tea. As the big guy went to sit down the host became alarmed and said, “Oh, no, no, no. Don’t sit on that pillow. Don’t sit on that pillow.”

The Big Guy stopped where he was and politely said, “Ok.”

“The Maharishi Yogi gave us that pillow.” Explained the host.

"The Maharishi Yogi?" Luco asked, "You mean the 13-year-old boy that's kind of big and all over the news?"

"Yeah, he is an incredible, incredible person. We give money to the Maharishi Yogi, and we are devout followers. We are going to spread the word by this herb."

The Big Guy and Brooklyn Boy looked at each other and started to get a little twitchy, but I really didn't think too much of it.

Finally the Brooklyn Boy asked, "Well? Where's the hookah?"

The host loaded up the hookah full of a combination of hash and weed, and we started smoking. It didn't take long to feel like Coconut Grove and Key West. It really felt good, and I got high as a motherfucker ... I was loaded.

All of a sudden the guy who hadn't said much – not the guy that got burned but his friend – started to give this spiel about the Maharishi Yogi and his teachings. Now I was high enough that I started to get caught up in it. I was a little mesmerized when he said, "Life is really nothing but a dream, and we're really not in a state of reality."

It seemed so peaceful and made so much sense to me. Then all of a sudden The Big Guy yells out, "Hey! Shut the fuck up, you flaming fucking asshole!"

It was so sudden that it scared the shit out of me.

The Big Guy continued yelling, "You fucking idiot! No one has the answers in this life. You stupid cocksucker. And if you take our merchandise and give any of that money to the Maharishi Yogi or steal from us, we'll come over here and put this Brooklyn Boy on your ass. Have you lost your mind, you hippie fucking shitbags?"

This snapped me back to reality. I was actually listening to the rap because it sounded kind of fun and good, but when I realized that Luco was right. I looked at the guy and said,

"He's telling you the truth. Don't fuck with us, or that pillow will be the one they use at the hospital."

The two guys looked at us and didn't say another word. We all stood up and walked out the door.

They sold all of the weed and paid in full, but I will never forget that pillow.

Chapter 18:

Burning Down the House

The Big Guy, the Brooklyn Boy, and I were still working our way up the ladder. We didn't have all that much money, but we were doing okay because we were working hard every day. Well, a friend of ours got knocked off for like 100 pounds of pot. They had him locked up, and he needed money for attorneys, bail, and the whole nine yards.

We wanted to help this guy because down the line we knew we were going to need him as another smuggler. I liked this guy because he was a sailor and a Vietnam veteran, and his old lady was always kind and sweet. They were just good people, so we went to work trying to raise some extra cash. And of course ... we had access to cocaine.

Now let me make something very clear here – the cocaine business is always a nightmare. It's very rare for everything to go the way it is planned. Well, this time we bought one pound of blow relatively cheap. It was still in the $7,000 range, but that was pretty cheap at the time. This pound was extra to our normal load so we could get the cash to help out our friend who got busted.

In order to flip it quick we decided to front it to this guy named Marcos. Now Marcos was a good guy, but not one of the guys that you wanted just to go around fronting dope to. But we needed the cash and felt like if he didn't pay us we could intimidate him to make him pay.

So being in the bind we were in and needing the extra cash, we went over to his house. After he let us in I said, "Hey – now listen. We've got a guy in trouble, and we need money for those fucking lawyers. We need money for the bond ... we need money. So we'd like to front you two pounds of blow, and we'll give you a good deal on it."

We had cut the original pound so we now had two pounds that we offered to him for $7,000 a pound which was doubling our money.

Of course he accepted our offer, but I was concerned that there might be some bullshit so I tried to pin him down, "How long is it going to take you to flip this?"

"Well ... give me a couple of days."

"Ok," I said. "We'll leave you alone for a couple of days, but get the money as fast as you can so we can take care of our friend and his old lady. We want to get him out of fucking jail and grease the attorneys."

"Ok."

Well a couple days went by, and we didn't hear from him. So I started to beep him, but he didn't call back. I kept beeping him and beeping him for another entire day, but there was still no answer.

Now I didn't want to just up and go over to his house. I wanted to talk to him first because it was bad manners to show up unannounced. No one ever did that. I was starting to get real upset when around 1:00 or 2:00 in the morning he finally beeped back.

I was all fucked up on dope, but I ran down to the local payphone and called him at the number on my beeper.

"Bro, what the fuck's going on?" I asked when he answered.

"Well, I'm having a little trouble," he said.

"Well, Jesus Christ – you know how important this is," I said. "We've got to get this guy out of the fucking can. We've got to grease those fucking lawyers. You know the attorneys won't do shit unless we grease them."

"Hey, I'm doing the best I can. Get off my fucking back."

"Hey, motherfucker!" I shouted into the phone. "You know what this is all about – what the fuck? Listen, I need that goddamn money!"

He paused for a second and then said, "Let me tell you something. You know where my house is, and you know where I live. I live right behind my mother," and he hung up.

I was so shocked at what he had just said that I continued as if he were still on the line, "You live behind your mother?" but there was no response.

I wasn't sure what he meant so I called Luco, "Hey, fuck face said that he didn't have the money. He got lippy, sassed the shit out of me, and said he lives next to his mother."

"What the fuck's that mean?"

"I don't know," I said.

"What the fuck does that mean?" He repeated. "Let's go over to his fucking house and find out."

So we drove over to his house, and he lived in a small one-bedroom cottage that was behind his mother's three-bedroom house. You had to walk down this long driveway to get to it. Well, we get almost all the way to the end of the driveway, and Luco just took off running. I pulled my gun out, but before I could say anything, he hit the door with his shoulder and it exploded into splinters. That's all it took to get inside the house.

As I entered the house behind Luco I shouted, "Hey, fuck face."

There was no answer – he wasn't home.

I looked around the room. We had walked right into the living room-kitchen. It was like a combo with the bathroom off to the extreme-right corner of the house, and then to the left was his bedroom. I walked into the kitchen and I start tearing it apart. When I was done with the kitchen I started ripping the living room apart. I looked through the couch and some kind of desk, but didn't find anything.

I could hear The Big Guy tearing the bedroom apart. I walked to the door of the bedroom and watched him dump the contents of the last drawer of the dresser onto the floor. Nothing but a pile of clothes. He looked around the room in disgust. He thought for a moment and then looked at the ceiling. It was one of those drop-down ceilings, and he got a smile on his face as he climbed up on the bed. All of a sudden he said, "Ahhhh," and he reached up. He started to pull down one of the tiles, but the whole ceiling came down instead. It scared the shit out of him and he screamed, but it really didn't hurt him.

As the dust settled we had a clear plastic bag full of coke and a bag full of money. We put them both in a pillowcase and left. As we walked out the back door we saw the Sunday paper on the steps.

Luco picked up the paper and said, "I'm going to burn his fucking house down."

"No, no, no," I said. "We've got to get the fuck out of here. What are you? Nuts??" I said laughing.

But he just ignored me and walked back into the house. He started wadding the paper up and tossing it onto the bed. When he was done with the paper he pulled out his lighter and lit it on fire. We walked out of the house, got into the car, and drove off. We just went down the street, hit Lejeune Avenue, and bang! We were gone. I later heard that the fire burned his house right to the ground.

When we got home we discovered that we had $60,000.00 and a half pound of blow in the pillow case.

Now tell me, if he had all that money in his house, why the hell was he being such an asshole in giving us our $14,000? We needed it, he knew we needed it, and he had five times what he owed.

Some people are just assholes on purpose.

Chapter 19:
Jack's No Hippie

The cocaine business was violent and nasty, and there was all kinds of trouble. Many of the people involved would lie, and they were cheating motherfuckers.

The weed game was a little different at first. It was hippie-ish. People thought they were doing good and promoting peace, love beads, music, and Woodstock. It was hippie-fucking shit, and we never really did business that way. We took business very seriously, and we only did the smuggling business for one reason – money ... that's it. It wasn't the glory, the excitement, and all that good shit. (Well, there was that from time-to-time, but that wasn't why we did the game.) We were in the game for the money.

One day I got this call from a guy who I will call "Julio" who I had done business with in the past. Julio said he had 8,000 pounds of weed, and he asked me to do him a favor.

"I need to move this merchandise," he said. "Some other shit has happened to my connections. I won't go into it, but I need to move 8,000 pounds. Will you help me out?"

"Well, of course," I said.

"I have a sample."

"I really don't need a sample. Just put the 8,000 on me, and let me take a look. If it's good I'll front it, and we'll get paid."

"No, no, no," he protested, "the sample's all set up. There's a 250-pound sample in the trunk of a '75 classic Chevy Caprice that you'll need to pick up in the grove."

Luco pick up the vehicle and deliver it to our connections, but when they looked at the merchandise, it was soaked in diesel.

Our connection said that they would take all of the merchandise we could get except the merchandise that was soaked in diesel. No one could sell that.

So I returned to talk to Julio. By the time I got back to his house, he had sold 4,000 pounds.

"Wait a minute," I said. "Here's your sample back. It's soaked in diesel, and you sold 4,000 out from underneath me after you called me and asked for a favor?"

"Well ... yeah."

"Who is responsible for bringing me the sample?"

"My brother."

"Your brother's a drunken fuck!"

"Well, he does drink a little bit."

I was shocked at his attitude, "So your brother brings me a sample of diesel soaked weed. What am I supposed to do with that? Am I supposed to say, 'Oh, what a shame? Oh, you guys are really good just because you're hippies?'"

He didn't say anything but just looked at me like some dumb hippie.

"We're gonna need your brother for that, and we're gonna have to break him a little bit just to teach him a lesson. And, quite frankly, to teach you a fucking lesson for fucking up."

He thought about what I said for minute and said, "Well, I can't give you my brother."

"You can't give us your brother?" I said. "Well, what about you? We'll just take this out on you, and you can pay for both you and your brother."

He turned white as the blood drained from his face, "Can you just sell the 4,000 I have left and let it go?"

"Yeah." I said, "No problem.."

So I took the 4,000 pounds of weed and sold it. It wasn't the best merchandise, but we made a decent profit from it because I kept it and didn't pay him a dime.

This was all part of the game. He was weak and didn't do business the right way, so we took what he owed us plus extra to teach him a lesson. If you did business the right way then we'd do anything to help you out, but if you fucked with us like this guy did you were going to have to pay for it.

Chapter 20:

A Little Bit of Turkey, A Whole Lot of Cocaine

Thanksgiving Day

An acquaintance of my wife invited us to Thanksgiving dinner. I really didn't want to go because the guy was a sleazy junkie, but my old lady was friends with his old lady so I went. Now Thanksgiving dinner in the early '70's meant a little bit of turkey and a whole lot of cocaine. There were a few other people there as well including my friend Luco. We had our turkey with the stuffing and all the trimmings, but not too much because we wanted to leave room for the blow. And it wasn't too long after dinner that we got right into the blow.

At the time Quaaludes were a big deal so we were doing coke and Quaaludes. Our acquaintance and his wife, who I will call "David" and "Jacline", had gone into the bedroom. Somewhere around 10:00 or 11:00 p.m. my wife and I heard somewhat of a ruckus, and at first we just joked about how wild they were in bed.

But then the ruckus led to screams, and Jacline came out of the bedroom with her blouse all ripped up. David had slapped her around. He came stumbling out of the bedroom behind her, and he was having a hard time standing up – he was just all fucked up. Now this guy could snort cocaine. I mean, this was before free-base days and before crack. This was snorting and eating Quaaludes. It's hard for me to tell you how many Quaaludes this guy could eat at a time because you'd just say, "Jack has lost his mind." But this motherfucker could eat Quaaludes. He started with three or four at a time, and eventually worked his way up to eating 15 – 20 Quaaludes. I remember seeing him eat 27 quaaludes.

Why he didn't die from an overdose on Quaaludes, liquor, and cocaine, I have no idea. But anyway ... he was all fucked up. Now even though he could eat a lot of Quaaludes, they made the guy mean, and he walked across the room and started beating and slapping his old lady. In those days and in the dope game, if somebody had a problem with his old lady, it was best to stay out of it. It wasn't your business.

But for some reason I just couldn't stay out of it that day. I stood up and said, "Hey, what the fuck?! Our old ladies are here. It's Thanksgiving, and we're all fucked here. You can't be beating your old lady in front of everybody – it looks bad. C'mon!"

He stopped hitting Jacline and looked at me. After a few seconds, he turned and stumbled his way back into the bedroom and slammed the door. Jacline fell to the floor and was crying. And by the way, his old lady was from Australia – blonde and beautiful! Why she was with this fuck, I have no idea.

As I mentioned earlier, David was kind of a sleazy junkie, but he knew everyone. He knew tons of dope dealers and smugglers, but he did business piss-poor. That's why I didn't want to go in the first place. But like I said, my old lady was friends with his old lady, and you know the deal. Well, my wife went over and consoled Jacline.

I walked over to her and said, "Listen – I'm sorry, baby, but we gotta go."

My wife wasn't happy about that, but she let Jacline know that everything was going to be all right, and then we left.

Well the next day about 4:00 p.m. in the afternoon, I got a beep. I go to the nearest pay phone, call the number, and it was Jacline.

"Jack, I need to talk to you."

"What about?"

"I need to talk to you right away. Do you trust me?"

"Yeah, I trust you," I said. I could tell there was something in her voice that just wasn't right.

"Meet me at the Easy Quick on the corner of 27th Avenue and Bird Road in Coconut Grove."

"When?" I asked. "In an hour?"

"No, come right now. Right now! I'm there right now."

Well, I lived all the way down in the southwest part of town, so it was probably a half-hour from where I was. But I could tell there was something in her voice that just wasn't right. I didn't have a fear that I was getting set up or anything. I thought it was something pertaining to her getting the shit slapped out of her the night before. About 45 minutes later I pulled into the Easy Quick – which we liked to call the Sleazy Quick – and she was standing out front by the pay phone with two shopping bags.

The shopping bags were Burdines bags.

"Jesus," I thought to myself, "that's kind of weird. It looks like she has her clothes."

As I pulled up, she came right over to the car and got into it.

As she got into the car she said, "Jack, I've got eight pounds of cocaine in the bags – four pounds in each bag."

"What?!" I said surprised. "What do you mean you've got eight pounds? What's going on?"

"That motherfucker has slapped me for the last time," she said with determination. "Will you sell the eight pounds of blow for me?"

"Are you sure?" I asked.

"Yes, I trust you, Jack. I know you're a rotten fucker. I know all kinds of bad stories, and I've heard rumors about you. But I trust you because you stood up for me last night. When that fucking clown was beating on me, you stuck up for me."

"I got eight pounds of blow," she continued. "It's his. You sell it for whatever you feel is right, and then give me half of the action."

"I can do that." I said.

"Right now! Take care of the merchandise, and then would you please give me a ride to Fort Myers, Florida?"

"No problem, sweetie."

So I took her down to the Mini Diner which was just south of Kendall Drive on Dixie Highway. It was on the right hand side heading south.

I pulled in and said, "Baby, you just wait right here while I take care of the merchandise."

Well, Luco lived right around the corner so I went to his house. Now it was kind of rude because I didn't beep him, and I didn't call. I just showed up. He was obviously surprised when he came to the door.

"What's going on?" he asked.

"Listen, I got eight pounds of blow. Fuck face's old lady stole it from him."

"What?! Are you shitting me? Is it any good?"

"I don't know," I said. "I didn't even look!"

"Well get the fuck in here."

“Where is she?” he asked as I walked into the house.

“She’s over at the Mini Diner.”

So we opened up the blow and looked at it.

“Holy shit!” Luco said excitedly. “This is from fuck face beating on his old lady in front of us?”

“Yeah,” I gave him a wry smile. “Good Karma for standing up for her.”

We both started to laugh.

“Well ... what the shit?!” he said. “Fuck it! Let’s sell it.”

“Ok,” I said, “but listen – I gotta take her to Fort Myers.”

“When you gonna be back?” he asked.

“I don’t know. Maybe tomorrow.”

So I went back to the Mini Diner, picked her up, and drove her to Fort Myers. When we got there she had me take her to a friend’s house and drop her off. She asked me to come in and meet her friend, so I parked the car and went in to meet her friend. Well ... one thing led to another, and I ended up spending the night in Fort Myers with these two gorgeous women. We had a great night the three of us.

The next morning I drove back to Miami. Luco and I flipped the blow in a couple of days, and a few days later I gave Jacline her end.

Chapter 21:

In a Killing Mood

Miami 1973

Once the money started to roll in, I rented a house. It was perfect because it was a secluded place down in the southwest part of Miami. It had five acres of land and a giant fence with three strands of barbed wire at the top. It even came with two German Shepherd guard dogs. I had a very well trained Doberman pinscher that I had owned for a couple of years. I knew a marine who'd worked with dogs in Vietnam and asked him to help me train her. Not only was she trained in obedience, she was also trained to bite. She would heel, come, sit, and stay – she did all of it, and she was just beautiful.

I got rid of the two German Shepherd attack dogs and instantly set up shop. I was doing all sorts of action in this house – I was making PCP pills, flipping kilos of blow, and in the middle of smuggling operations.

It was around Christmas time, and I, of course, was running in and out and doing business. My wife had gone to the doctor and had taken the dog. The only drawback to the house was it was across the street from a huge complex of blacks. It was a large ghetto project – the only one in the neighborhood, and it ran for blocks and blocks. All the rest of it was basically white, single, double-family houses, but there was this one project.

When we came home, the house had been robbed. They got $4,000 in cash, a 9mm pistol, and all of my wife's jewelry. Now my wife was big into all that turquoise shit from New Mexico and Arizona, and a lot of it was beautiful

... I mean beautiful, so of course she was terribly upset. Well, I was a convicted felon so I didn't know what the fuck to do. I decided to call my attorney, and he said, "Don't worry. I'll send over a detective."

A short time later two detectives arrive. When I answered the phone they got right to business and said, "We understand that you're a friend of Lee George, the attorney."

I answered that I was. The detective then said, "He's a friend of ours as well. What did you lose?"

I didn't say anything about the money, but of course I had to report the pistol because it was in my wife's name. I told him a Browning 9mm and my wife's jewelry was missing.

The Detective took some notes, and when he was done he said, "You can forget about that gun, and more than likely you can forget about the jewelry. Who do you think did it?"

"It kind of points to the black guys from the ghetto down the street."

"How do you know that?"

"Well ... look how they came in through the screen over by the pool. And if you walk to the fence in that same direction and keep going, you get to the ghetto project."

The Detectives and I walked across the property, and when we got to the fence, we found some Popsicle sticks.

As one of the detectives picked up one of the Popsicle sticks he said, "Oh, Jesus Christ. Yes, it's them."

We went back into the house, and the detective that had done most of the talking said, "Would you mind stepping outside with us a little bit? We'd like to talk to you."

"No problem."

Once we were outside and out of earshot of my wife, he turned to me and said, “Hey, do you want to kill those fucking niggers?”

“Oh, fuck, yeah, I want to kill them. I want to kill them real bad.”

He just nodded and said, “We can set it up. Every day, move your car somewhere else. You come back late at night, 2:00 or 3:00 in the morning so your car is not in the driveway. And then every morning at 9:00, have your wife take the dog out. You put a little mattress down right behind the couch facing the sliding glass door the same way they came in. Can you get your hands on a shotgun?”

“Yeah,” I said, “my friend’s got a 12-gauge.”

“Good. Double 00 buck five shots. Let them come through the door and just give it to them. Fucking take them the fuck out.”

After they left I called my friend and asked him if I could borrow his 12 gauge. He wanted to know why and I told him. He just laughed and handed me his gun with a box of shells.

I sat in that house for more than two weeks waiting on them. Do you think they came back? No – every day my wife took the dog out. I was trying to get them. Oh, was I trying to get them! What really pissed me off was that I could hear them rattle that 9mm, boom-boom-boom, every fucking night. It drove me crazy.

I never did get them.

Chapter 22:

Moving to California and Meeting the Drummer

California 1974

In 1974, problems came up among the different groups that were smuggling and dealing dope. It started to get too hot for us, so we decided to move until things cooled down. I knew a few people in San Francisco so we moved to California.

I hadn't been there but maybe a month, and I ran into this guy that was with a household name rock-n-roll band. He was the drummer, and I clicked with this guy immediately. Through cocaine, shooting the shit, and drinking whiskey, this guy became a great friend of mine.

Over the next several years we spent many a night at the clubs – drinking, snorting cocaine, and chasing pussy. It was unbelievable. He was a New Jersey boy, and he had served in the Navy as well.

He wasn't just one of those rock-n-roll guys that was some little faggot pussy motherfucker; he was a bad-ass Jersey boy. I liked this guy, and we started doing a little business with him. The next thing I knew, he was selling Quaaludes, cocaine, and heroin. I didn't really involve him in any smuggling trips, but certainly drug dealing. Oh boy, could this guy move some merchandise!

And pussy ... pussy just seemed to hang on him. I mean everywhere he went everyone knew who he was, and pussy would just come. We banged a lot of girls during that time.

We were doing very well, and I had a number of new cars including a brand new Benz, and a Trans Am. I just traveled around with this guy. I wouldn't see him every night of the week, but certainly no more than ten days, two weeks would go by, and I'd be craving some of that action. We would travel all over Northern California – Fairfax, San Anselmo, San Francisco, and back and forth to L.A.

In 1980 I left California and moved back to Florida, but I stayed in very, very close touch with the drummer.

I guess it was about a year or so later when I got a call from this guy. He was still in Los Angeles, and it turned out his band really fucked him over. He wanted to get even with them.

"Hey," he said, "you know that band that fucked me over?"

"Yeah," I said. "You got any problems?"

"Well," he said, "I did a little move on 'em."

"What do you mean?"

"They really hung me out to dry – really stuck it up my fucking ass, and they treated me like a little fuck boy. They just did me wrong, and cheated me out of millions of dollars, and I mean millions. So I didn't get a lot, but I got a little bit of payback."

"What did you do?" I asked.

"I used this girl, and she robbed them."

"Of what?"

"Cocaine."

"Cocaine?" I said a little surprised. "Ok, buddy – how many?"

"I got 'em for 17 kilos."

"Really? You got 17 kilos of blow?"

"Yeah, but it's been some time since I sold any of this shit." He said, "I'm not sure how to sell it, and I really don't want to cause any trouble. I don't want to draw any attention to myself. Can you help me out?"

Now if you're not in the dope business, 17 kilos is a lot. Any dealer in the business would know that moving this amount of dope could get you knocked off by the man. I was always cautious, but I knew I could help my buddy out.

"Fuck yeah," I said. "I'll come right out. We'll bring it back to Miami, and I'll flip it."

"Oh, man – that would be great!"

"Now listen," I said. "I'm going to have a driver so I'll come out with the boys. I'll come out with The Big Guy – you remember Luco. We'll have the driver take it back to Miami, and you, Luco, and myself will fly back to Miami, and we'll flip the merchandise in town."

"Fantastic," he said. "I have to get out of this fucking town anyway."

So Luco and I flew out to L.A., and I had the Packer drive the van out. When he arrived, we packed it all up and sent him back to Miami. Then we got on the plane with the drummer and flew back to Miami.

Everything was going good – we started flipping the merchandise and making some serious cash off of it. We were almost done when the drummer said we should celebrate.

"Shit," he said, "let's grab a half an ounce and chase some pussy."

Now Miami's my town, and I know where to get the girls. So we got the girls and had our party. Of course these were working girls, and the best thing about a working girl is when she leaves in the morning.

Well ... after we played with these girls for a few days, Luco says, "Fuck it! Let's keep snorting blow, go over to Miami Beach, and shoot some pool."

Now it was almost midnight, but we were so fucked up from the dope and banging these girls for three days that it just seemed like the right thing to do. We also had money up the ass because the blow was going good. Blow was going for like $30,000 ... $30,000 plus. The drummer boy had cleaned the band's clock for over a half a million dollars. My end of that deal was $170,000– just for flipping it for him.

We went to this little bar off Washington on Miami Beach. We were all high, but Luco was really messed up. He had eaten too many Quaaludes that night. We had a rented a Pontiac, and Luco was in the back seat.

As we pulled up to the bar Luco said, "Hey listen! You guys go in, shoot some pool, and have some drinks. I'm just going to crash out – I'm all fucked up."

So the drummer boy and I went into the bar and left Luco sleeping in the back seat of the car. We started drinking and shooting pool then after a few rounds, we went in the bathroom and started snorting blow. Now it was the early '80's, so anyone coming in didn't give us a second look. But these two guys – regular white boys – walk in and see us. They talked to each other for a few seconds, and then one of them said, "Hey! You guys want to shoot a game of pool with us?"

We looked at each other and then said in unison, "Sure!"

So we shot a game, and oh how the drummer boy and I were on the money because we didn't give a fuck. We were drunk and high as shit, but the drummer boy made the first shot – cross-cornered. I mean it looked just sweet. I was making cross-sides, and we were just pounding them.

Then they stopped the game and said, "Hey! Do you want to shoot for some money?"

Well, the drummer and I were just in t-shirts, jeans, and cowboy boots. I mean we looked like we could have had $20 million, or we could have had $20 – you just couldn't tell.

I looked at the drummer, and I knew he was thinking the same thing. These guys have got to be the stupidest fucks in the world. We were pounding them into the ground, and they wanted to play for money.

"Well ... sure," I said.

I think we decided on $5 or $10 a game ... some nickel-dime shit, but we couldn't lose. I mean the drummer boy and I were on, and it was back and forth. We were really having a good time, and we weren't running a game down on these guys – we were just having fun. We were laughing, but we weren't making fun of them or laughing because we were whipping their fucking asses – they just didn't have a chance ... they didn't have a fucking prayer.

It was one of those rare nights where everything went our way ... one of those nights when you get really, really on. And I mean I can't say enough about the drummer boy; he was playing Willie Mosconi fucking bullshit. He was great, and we were cleaning their clocks.

We played several games, and we probably had them for a couple of hundred dollars. I think what broke their back was this amazing shot by the drummer. The cue was right down in the corner, and the drummer boy ran it up the rail – right from corner to corner up the rail.

It was so amazing, and I said, "Hey, great shot! Un-fucking real!" I smiled, and it was kind of like those two motherfuckers didn't even count.

And they got pissed.

I don't know why. It wasn't like I had bad manners or anything. They just didn't count – they were just a couple of shmucks. And a couple of hundred dollars to the drummer boy and me didn't mean a fucking thing anyway. We were just cleaning their ass.

"Hey," one of them yelled at me. "You two hustling us?"

I looked at them and said, "What? What the fuck are you talking about?"

Now the drummer boy and I are not great big strapping country boys or rednecks, we were just city boys. And it doesn't take much to get us going. Both of us got some mouth on us, but both of us can back it up.

Now me personally ... in 1981, I would shoot your ass just like that. The drummer boy wasn't so quick with a gun, but he was quick with a knife. He'd cut your balls off just for the hell of it.

I said, "Fuck you, you mother fucks. We're not hustling anybody. $200? What? You motherfuckers don't have $200? Get the fuck off the beach, and get the fuck over to Liberty City. Go somewhere else you fucking pussy cocksuckers."

"Well try this on for size. He said as he grabbed a beer bottle and smashed in on the bar.

Now I didn't want to shoot 'em, and the drummer boy didn't want to cut 'em, but reality set in. We realized that we were both fucked up, so we started edging our way towards the door.

That's when they start coming towards us – one of them had a pool cue, and the other one had a bottle. It's like a Mexican movie where he smashed 'em all, and now he was gonna cut us.

We moved outside through the front door with these two white boys right behind us ready to attack. As soon as the drummer boy was on the sidewalk he started shouting, "Get the Luco! Get the Luco!"

Both of the white boys stopped, and one of them said, "Get the Luco? What the fuck does that mean?"

I yelled, "Luco! Luco!"

And out of the car came 345 fucking pounds of Sicilian with his hair all disheveled and completely fucked up. Now that's a motherfucker you do not want to wake up on a good day! He came out sweating with a stain of some tomato sauce on his goddamn Dago t-shirt.

He screamed out of that Bonneville, "What?"

I pointed at the two white boys and said, "We got trouble with these two motherfuckers."

Luco came running across the street screaming, "I'll kill you, you dirty fucks!"

While he was screaming, the two white boys threw down their weapons and then threw their hands into the air and started yelling, "We're sorry! We're sorry, bro!"

As Luco stopped next to us, one of the white boys reached into his pocket, pulled out a wad of cash, and said, "How much do we owe you?"

The drummer boy and I just started laughing.

It still makes us both laugh to this day.

Chapter 23: Fingers, Pills, and a .45

California 1975

As I mentioned earlier, I had a little problem and had to move to California in 1974. In the later part of '74, I decided to call Bobby. He was still living in New Jersey.

"Hey, what are you doing?" I asked.

"I'm working for UPS." (I don't know if UPS was started, but it was one of the mail services ... maybe it was even the post office ... whatever. The point is, he was driving delivery trucks.)

"You're a packer, huh?" (And that is where he got his nickname.) "Well, fuck that," I said. "Quit, and come on out here. We'll start you right away at $1,000 a week, all expenses paid – rent, house, food, money, dope. I even know some girls, and I'll introduce you."

"Are you shitting me? Really?"

"Yeah," I said.

"What else?"

"I don't know," I said. "Get the fuck out here, and we'll talk about it."

So he came out to California, and as soon as I saw him he asked, "What do you do?"

"Well," I said, "I do all kinds of shit. You know ... I'm in the dope game. I sell dope. I sell coke. I sell pills. I sell anything. I don't give a fuck what it is."

"Sounds good. Let's get to work."

So Bobby started working with us, and he would wind up being with me for the next 30+ years.

You know, some guys say they've got a friend. Well ... this guy's my friend. This guy is still my friend today whether I've been up or I've been down, whether I've been in the penthouse, the basement, or prison; whether people turned on me, shit on me, or caused me all kinds of trouble – if I lost my homes, my houses ... lost everything, had nothing, and was in the street ... he's still my friend. Fuck, he's my brother. I love him, and I love him because he is my real friend. Fuck with me, no problem. But you fuck with him, and you deal with me.

Now I told you a story earlier about a friend in the hog tranquilizer business. Well, we had nicknamed this guy Fingers. He was a guy that was never happy, and he always had a scowl. But I don't really want to badmouth him because in a way, I kind of liked the guy. He just had a few idiosyncrasies.

He lived off of 117th Avenue in Miami, and before I moved to California, I went to see him. I pulled into his neighborhood, and I saw a big cloud of smoke. "Oh, Jesus – I hope it's not him," I thought to myself. But as pulled up to the gate, I saw that there was a pretty good size fire going on in his driveway.
"Open the gate," I yelled up.

He opened the gate, and I drove up to where the fire was. As I got out of the car I saw that it was a pile of lady's clothes including boots, pants, and shoes. Fingers was just standing there watching the entire pile burn.

"What's that?" I said as I walked up to him.

"Oh, that's just my old lady's clothes and the rest of her shit."

I then realized that it wasn't just her clothes that were in the middle of the driveway on fire, but it was everything she owned including her guitar.

"What the hell's going on?" I asked.

"Oh, that bitch is causing me nightmares. You can't believe what the bitch has done – she's run off. And I just said, 'Fuck it. I'm tired of it', so I set all of her shit on fire."

Now that should give you an idea about this guy. He was sort of in and out of it. He could flip out easy, and he was very anti-guns. He never owned a gun and never wanted one.

But he did have some of the finest weed. He had those round 25 block cylinders ... Santa Marta Gold. He always had great cocaine and heroin as well.

Anyway ... Fingers had moved to California roughly at the same time as I did, and shortly after we got there, I did one deal with him for a million hits. But then two months went by, and I didn't hear from him. That really bothered me.

When I tried to call him, all of his numbers had been changed. I thought that was kind of odd because he was sort of like clockwork on turning thousands and thousands and then eventually millions of hits of PCP and THC. It was very strange that I had lost touch with him.

Eventually he called me, and he said, "Listen – I've got a new number, but I've been out of operation for a while. I've had a couple of little medical issues, and I'd like to come over and see you."

"Sure, come on over," I said.

When he showed up, he has a very strange concoction. I've never seen anything like it before or since. He had a wire that went through his fingernail on his left hand then stretched back and was actually hooked into the bone of his elbow.

I was more than surprised.

"What the hell happened?"

"Oh, I got all fucked up," he said, "and I yelled at the old lady. We got in a big fight, and I decided I was going to shoot her cat."

"What old lady? I thought that she left you, and you burned her shit?"

"I got a new one."

"You don't even have a gun," I said.
"Well, I started buying some guns."

"But you never had any guns," I said. "You were always anti-gun."

"Yeah, but once I got to shootin' 'em, I fell in love."

Fingers was one of those guys that never grew up with guns as a kid, but came into a great deal of money because of dope so eventually he bought up every gun he could get his hands on.

Fingers told me that he had the cat in his right hand, and he was threatening to shoot it. Whether he did or did not, I do not know. But somehow – because he was all fucked up on dope – he had his middle finger up near the action of a .45 pistol. When he fired the gun, the action came back and literally cut off the middle finger of his left hand. They had to sew it back on, stitch it up, tape it, and run those wires up to his elbow.

Subsequently he came down with the name Fingers.

"That's an interesting story," I said, "but what about business?"

"I'm gonna have to postpone that. I've got some family issues I've got to take care of, but I've got some weed."

He had a few hundred pounds of weed that he'd brought out from Miami. He fronted it to me, and I flipped it for him. I didn't really think too much of that except that it was kind of weird because he was sort of like clockwork on turning those multiple hits of PCP, so I was suspicious.

About two weeks went by, and I got a call from a Dr. Quack from some mental institution north of San Francisco. (And I'm not making that up. His name really was Dr. Quack.) If it hadn't been so early in the morning, I would have died laughing. But it was close to 7:30 am, and the call had woken me up.

After he introduced himself he asks me if I was Jack, and I said, "Yeah, I'm Jack."

"Jack, we have Fingers up here in the mental institution."

"For what?"

"Well, his wife had overdosed on PCP, cocaine, and Quaaludes so he called an ambulance. When the ambulance showed up, the police came. And when the police came, they found all kinds of PCP – actually, pounds of it and a couple of pill machines. It looked like he had a setup to produce and manufacture PCP pills."

"Ah ... and he is asking you to call me for what reason?"

"Well, his bond is $250,000, and he wants you to come bail him out."

As soon as I hung up the phone I woke up the old lady and said, "Ok, pack up this shit right now. We've got to get the fuck out of here."

So we got up, went right upstairs, packed up all our stuff, and split. We ended up in a motel, and as soon as we were settled I called a couple of my boys and had them move the rest of the house into storage.

I waited about a week, and then went to a payphone to call his house.

When his old lady answered I said, "What the hell's going on?"

"Jack, he got all fucked up, and he decided that he wanted to cut you out of the action and go into business for himself. On the first night of business I overdosed, and the ambulance came and busted him. He never actually sold a hit."

"What the fuck?" I said. "I never did anything wrong to him. In fact, I know he's always been weird, but I never did anything wrong to him."

"I know, Jack. I know," she said quietly. "There's another thing. I need your help."

"With what?"

"He's got a safety deposit box in Miami. I have the power of attorney on the box, and there's $220,000 in it. I just want $100,000, and I'll sign over the power of attorney to anyone you want so you can get the money. If you will go down to Miami, get the box, and take care of the attorneys, you can keep $120,000 and give me $100,000."

"No problem whatsoever," I said, even though I knew right then and there that I was going to keep the entire $220,000 when I got it.

Then she laid it out, "I've got his connection with me right now."

"His connection?"

"Yes," she said, "He'd like to talk to you about doing some business."

I was very leery about this. I was sure it was some type of set up. Before I could say no the connection came on the phone and begged me to please continue to do business with me. I asked him a million questions to try to determine if he was working for the police, but he didn't come across as someone trying to hide something. My gut feeling was that he was ok, but I wanted to be sure. So I ran him through all kinds of games to make sure he wasn't working with the police. Once I was sure he was ok, I decided that Finger's old lady wasn't so bad and I wouldn't steal her money. I asked the connection to put the girl back on.

"Ok," I said, "We need to get the paperwork signed. When would you like to meet?"

Can you come over tonight?"

"Well, no. I'm in L.A."

"Well ... can you come up?"

"No, I can't", I said. "Why don't you come down to Los Angeles? I'll have a friend of mine pick you up at the airport."

"Ok."

"I'll call you back in exactly two hours."

In those days, PSA flew back and forth between L.A. and San Francisco –practically on the hour, 18 hours a day. So the following day, she flew into L.A., and I had a friend of mine pick her up.

At that time I had the right attorneys on retainer, and I had asked them how to work it all out. They drew up all the paperwork, and I took her to their office where she signed over her power of attorney. Then I sent her on her way, and I flew to Miami.

Once I got to Miami, I went to see Lee George, my attorney. Once he made sure all of the paperwork was in order we went to the bank and gave them the power of attorney. They brought the box right up, but there was a problem, there was a sticker on the box. Luckily one of my attorneys knew the Bank President. He handed him $5,000 and the Bank President peeled the sticker off. Once the sticker was off of the box they took out the $220,000 and put it into a briefcase that we had brought with us.

The attorney took me to his house in Miami. I gave him $40,000 and kept $180,000. We sat down and had some drinks and thought everything was good. At the time he was married and he lived in a townhouse in a place out on Kendall Drive called Kendale Lakes, and it was very nice. When you walked into the townhouse you walked into the living room and to the left was a staircase that went up to a couple of bedrooms. Straight ahead through the living room was a kitchen and then you could walk out onto kind of a yard. It was fenced in and had a grill.

At roughly 6 o'clock that evening Lee was grilling food and the doorbell rang.

His wife was in the kitchen and said, "Don't worry, honey. I'll get it."

She walked through the kitchen and answered the door.

A few seconds later she said, "Honey, it's the IRS."

I looked at Lee and he looked at me. We didn't say a word. I grabbed the briefcase with the money in it and we just ran straight out through the sliding glass doors, across the yard, past the grill, climbed right up over the fence and into the street out back. Lee had a Porsche that he always parked in the back. We went over the fence, jumped into the Porsche and we left immediately for Palm Beach. Once we got to Palm Beach he dropped me off at a hotel. The following morning I caught a flight out of Palm Beach. I think it went through Atlanta and then on to San Francisco.

When I got back to San Francisco I gave the $100,000 to Finger's wife, and I kept $80,000. That was the last day I was in the pill business with Fingers.

Fingers, if you're out there right now reading this, get a hold of me. I never did a fucking thing wrong to you, man.

Get a hold of me just to say hello, and let me know that you're still alive.

Chapter 24: Through the Roof

California 1975

Sometimes what happens after running a load or a smuggling trip can be just as dangerous as the smuggling itself.

A friend of mine called me from New York City who I hadn't seen since I left Coconut Grove. He was coming out to California and wanted to know if we could get together to have lunch and talk business.

So he flew out, and we met up in the Marina district of San Francisco. While we are eating lunch he told me about a smooth little weed smuggling operation that he had going with the Colombians. The weed was grown on the west slopes of the Andes and then loaded onto a freighter on the island of Gorgona, just off of the coast of Buena Ventura, and then smuggled into Seattle.

"Jack, I need your help."

"Sure, what do you need?"

"In the last shipment the Colombians brought up 12,000 pounds," he said. "Something happened. I don't want to get into the details, but I've got 8,000 pounds left. There's just one problem."

"What's that?" I asked.

"This weed is strange."

"What do you mean it's strange?" I asked.

"It's not Santa Manta Gold. It looks like a small version of Jamaican collie, like collie buds, but only about one fifth their size. But it's good herb."

"That is strange," I said. "What do you need me to do?"

"If you can get the right boys to drive it back across the United States – 4,000 pounds to New York City, and 4,000 pounds down to Miami – I'll kick you $50 a pound, plus I'll pay each one of the drivers $40,000."

"All expenses included – airline tickets, hotels, and meals?" I asked.

"Yes."

"Ok," I said, "when do you need the transport?"

"As soon as you can get everything together. Just come up to Seattle and walk us through what you want to do and how you want to pack it."

"No problem," I said. "We can be there in three days, but I'll need some cash up front to pay the expenses."

He handed me $12,000. That afternoon I called a couple of my boys from Miami, and we went up to Seattle. We met my friend at the address that he gave me. After some small talk he took us to where he kept the weed. He was right – it was very, very strange looking shit ... very weird. But that was none of my concern. It was just $50 a pound to me.

We had rented a couple of Ryder trucks to transport it. In order to hide the merchandise, we come out about 2½ feet from the back of the truck with 2"x4"s, and then built false walls out of plywood. We painted them white because the insides of all the Ryder trucks in those days were painted white.

We put 4,000 pounds behind each false wall in each truck.

Next, we had to find some furniture, so my friend took us down to a used furniture store. I remember the main sales guy because he was a nice, nice guy.

I walked up to him and said, “Hey, listen! I’m gonna need enough furniture to take care of a couple of small rentals.”

“Where are the rentals?” he asked.

“I don’t really want to say. Just give me a price.”

“Well, what do you want for your rentals?”

I told him I wanted beds, a refrigerator, a stove, a couch, and all the other furniture I would need to fill a small rental unit.

Now the furniture was just shit –it was junk. And as the boys are loading the furniture into the trucks, I looked over in the corner. There was a lawnmower there, and I said, “I’ll take that lawnmower too.”

The whole idea was to fill the truck full of furniture. If you opened up the back of the truck, it just looked like any moving truck. We ended up spending about $5,000 for each truck of used furniture. I stuck the lawnmower right in the back – right where you lift up the back of the truck. I emptied all the gas out of it and cracked the cap. If the drivers were stopped on the way across the country by the police for whatever reason, the cops would get a nice whiff of gasoline.

We loaded up all the trucks and they took off – one to Miami, and one to New York. As soon as they were gone I said goodbye to my friend, and I flew back to San Francisco to celebrate.

When I got home I called a friend of mine to come over, and we started snorting cocaine. Once I started snorting coke, I didn’t stop until it was gone. After doing dope for a bit, I went and played cards with some other friends. While I was there I started drinking, and I was in a real good mood. I had just done a job for $400,000, and I really didn’t have to do anything. I decided I liked brokerage fees.

So I was drinking, playing cards, doing more blow, and they even had a couple of girls come by for added entertainment. We drank, snorted, and fucked all night. When I left it was just about daylight.

Now I lived up on top of the mountain in Fairfax. On the way home, the last stop I made was at this bar called River City which was right downtown. Nice place, and a nice guy who owned the place. I continued playing cards, drinking, and snorting blow for another couple of hours before I got in my car to head home.

A few weeks earlier I had bought a brand new Mazda. The ads all bragged about how fast they were with the rotary engines, etc. I had never heard of that before. I just remember that I spent $5,400 for a brand new car and paid cash. Back then that was a lot of money for a car, and I soon learned that it was a quick car for its time.

I started for home drunk and completely fucked up. I was going right along, and there was a 90-degree turn you had to make to go up over the top of the mountain where I lived. Just before I got to the turn I got this amazing idea – I was going to take the turn like they did in the movies, so I shifted into low gear and floored it.

I didn't even come close to making that turn.

I lost control of the car and flew off the road right onto the roof of a man's home.

I didn't just drive onto the roof. I drove right through the roof and into the kitchen. The front part of the car was literally inside his kitchen.

I can still remember touching myself and saying, "Damn! I didn't even get hurt out of this."

I was so discombobulated that I thought I could get out of there before anyone noticed. So I grabbed the stick, stuck it in reverse, and floored it. I was blowing shingles like 30 feet up in the air right off the man's roof.

I couldn't understand why I wasn't going anywhere and said out loud, "Oh, for Christ's sake! Where am I?"

Then I opened the door and fell out. I landed on the roof, bounced off, and fell down into a flower garden. Now that did fuck me up – I was hurt then.

But I remembered that I had dope and a gun in the car, and I had probably $12,000-15,000 cash on me.

"Oh, no!" I shouted.

As I tried to get up, I looked up and there was a man with his wife and his little children all standing there in their pajamas looking at me.

"Oh, my god," I half said. "Sir, I'm terribly sorry – I lost control. I'm sorry, sir. I'll pay for your roof ... please don't worry about anything. I'll pay."

He walked over to me and said, "No, don't worry about that. Are you okay?"

He was more concerned for me than his home.

"Yeah, I'm all right," I said as I half attempted to stand up.

"Well let me help you," he said.

He sat me up next to the side of the house and asked, "Would you like to have a drink of brandy?"

"Yeah, that would be nice."

He disappeared for a minute then came back out and handed me a small glass of brandy. I could hear the sirens in the distance as I shot down the brandy. I looked up, and there's the car stuck right through the roof of this man's home. It was a terrible looking situation, but the man said, "Jesus, this is really, really exciting!"

All I could do was keep saying I was sorry. Then the police showed up, and you can imagine what they were saying. I could hear them talking and whispering to each other – drunk ... high on dope ... dope dealer, etc.

Finally, one of them said, “What are we gonna do with this motherfucker?

That’s when the home owner stepped up and said, “Oh, no. Hey! The only thing this man’s guilty of is he can’t drink. He was cold sober when he hit my house. I gave him one glass of brandy to calm his nerves, and he just got drunk.”

I was so shocked, or maybe I was just so fucked up, that I just sat there listening to the conversation.

The man continued, “He’s my neighbor – he lives up on top of the hill. He lives right next to Phil Lesh of the Dead up on top of the hill. He’s a nice guy, and I just want you to tow his car home and take care of him.”

“Jesus,” I thought, “what a guy.”

Of course I didn’t know he was a big time Marin County attorney. I didn’t realize that because I had never met this man. All I could say was, “Jesus, sir – I’m sorry.”

“Don’t worry about it,” he said. “I’m not going to be pressing any charges.”

So I was never arrested, and the police didn’t say anything. The wrecker just pulled the car off the roof. It was smashed all to hell – completely totaled. After they dragged my car up over the bank and I got in the wrecker, he took me and the car home.

As I got out of the wrecker my wife came out and said, “Jack, what happened?”

“I lost control of the car and drove through a roof. Just as soon as the wrecker gets out of here there’s some shit in the car I gotta get. There’s a gun in there, and there’s some dope. Everything’s good ... just let me get that shit out of there, and I need to go to sleep. I’m tired.”

As soon as the wrecker drove down over the hill I grabbed the gun and whatever little blow was left, went in the house, and went to bed.

When I woke up the following morning I was in terrible shape. I could hardly move so I just laid up and rested for a few days. When I started feeling better, I went downtown to get a drink at a little bar in Fairfax called Naves.

I went into Naves and ordered a double shot of vodka. And as I'm waiting for my vodka, I looked down at the end of the bar, and there's the attorney whose roof I had driven into.

He was sitting down at the end of the bar with Phil from the Dead. I had never met Phil even though I lived next door to him, but everyone knew who he was. I didn't want to look like a groupie or say anything because I knew he wouldn't like that so I respected his privacy and stayed away.

The attorney nodded to me, so I strolled down to the end of the bar.

As I sat down on the bar stool next to the attorney he says, "Hey, you owe me $100."

So I broke out the roll, whipped out a hundred and said, "Here you go."

"Don't you want to know why?" he asked.

"No, I don't care," I said. "After all the trouble I caused you, it was unbelievable."

He laughed and said, “Well, I got a $100 deductible on the house.”

“No, shit,” I said.

He nodded and then introduced me to Phil. It was nice to finally be able to talk to my neighbor. As we had our drinks and talked, I realized my luck of the devil had saved me again.

From that point forward I didn’t worry about much. I just did my job knowing that it would all work out … and it usually did.

Chapter 25:

Falsely Accused of Murder

1976

In 1976 a friend of mine, and I mean a really good friend, was murdered in Coconut Grove. It was tragic because this man was really a sweet, sweet guy.

I had needed some money and had been doing some business down in Florida a few weeks before this terrible thing happened. I had put up a large sum of money and needed about $100,000 more, so I went over to his house. This guy was a junky, but not in the traditional sense where he was just a fucking dirty slob who didn't do anything and was a sleaze ball. No, this guy was a health nut. He loved to surf, he loved the water, and he loved to dive. But he also liked to shoot heroin, snort cocaine, take pills, and smoke marijuana as well – he did it all.

Well anyway, I went over to his house and told him that I needed some money to make a purchase on some weed. I needed the down stroke, and I was light about $100,000. When he asked me where I was going to be taking it, I told him I was taking it to New York City. After I explained what I needed, he said it would be no problem and asked me to follow him up to his bedroom. So I went up to his bedroom with him. He pulled down a fake wall panel, and he had $600,000 in the wall in 100's, 50's, 20's. He counted out $100,000 and gave it to me. We didn't discuss terms because it was understood that I would pay him back with interest in either cash or some of the merchandise I got.

After I left, I immediately started to flip the weed. Originally I was planning on taking the weed to New York City, but I ended up taking most of it to Gainesville, Florida, where I ran into some problems and couldn't sell all of the merchandise. Since I couldn't sell all of it, I did not get back the initial amount he had loaned me.

Normally I would have never treated this guy like this. I would have called, given him an update, and told him what the hell was going on. But I just didn't want to hear any shit, so I didn't call him.

After a couple of weeks of frustration I finally took the merchandise to California. I hadn't been there two days when I got the word that my friend had been shot, and he was dead. He had been murdered.

I was able to move the merchandise in California, and eventually, I sold all the weed I had purchased. A couple of weeks went by without any issues, but then one day I got a call from my attorney in Miami.

"There are people looking for you," he said. "They're looking to blame you for the thing that happened in the Grove."

"What the fuck?" I responded. "I didn't have anything to do with that."

"No, but the families have gotten together and hired a private investigator. He wants to know if I will come out to California with him and do a polygraph on you."

"No," I answered immediately.

"Jack, listen. They're applying a lot of heat."

I thought about it for a minute and then asked, "What's this gonna cost me?"

"I've got a client out in L.A. So if you pay me a couple thousand dollars, I'll come out because I have to see this other client. I'll only be there while this private detective administers the polygraph."

"No problem," I finally said.

"Good," he responded. "Of course you're not going to take it if you had anything to do with it, so I'm going to ask you straight out. Do you know anything about it?"

"Absolutely not. Not a thing."

"Ok, and just so you are aware of the situation, the reason they're trying to put this on you is because you borrowed $100,000 from the guy a couple of weeks ago."

"Well, damn," I said. "I know that looks bad, but son of a bitch, I loved this guy. He was my friend, and I did not have anything to do with it whatsoever. I don't even know anything about it."

"Ok then, don't worry about a thing. I'll be there when he conducts the polygraph, and everything will work out all right."

I figured that I'd need some security so I went to speak to a friend of mine who lived in L.A. because a friend of his was a biker. He didn't have a large biker club, but they were established in the area and had a substantial following. There were about 40 bikers in his group, and this guy was the president. But he wasn't a traditional biker. He was clean and neat – a real businessman and a serious motherfucker. He was Sicilian, about 5'10", 180 pounds, and he had an un-fucking-believable weightlifter body – I mean from top to bottom. He had been locked up in Folsom prison for about five years in the early '70's. He had gotten out just a little bit before I met him, and we clicked off real good right from the beginning.

After some friendly, get-to-know-you chit chat I got down to business. "Hey, listen. Would you help me with security?"

I told him the story and said, "I did not have anything to do with this, but I don't trust this private investigator that's coming out. It doesn't feel right. Maybe it's the move, maybe they're going to put a move on me – I'm just not sure what the deal is. Would you guys pick 'em up at their hotel and bring them up to Beverly Hills? There is a real exclusive hotel where they can do the polygraph on me, and that'll be that!"

Now when I say "bikers" ... they didn't just show up on a bunch of Harley's, wearing colors, and acting all mean and nasty like the traditional biker you see on TV. No – these guys – they were very cool. They were in jeans and boots, but nice shirts, and they were all clean and neat. They picked up the attorney, the polygraph guy, and the private investigator, and they brought them up to Beverly Hills.

Well, Jesus! It was terrifying for me because I didn't want to rehash it. I really, really liked the guy that got hit.

So I went across the street and started drinking Stoli and snorting cocaine. When it was time I crossed the street and went into the hotel. After some introductions the guy administered the polygraph. He asked me a bunch of questions to see if I was who I was and to see if I was lying or not. Then they ran down a list of questions and mentioned a bunch of shit that didn't mean anything to me.

When the polygraph was over, I looked at him and said, "Well?"

He looked at me and said, "Well, I have to take this back and do a final analysis, but I don't think you had anything to do with this murder."

"Well, great," I said relieved. "Everything straight then?"

As I started to get up the private investigator said, "There is one thing. We want to know what you're going to do about the $100,000 that you borrowed."

"What?" I thought defiantly. "What are you talking about, man? You come out here, and you put me through all this fucking shit. You make me run around, and cost me all kinds of fucking money. Now you want to talk about money? Go fuck yourself! And tell everybody in Miami to go fuck themselves, too. Fuck you! You know, I didn't have anything to do with this. I loved this guy, and it's insulting to me for you to talk to me about money. Fuck you! Like I would admit that I even had any money from this guy. You're a motherfucking piece of shit, go fuck yourself."

All of this went through my head in just a brief second. But I just looked him straight in the eye and said, "I'll pay him just as soon as I see him."

I didn't wait for a response. I just turned and walked out the door and across the street. A few days later the attorney called me and said that I didn't need to worry about anything because the polygraph report came back clean. He had taken care of everything else.

I thanked him and hung up the phone.

I can tell you that even after 30+ years, being falsely accused of murder is fucking horrible.

Chapter 26:

A Thief in the Trunk

1976

In 1976 I was living in San Francisco. One day I got a call from The Big Guy who said, “I have something interesting here. Would you fly down to Miami?”

“Well ... give me a little hint what’s goin’ on,” I said.

“Well I met a guy with a boat.”

“Ok, great,” I said. “I’ll be down in a couple of days.”

A couple days later I flew into Miami. Luco picked me up, and we went back to his apartment.

After I put my stuff away he told me the following story.

“I was down in Key West visiting my girl and had this great big mother fucker come over who said he owned a shrimp boat. Well, we started snorting cocaine and drinking whiskey, and that went on for the better part of a day – day and a half. The bottom line is he’s got a shrimp boat that will hold 20,000 pounds, and he said he’d like to do a load. So I worked out the numbers with him, and I think we can do pretty good if we get him loaded for 10,000 pounds.”

“This is great,” I said. “I’m not sure that we can swing the 10,000, but I’m certain we can swing 5,000 pounds with the guy.”

We had worked out all the details to make doubly sure, then we took off for Colombia. In those days Colombia wasn’t the center of the drug world like it later became. This was before the cartel boys moved in and before the big-time Colombians. We were dealing directly with the Indians. The Indians were good, and they never gave us any problems. But they didn't really speak Spanish; they spoke a mixture of Indian and Spanish. It was very, very difficult to understand them, so we had to play charades to try to understand each other. We would draw on the ground, use hand gestures, and jump up and down if we had to. We would do anything we could do to get our message across, and somehow it worked.

We actually got it across where we wanted to load the merchandise.

They said "la playa" which we found out meant down on the beach. So anyway, we played charades, tap danced, and made drawings in the sand. It was really crazy, but we ended up cutting a deal for 5,000 pounds.

We flew back to Miami with all the details. We let the captain know where to make the pickup, and that we were going to unload it up in New Orleans. We knew a guy that had a fish house down in Plaquemine's Parish, so we made all the arrangements. All the boat captain had to do was pick up the merchandise and deliver it to the fish house in New Orleans.

Once everything was set we flew back down to Colombia. He showed up on time, and we put him up at the Santa Marta Airport. The airport runway actually dropped down a little cliff to the water, and there were a bunch of houses along the line there, right along the shore. We had it all worked out with the Indians, so they brought the merchandise down and loaded 5,000 pounds of weed onto this guy's boat.

Before the captain left we all went over the charts, and he knew exactly where to go. Once we were satisfied, we flew to New Orleans and waited.

Ten days went by, and he didn't show up. Then another day went by, and he didn't show up ... then another day, and another day, and another. Of course we're down on Bourbon Street acting like fucking tourists – drinking, and … well, you can imagine if you've ever been to New Orleans. Finally on the fourteenth day we said, "Well, what the fuck?"

So I called my girl down in the Keys, and I said, "Hey, have you seen numb nuts?"

Now she had set the deal up with The Big Guy. I was not there when they made the arrangements, but they had set this deal up. She's a good girl, smart as shit, and she said, "Yeah, the guy's over La Concha acting like a drunken sailor. He's loaded and snorting cocaine – he's having a hell of a good time."

"You got to be shittin' me," I said. "We're in New Orleans, but we're headed for Miami right now. Why don't you get over there and promise him anything, and you know what I mean by that. Just go over there and start hanging out with the guy."

"Ok, sweetie. Don't worry – I'll get his attention."

"That's my girl," I said. "It's noon right now. We'll head that way, and I'll call you at midnight no matter where we are."

We took the first plane out. We didn't give a fuck where it went, but I believe it went to Atlanta. When we got to Atlanta we rented a car and drove the rest of the way to Miami. We got to Miami between 11:00 and midnight then we went to see Rocky. He was a friend of mine who had some guns.

He was surprised to see us, but when we explained that the piece of shit had stolen our merchandise and we needed a couple of good guns, he was more than accommodating. I think we got a Walther, a

.38, and a Browning 9mm.

We put a little package together of guns, duct tape, and handcuffs, then off we went for the Keys. We drove to the Last Chance Bar which is down at the end of Homestead right before the tip of the Keys, and I called my girl. She was waiting for my telephone call, and I told her we were at the tip of the Keys at the Last Chance and were headed her way. I figured it should take about 2½ hours or so to get there.

"Is the guy still there?" I asked.

"Oh, yeah," she said.

"Ok, make an excuse and in 2½ hours we'll meet you at your house. I'm gonna fuckin' drive as fast as I can without getting stopped, and we'll formulate the game plan and go from there."

As we drove we had all the windows down and were snortin' cocaine and drinking all the way to her house. She lived on this little tiny lane, and there was shrubbery all around the house that opened up into one of those little conch houses. It was really nice and secluded.

When we got to her house I explained everything. "Ok, here's the plan. We want you and another girl to go over to La Concha. Get that big piece of shit and bring him back to the house. When you're coming down the lane, give a code word and say 'many a drunken sailor has gone down this path.' When you say that, we'll know he's with you, and we'll all be ready to go from there."

She left, and we waited in the house. It wasn't 15-20 minutes later when we saw three people walking down the lane and heard, 'many a drunken sailor has gone down this path'."

I was in the kitchen, and I had the Walther on me. The Big Guy and Rocky were in the back bedroom.

The Captain stumbled into the house and he said, "Oh, Jesus Christ, am I thirsty!"

"Well," my girl said, "just go right in the kitchen and help yourself. Get a drink."

When he came in the kitchen I was standing there with my gun drawn down on him. He saw the gun and froze. He looked at me started to say something but just as he did – "whap". The Big Guy hit him with a board.

They were building a deck onto the house, and there were all kinds of 2"x4"s and boards outside, and Luco hit him right in the back of the head with one. It was like smacking a watermelon, and he went right to his knees. The minute he went to his knees we were on him. We had him handcuffed and duct taped his legs in no time.

Once he was secure, I looked at the guy lying on the ground. I didn't realize how big he was, but he was a monster about 6'5"/6'6". He was a bit groggy, so I went into the kitchen and got a cup of water and threw it in his face. He shook his head and looked up at me and said, "Now what, you fuckin' punk?"

I didn't say a thing. I walked up to him and kicked him square in the head, and his entire right eyebrow ripped right off. It looked like I kicked his eye out. It was a terrible, fucking mess – it was a mess all over the fucking place, but I was caught up in the moment.

This piece of shit had just stolen 5,000 pounds of weed from us. I'd been back and forth to Colombia a couple of times, and I was fucking hot. I couldn't stand to look at him, so I had Luco blindfold him. Instead of beating the living shit out him right there, we decided to take him to Miami.

We had rented a big green Chrysler, so we backed that car down the driveway. We managed to rifle him out through the door, across the lawn, and tossed him into the trunk. Then we got in the car and took off for Miami.

We got right up to Seven Mile Bridge, and the road was blocked off. There were six or seven state trooper cars there.

One of the Troopers saw us and started to walk towards us. Rocky, who was sitting in the middle of the car, started to freak out on us.

"Oh, no! They got us," he said.

"No, no, no!" Luco said.

"Hey," I said, "everyone just be quiet. Nobody knows a fucking thing. Those girls haven't said a word."

The Big Guy grabbed Rocky's leg right up close to his nuts, squeezed it, and said, "Hey, don't say a word. Let Jack talk to 'em."

As the officer approached the car I rolled down the window and the highway patrolman said, "Hey, boys – we got a convoy of water coming down. Five or six trucks. You boys wait right here if you would, please. Once the convoy goes by you will be good to go."

"How long do you think we'll have to wait, Officer?" I asked.

"You've got about 15 minutes. We're sorry to disturb you, but no problem, right?"

"No," I said. "No problem, sir. We'll wait right here."

The officer nodded and walked back to his car. Well ... sure as shit, about 15 minutes later the convoy went by. After the last truck passed they opened up the road and let us through then we took off as fast as we could.

Once we got up into Homestead there was a little barbecue joint on the right side of the road – Shrivers, I think it was called. I pulled into the parking lot, walked over to the payphone, and called a friend.

"Hey, listen," I said. "I've got a piece of shit with me. This guy stole 5,000 pounds of weed from us."

"What?" he said, surprised. "Where is he?"

"He's with me right now."

"Well, bring the motherfucker over."

When we got there and walked in he asked, "Where is he?"

"He's in the trunk," I said. "This is worth $10,000 to you as well."

He nodded and went to work moving the furniture. Once the furniture was moved he rolled up the living room rug.

"What's that for?" Rocky asked.

"You'll see," I said.

We took the rug out to the car, rolled the captain up in it, carried him in the house, and dropped him on the floor. We unrolled the carpet and put him up against the wall. He was still all duct-taped up and blindfolded.

Everyone knew that I was the only one that was going talk to him. No one else was to say a word.

"Listen, motherfucker! You stole 5,000 pounds of weed. When I take the tape off your mouth, just tell me where my merchandise is and who else helped you steal it. Then we'll go from there and see about getting it back."

He didn't say or do anything.

"If you don't," I paused for a few seconds, "well ... you're gonna have a problem."

So I ripped the tape off, and he nearly shouts, "Yeah! I stole your merchandise, I'm sorry! I've got it over on an island between Naples and Tampa. I'm from Tampa, and my brothers and I took the merchandise. You know? You were supposed to get ten, but you only got five. You got short loaded. We got mad, you know, snortin' cocaine, and we just looked at The Big Guy and didn't think he'd do anything anyway, you know? He's sort of a happy, jovial guy, you know? I'm feeling kinda weird right now, and I'm worried that you're gonna hurt me."

"No, no, no," I said. "Get the guy some donuts. Let's get a washcloth."

He looked terrible from that eyebrow mess. He had blood all over his face, and he smelled just like death – he was in terrible shape.

"Take it easy, buddy," I said. "Just take it easy. All we want is our merchandise back – do you understand?"

He nodded.

We cleaned him up and got him some donuts and coffee.

By the time we got him cleaned up it was early morning. Once he was cleaned up I said, "Ok, we're gonna take you to the street." We got him a new shirt, and we cut out some black tape and covered a pair of sunglass. Then we took him right out into the street to a payphone.

We had him call his brothers, and he told them that him he had all the merchandise sold. They needed to deliver a U-Haul truck with the weed that night at the Dadeland Shopping Mall at midnight. There was a J.C. Penney tire store all the way on the corner of Kendall and Dixie, and they were to leave the truck there. Put the keys in the ashtray, get out, and drive away. He assured them that it was all sold, and that he had it all done, and everything was nice and tight.

Sure as shit, that night at midnight a U-Haul truck pulled up in front of the tire store followed by a smaller car. I was there with one of my guys to make sure that everything went off like it was supposed to. The driver got out of the U-Haul, got into the car, and they drove off.

Well, I had previously sold the merchandise to the Jew from Miami Beach. (I told you a couple stories about him in the chapter titled "Cocaine 101".) I told the Jew that we'd have the merchandise at the Dadeland Shopping Mall at the tire center, and he could pick it up a little after midnight. So we waited, and about 20 minutes after midnight another car drove into the parking lot. It stopped, and the Jew stepped out of the car and climbed into the U-Haul. After a few minutes he got into the truck and drove off.

Four or five hours later, it was close to dawn when the Jew brought the big down stroke for the money to where we were staying at the Marriott over on Lejeune next to the airport. About four days later he paid the whole thing off.

The money was great, but what a fucking mess the captain and his brothers had made of everything.

Chapter 27:

Colombian Whorehouse

1977

Very, very seldom did any of the deals go off without a hitch. There was always trouble, and we were amateurs who were usually winging it. We were just trying to make a lot of money and work our way up the ladder.

We had a guy with us who grew up in Tucson, Arizona. At the time I was 30, and he was 42. He'd been smuggling people, guns, and weed on the Arizona-Mexico border, and he spoke fluent Spanish. We called him The Pony because he was kind of like a little miniature pony.

He was probably 6'3" and 240 pounds. He had a bald head on top with long blond hair around the edges that he drew into a pony tail at his back. He also had a dark brown beard – he was a very, very nice looking man and very meticulous. It took him an hour to primp just to get ready to leave in the morning. He'd soak his head down with this kind of lotion like you what can get at the barbershop. He wore Lucchese Cowboy Boots, jeans, a belt buckle, a t-shirt, and a safari jacket just like the rest of us.

We started working together smuggling weed out of Santa Marta, Colombia. Santa Marta Gold is what it was called, and it was the best weed in the world at the time. We were in Colombia, and we were going to load up 12,000 pounds of Santa Marta Gold. We were staying on the top floor of a hotel called the Porto Galione that had just been built. It was 15 stories high, and it came around in a half circle right on the water just west of the airport in Santa Marta. Out in front of the hotel they had built a replica of a

Spanish galleon which acted as a restaurant and bar combination.

I had the Luco – The Big Guy – and The Pony with me. It wasn't a suite, but we had a couple of adjoining rooms on the top floor. We always gave Luco his own room because he snored so loud, and the Pony and I always had the girls up.

When the time came to talk to the boat, I suggested that I go down to the bar and have a drink while Luco and the Pony got the captain on the radio. We'd get him ready to load, and he would be on his way in a couple of days. Luco and the Pony agreed so I went on down to the bar.

Now in those days there were no Americans around. When I walked into the bar, there were only Colombians there. I could see them and their families, and I looked like an alien. I was the only American sitting there – it was just me, and I'm terrible at Spanish. I managed to get a Rum and Coke and then sat down.

All of a sudden I hear, "Morgana One, Morgana One, Morgana One – Evening Star, over."

I looked around and said, "Jesus Christ, what's that?"

"Morgana One, Morgana One, Morgana One – Evening Star, over."
Then it hit me – those are our call signs.

"Morgana One, Morgana One, Morgana One – Evening Star."

"Evening Star, Morgana One. Evening Star – come back."

"Oh, fuck!" I knew we were in trouble. The whole bar, the whole galleon, the whole hotel was listening to Luco broadcast out the window.

I wanted to run across the lawn to the hotel, but I didn't want to draw attention to myself. So I stood up from my chair, walked quickly to the elevator, and hit the top floor button. It seemed to take forever to get there. As soon as the door opened, I ran down the hall and started to pound on the door.

The Pony answered and said, "What the fuck? What's the matter?"

As I walked into the room I could hear Luco talking to the Captain, "We'll be out tonight. Let's talk this over at 8:00 o'clock."

I ran across the room yelling, "Stop it! Stop it!"

Luco stopped talking and looked up at me like I was nuts. The Pony walked over and asked, "Hey, what the fuck's the matter? What's going on?"

I said, "The whole goddamn bar – the whole fucking hotel can hear you."

They both looked shocked, but Luco remained calmed and told the Captain we'd call him back at 8:00 o'clock. As soon as the Captain acknowledged, we didn't hesitate to bring in the antenna in and turn the radio off.

As we were bringing in the antenna I said, "Somebody's going to call the DOS. Get it in, get it in."

Later that evening we met the Frenchman. Down near the water there was a tiny little house that he owned. He didn't speak English, but he spoke French of course, and fluent Spanish. Luckily the Pony knew French and Spanish, so that's how we communicated – no English, just Spanish and French.

Through a contact we knew, we had bought off the local authorities. The idea was that they were going to come down to the Frenchman's house and keep people away while we loaded up the merchandise. This part of the deal went smoothly with no problems. We got the merchandise down to the boat and loaded in just a few hours.

When we were done I said, "We might as well go celebrate a little bit. Let's go down to the local whorehouse."

So we went down to the local whorehouse. There were probably 12-15 girls there, and before long, we each had girls sitting on our laps. Now whorehouses in Colombia are a bit different, and Colombians don't act like Americans when they go to the whorehouse. Americans just want to go in and wham, bang, thank you, ma'am. Colombians like to make it a social event – talk, drink, do some cocaine, and be nice to the girls. We had picked up those customs because we had been back and forth between there for years.

Luco spoke a little Spanish, and he was doing his best to talk to the girls sitting on his lap. But, like I said, the Pony spoke very good Spanish. It wasn't surprising that the girl sitting on his lap was really, really nice. Even though I didn't speak any Spanish, I had a couple of nice girls with me.

As we were talking and doing coke with the girls a song came on. The song was "Gloria". Now the girl that was sitting on the Pony's lap was named Gloria. We all had a little buzz, and we were in a real good mood so the Pony stood up and started dancing with this beautiful girl. He couldn't dance worth a shit, but he was dancing with his whore. I'll never forget it.

All of a sudden this big Colombian came through the door. As he stepped through the door he stopped and looked at the Pony dancing with the girl. After a few seconds he looked over at the owner and nods.

The owner of the whorehouse walked over to where the Pony was dancing and said something to him in Spanish.

The Pony stopped dancing and looked at him and asked, "What the fuck are you talking about? She's with me."

The owner pointed at the Colombian who had just walked through the door and said something else in Spanish.

The Pony looked at the guy and said, "I don't give a fuck if her boyfriend's here or not."

The owner looked at the Colombian and started to fidget. Finally he looked at the Pony and said something in Spanish that ended in "Policia."

Now this entire conversation was in Spanish so I had no clue what was going on. I only knew that something was wrong because of how nervous the owner was, and he had just said police in Spanish. I moved the girl off of my lap, stood up, and walked over to the Pony and asked him what was going on.

When he was done I said, "Listen, get rid of that fucking whore. Get another one."

I was surprised when he didn't answer.

"Hey, bro, listen. Listen! We don't need any goddamn trouble down here with the Colombians. Fuck ... think about it. We've got dope dealer costumes on, and we look like fucking aliens. If we fuck with the Police Chief's son, we don't have enough money to keep him from locking us the fuck up or killing us. The only thing good thing that can happen is they take us to jail, and then we'll have to pay. It's going to be a bunch of shit, so get rid of that fucking whore."

He stared at the Colombian for a good long while and then said, "Ok."

The Pony kissed the girl quick, and we went back to our table and sat down. But then the police chief's son came over to the table and started to rap in Spanish. He was right in the middle of saying something when all of a sudden the Pony jumped up and backhanded him. He hit him so hard that the guy stumbled back a step. The Pony's next swing caught him square on the jaw. The Pony flattened him, and he didn't hesitate to put his cowboy boots to him right away with four or five good kicks. Wham, wham, wham.

I jumped out of my seat alarmed. In the United States that shit goes on and you can always walk away, but we speak the lingo. We can bribe ... we can pay. We'd get away there, but here? We're in Colombia here.

I grabbed the Pony and said, "Oh, jumpin' fucking Jesus."

He stopped kicking the guy and sat back down.

I didn't sit down. I looked at the guy bleeding on the floor, turned to Luco and the Pony, and said, "Ok

– now let's get the fuck out of here. This is going to be a problem."

But the Pony still wanted a fight, "I'm not taking any shit just 'cause this cocksucker happens to be the police chief's son. This is bullshit."

While we were talking the police chief's son got up, and he kind of half-ass wobbled around the room not saying anything. He stumbled across the room to the corner where there were six or seven guys all holding a girl. I couldn't really tell, but they didn't look like Colombians. The Police Chief's son stumbled over to them and started talking to them.

Well the owner saw what was going on and came over to our table and said, "Hey, you guys better leave."

I was upset because, you know, I was in a whorehouse. I wasn't there to get a fucking beating. I was over there just to have a good time.

I didn't want any trouble, so I said, "Ok, let's go."

As we got up to leave I looked over just as the guys on the other side of the room stood up, and I saw they all had knives.

The police chief's son turned around and started coming towards us.

"Oh, Jesus Christ," I said as we backed up defensively. We backed around the bar, but we were caught in the corner.

The Pony had pulled out his K5 knife and said, "Luco, get behind me. And Jack, you get in the back because you're the littlest. I know you've got heart, but get in the back. Right away – they've gotta get through me."

Luco had pulled out a Buck knife, and I had a Buck knife as well.

The Pony turned to the Colombian and said, "Hey, Puto y maricona, you fucking maricone. You faggot fuck."

"Jesus," I said, "what are you doing?"

"I'm going to kill this motherfucker. I'm going to stab this fucking piece of shit, and I'm telling him he's a fuck boy. Maybe I can scare him off."

Well ... they started coming towards us, but they were not taking great big giant steps in to kill us. I felt like we were surrounded by a group of hyenas that were getting ready to move in for the kill.

Then The Big Guy steps right out in front and starts to egg them on, "Come on. Come on, you motherfuckers."

I thought, "Oh, fuck it. Maybe I can defuse this situation."

"Guys, let me through."

The Pony and Luco opened up, and I stepped in the middle and said, "Hey, come on! Come on, guys. What the fuck? There's no sense in doing this. The girl ... we didn't mean any disrespect. Shit, this is just business. Come on ... what's the deal?"

One of the guys from the table – not the police chief's son – looked at me and said, "I hate fucking English."

"Oh, that's okay," I said. "I'm not English. I'm a fucking American – I'm American."

He looked at me for a minute and said, "You speak English ... you English."

"Well, fuck you," I said. Now I was fucking mad, and I said as I pointed to the Police Chief's son, "Pony, you make sure you stab that cocksucker – that fucking goddamn police chief's kid. You get that piece of shit ... he's the whole trouble. I don't see the rest of these motherfuckers doing anything without him."

So the Pony started taunting him, "You maricone ... you woman. You're a whore ... a woman lesbian."

He was saying all this in rapid Spanish that I didn't understand at the time. He was saying all kinds of shit.

We worked our way towards the door at the back, but when we got there it was locked. With no other choice we turned our full attention to our attackers. They were coming closer and closer, and it was like one of those Boris Karloff movies. You know – where all the townspeople are coming? And strangely enough, I was scared. But I wasn't scared to the point of like, you know, wanting to suck my blanket. I knew I was gonna get hurt and fucked up, but I knew I was going to get a chance to do some stabbing as well – all three of us.

Now Luco had gotten really mad, and he came close to losing control of himself. He wanted to charge, but I just kept saying, "No, no, no. Wait. Wait until they get closer. We can at least put the fucking knives in some of these pieces of shit."

The doors to the place flew open with a bang and standing by the doors was the owner. He didn't want any trouble with the police chief's son, so he pointed out the doors to the alley. I looked through the door and could see that there was a cab waiting with its doors open. We didn't hesitate. We exited through the door and jumped into the cab, and the taxi driver didn't wait either. As soon as we were in, he drove off before we could even get the doors shut.

As I peered out the back window I could see all the Colombians shaking their fists at us as we drove off into the night.

That was a close one.

I don't know why, but the luck of the devil had saved me again.

Chapter 28:

LSD and the Racist Honeymooners

1977

When the smuggling business out of Colombia really started to pick up, I purchased a mansion on a small island in the Caribbean. It was a very nice beach house that was on the extreme east coast of the island and right on the Atlantic Ocean. It was huge, and it was beautiful. It came with 6 acres right on the ocean and sat outside this quaint little town. I picked it up for a song – just a song.

We wanted to make it a real nice place so we started throwing money into it – trying to make it better and better. On the north side of the property was a state park that stretched for six miles. You couldn't build on it so there were no further developments in that direction. Most of the state park was this long, beautiful beach. It started near the mansion then swung up and around in a quarter-moon shape. It was just beautiful.

To the south was a long stretch of great big rocks that were constantly getting pounded by the ocean. The beach and waves near the mansion had some of the best surfing in this hemisphere. It was so unbelievable that surfers and people from all over the world came to visit, and it was also a very popular spot for honeymooners. Adjacent to the beach house was this small inn that was always full of surfers and tourists. It was run by a man from Miami who was a nice guy, and we became good friends.

The inn had a great big mahogany bar with windows looking right out onto the ocean. He had jury rigged some tubing so all he had to do was flip a switch and fresh water would wash the salt buildup off of the windows. The place was all open, and the owner liked to cook so he put on these fantastic buffets. However, he didn't like surfers because they would come in and eat him out of house and home and then not even tip worth a damn.

We became very, very good friends with him over the years, and he is still a good friend today.

When the smuggling business started to pick up we traveled back and forth to the island all the time.

One time we were staying on the island at the mansion and The Packer turned to me and says, "Well, let's just skip over to the inn and get a drink."

So we went over to the bar, and when we got there, a girl was sitting alone at the bar enjoying a drink. She was fairly good looking with brown hair and a nice body, etc. We ordered our drinks and started to talk to her. She said she was from New York City, and that she was down on her honeymoon.

Well, we knew that was the end of anything with her. She was on her honeymoon, and that meant she was off limits. We were certainly not afraid of women because of the business we were in, and we had no problem talking to women. So if once you got to know them one thing led to another ... great. That was just part of having a lot of money, and part of the smuggling business.

Once she said she was on her honeymoon that was it. We weren't rude, but we weren't going to spend a lot of time getting to know her.

So we're drinking and looking out at the ocean, and she asked, "Hey, do you know the guy that owns this inn?"

"Yeah, we've seen him around. We're in here all the time."

She looked around and asked, "Well, did you see all these half black children?"

"What do you mean?" I asked.

She leaned forward and spoke a little quieter, "He's having sex with the local black girls."

I was a bit surprised by her statement and said, "Really? You know that for sure?"

She pointed at one of the kids playing in the sand and said, "Well, look at that child over there ... he looks just exactly like him."

"You don't approve?" I asked.

"God, no – that's disgusting! White boys are not supposed to have sex with black girls."

"Really?" I said. "Wow ... ok."

I paused for a moment before I asked, "You're from Manhattan, right?"

"Yeah, we're from Manhattan."

Her statements just hit me kind of weird, and I thought to myself, "Why you piece of shit. You racist fucking cunt." But I didn't say that to her face; I kept it to myself. But I was hot ... it really pissed me off.

We didn't say much after that. She finished her drink, got up, and went to her room. When we finished our own drinks we started to leave, but as we're walking out, our friend who owned the inn was coming up from the ocean.

We stopped and waited for him, and as he walked up to the inn I asked, "Hey, do you have a honeymoon couple upstairs from Manhattan?"

"Yeah."

"What do you think of them?" I asked.

"Well, the guy's a nitwit, and you know I don't really like white women anyway. You know what color of women I like."

"Well, that's strange," I said. "She just made a comment that you have some half-black bastard children, and that you should to be looked down on for maybe having sex with black girls."

"What? A racist?"

"Yeah, you know ... a Manhattan racist socialite. You know the ones that carry themselves like they're fucking something."

He smiled, shrugged his shoulders, and said, "Ah, fuck them."

"No, no – not fuck them," I said. "We can't let them get away with that. Let's teach them a lesson."

"Well, what do you have in mind?"

"You know that we usually come over and have dinner with you every night. I see that nitwit husband of hers, and he always comes down to the bar and has a double shot of Mountain Gay rum just before dinner. How 'bout tonight when he comes down and has that double shot of Mountain Gay rum, I put The Packer behind the bar. We'll distract the nitwit, and The Packer will put a couple hits of LSD in his rum, and we'll see where it goes from there."

He smiled and said, "That sounds like a fine idea."

We went over to the bar right around sundown. I took a seat at the bar, and The Packer went to work as substitute bartender. Sure as shit, just like clockwork, the pretentious couple came walking into the bar holding hands all lovey-dovey like. Now she was all made up with her makeup on, and sashaying around, she looked pretty good. I'm not gonna give her an 8 or a 9, but she was a solid 7. She looked good, and she had a tropical dress on. He was one of those guys you just don't like ... he was just a goofy fuck, just goofy.

So he went to the bar ... and The Packer has already crushed up two hits of purple sunshine (LSD - actually, in those days it had so many different names). We called this purple sunshine because it had a dark purple color. We decided to use it because the rum was a dark purple color so nitwit wouldn't be able to see it in his drink.

The Packer walks over to the couple and says to him, "May I help you?"

The girl ordered a Shirley Temple or a Banks beer or something – whatever the fuck.

But the guy says, "Oh, man, I'm hung over; just give me a glass of water."

The Packer put a glass of water up on the bar and looked over at me. I gave him the nod, and he dumped two hits of purple haze into the glass of water. It looked like a great big purple smear with trails going from the top down to the glass, but the guy did not even take a look. He took the glass of water, and he chugged it down.

"Well, shit," I thought to myself. "We'll see if the guy can handle of couple hits of LSD and see where this goes. We'll see what the guy feels like, what he looks like, and what kind of people they really are. Maybe it'd come out where they get all this racist shit that you shouldn't fuck around with the black girls in the islands."

Island black girls, by the way, are gorgeous. They are some beautiful, beautiful girls. I've always liked black girls ... always.

Well, it didn't take long. Within 20 minutes he stood up and said, "I'm going to town."

Now the island we're on is roughly 30 miles long and about 15 miles wide and had about 750 miles of paved road that intertwined through the sugarcane fields. There are dead ends, ups and downs. To the north it's all mountains, and then it flattens out down to the southeast.

If you don't know the island, if you're not familiar with the roads and it's night, you will get lost. You'll be in the sugarcane, and you won't have a fucking clue where you are – you're gone.

He stood up and said, "I'm going to town."

Now the main town is on the other side of the island, and to get over there at night (even today), you need a GPS.

He turned to his bride and said, "Ok, baby, let's go."

She looked at him for a minute and said, "I'm not going. You're acting weird."

"I'm not acting weird," he said. "I feel great – I feel the best I ever felt in my fucking life."

Then he started drinking beer, or more accurately, pounding beer. After his fifth or sixth beer he stood up, and said, "Well ... I'm leaving for the other side. If you don't want to come, fuck it! I'm going over to a club."

He didn't wait for his girl to answer; he just turned, walked out to his car, got in, and drove off.

I looked at The Packer. He just smiled, turned to the girl, and said, "Hey, honey, you want to shoot a game of darts?"

I don't know what it is, but Americans sure like to shoot darts. We had a big dart board up on the wall, and as we got ready to play, we had a little blow and started snorting rails. So we're shooting darts, we're snorting cocaine, and we're drinking Banks Beer.

And if you don't already know, Banks Beer tastes good, and it goes down like water. I mean you can pound the shit out of them. We were just pounding the beer down, and we're also drinking Mountain Gay rum.

So there we were ... shooting darts with this racist woman. The next thing we know, a few hours had gone by. Now the guy who owned the place had built this redwood deck on the backside of the inn, and it was beautiful.

It was close to 11:00 pm, and we were all fucked up. We went out on the deck, and the honeymooner came out with us. She was totally fucked up drunk now. Did we drug her? No, we did not. At least, I'm not aware of it. But it wasn't five minutes and The Packer had her dress up over her head.

I said, "Oh, shit! Jesus Christ! They're on their fucking honeymoon."

But The Packer just ignored me. He was mauling on her like a rabid dog while I was taking a piss off the back of the deck. Then I realized it wasn't only The Packer, she was mauling him back.

And it struck me ... the humor of it all ... here you've got this pretentious, uptight, snotty bitch saying racist shit about my friend. The next thing you know, The Packer's out there fingering her on the goddamn back deck.

I had finished my business, zipped up my fly, and turned to go back into the bar when The Packer lowered the girl's dress and said, "Hey, listen – we're going up to her room."

I was a bit surprised because like I said earlier, she was on her honeymoon. That meant she was off limits.

"Are you sure?"

He just nodded and said, "Yes, we're going up to her room."

I went back into the bar and told the owner that The Packer had taken the racist slut up to her room.

"Oh, shit," he said, a little alarmed. "What about the old man? What if he comes home?"

I thought about it for a couple of minutes and came up with an idea.

"We gotta play Paul Revere. You got a flashlight?"

"Yes, in my room."

"Good. I'll go out on the terrace of the room, and I'll look in and see how he's doing. You go keep a watch out of your window. If you see the nitwit coming, flash your light a couple of times and I'll get The Packer out of there."

"Ok," he said as he headed up to his room.

The guy that owned the hotel was a furniture nut, and he loved those great big four-poster beds. The ones they made out of oak and mahogany down on the islands. I believe the ones in the inn were made of mahogany, and it was just beautiful furniture – gorgeous.

As I started to climb up onto the terrace of the room that the Honeymooners were staying in, and it was clear that The Packer was pounding the bride. The bed had come a little undone, and it was squeaking loud as could be.

I reached the terrace and looked in, and sure enough, this was one of the four-poster beds. Only this one had a headboard, and they were headboard slapping. The Packer was pounding the bride ... I mean pounding her. She was screaming like she was being beaten, and I was fucking dying. I wanted to laugh, but didn't want to give away that I was watching them so I grabbed a washcloth that was on a chair just inside the window and bit into it to keep myself quiet.

The Packer never slowed down; he just kept going and going. I'm watching him just pound into her, and I'm thinking, "Jesus Christ!"

All of the sudden, I saw the "one if by land, two if by sea" flash from the owner of the hotel. I looked over, and he's leaning out his window flashing the light. I looked around the inn, and didn't see any lights. But then I heard the car coming.

I leaned in the window and said, "Hey, Packer, the old man's coming!"

But The Packer didn't even slow down. He just shouted at me, "I don't give a fuck ... I don't care, let him see it. Fuck him – he's a worthless piece of shit. He can't even get a hard on – he's a-"

I'm thinking, "Oh my God! This ain't good ... this is just not good."

"Packer, come on now! Listen ... we don't want any trouble."

He just kept pounding her, and she just kept screaming.

"No, I gotta get off. I gotta get off."

And he picked up the pace.

I wasn't sure what to do so I just climbed in through the window and said, "Get the fuck off that woman."

"No, I don't give a fuck about him. I don't give a fuck about nothing."

And then the girl started yelling at *me*, "Get the fuck out of here."

Well right down the hall was The Pony so I went down and pounded on his door.

The Pony opened up, and when he saw me asked, "What's the matter?"

"The Packer's in there pounding the bride."

"So what?"

"Well, her husband's coming! He's going to cause trouble for the owner, you know, and he's not going to like that."

"Oh, Jesus Christ ... you're right!"

So I bring down The Pony, and all he's wearing is his underwear. We walked down the hall to the room they were fucking in, and I opened the door. The Pony runs in, and just grabs the Packer. The Packer went out of his fucking mind and started swinging at us, and it was actually quite a hilarious scene. There he is ... he's got a hard on, and there's this naked bride in the fucking room. The Pony drags him out into the hall just as the shit-bag husband pulls up.

The Pony dragged The Packer down the hall to his room as the nitwit was getting out of his car. I stood by the stairs and listened as the nitwit walked into the hotel. The owner went down and greeted him, "Hey, how you doin' buddy? You have any trouble getting back across the island?"

"I've been lost for three fucking hours."

I went over to the Pony's room, and finally we straightened The Packer out.

"Jesus Christ Almighty," I said. "Are you nuts?"

"Jesus, that's the finest pussy I've had in a long time."

I looked at him and said, "Well, goddamn it, stay in the room!"

I cracked the door and watched down the hallway. In a couple of minutes the husband came up. He went into his room, shut the door, we didn't hear a peep the rest of the night.

The next morning we went over for breakfast, and there they are ... all lovey-dovey, and everything is good.

There are times I wonder how long that marriage actually lasted.

Chapter 29:

Tap Dancing on LSD

July, 1977.

The Packer, Luco and I were living in San Francisco. We had just brought out some weed and blow from Miami because the money was much better in California. When we had sold all of the dope, I asked the Packer, "Hey, would you come down to Los Angeles with me?"

"What for?" he asked.

"I'm going to buy a new Benz. Remember Joe Cline? He lives in Los Angeles and he's going to put the car in his name."

"Okay," he said, "I'll go."

So we flew down to Los Angeles and went to our friend's house.

We met Joe in the Navy. As soon as we got to his house we instantly started partying, snorting cocaine, popping pills and so on. Eventually we made our way to the Mercedes Benz dealership. I bought a brand new 450 SL convertible. With all the upgrades it cost $32,000. I gave my friend 20 grand in cash and he financed the rest of it. The deal was that I would pay it off in a year at $1,000 a month. I greased him down for the insurance and we drove away with a brand new Mercedes Benz.

We went over to his house and continued the party; we drank all night, we snorted cocaine and we got all fucked up. Eventually we left the house and made our way up into Hollywood to get some girls. Once we had some girls we continued partying. And, boy, did we party. We didn't get back to Joe's house 'til six or seven o'clock the following morning. We finally went to sleep and everything was good.

The Packer and I got up around noon, and I said, "I've got some business up in San Francisco."

So we took off. Even though we had gotten some sleep, we were still fucked up. It wasn't long before we started drinking again. We even stopped for a couple of snorts. After we snorted the blow we took off again. I was driving.

As we left LA our plan was to go up over the grapevine, come down over the other side and get onto I-5. We were going to make our way up towards the big cutoff, through the desert, before we headed over to San Francisco.

We stopped at a gas station and filled up. We also emptied out all the remaining beer bottles and shit. As we were cleaning out the car, all the partying finally caught up to me. I didn't feel good. I looked at the Packer and said, "Jesus Christ, I'm tired. Do you want to drive?"

He looked at me like I was crazy, and said, "Sure."

It was a nice day, so we put the top down before we took off. I fell asleep as soon as we hit the main highway.

All of a sudden the Packer is yelling, "They got us! They got us!" I thought I was having a nightmare, but as I woke up, the Packer was shaking me and repeating, "They got us. They got us."

I shook my head a little and tried to figure out what was going on. "What?" I said as I tried to clear the sand out of my eyes. I had been sound asleep. Even though the top was down, for some reason it was hot as a motherfucker. I was confused. With the top down while we were driving, it should be nice and cool with the wind blowing across the car. Then I realized that there wasn't any wind blowing across the car because we weren't moving. We were in the desert and it was hot as hell.

I looked at the Packer. "What's going on?"

He nodded toward the front and back of the car. A couple of cop cars pulled in front of us, and I could hear sirens behind us.

I looked at the Packer. "Well, they got us," he said. "They got us."

"What do you mean, they got us?" I was confused.

"This bitch was going 142 miles an hour when the first one pulled in behind me"

I was just about to say to the Packer, "Why the fuck are you driving my brand new car at 142 miles an hour? It's only a day old," when I saw the detectives get out of the cars in front of us. As they walked around their car and towards us, another cop car pulled in, facing right into the Benz. There were two or three cop cars in front of us, including the detectives, and there's another couple behind us.

The detectives came up to the car on the Packer's side and said, "Get the fuck out of the car. You were going 95 miles an hour."

"Well Jesus," I said, "that's not so bad. Packer said he was going 142."

As the Packer gets out of the car, the other detective came around to my side of the car and looked at me. "Whose car is this?"

He wasn't really rude, but he was kind of excited from the chase because I think in his mind he was sure that we had stolen the car.

"It belongs to a friend of mine." I answered.

He wasn't convinced. "It's a brand new car. You got any temporary tags on it?"

"Yeah, I do." I said.

"And your friend lets you drive a brand new $20,000 car?"

"Well, actually the car's a little more than that," I said, "It's a $32,000 car."

"Well, why in the fuck would he let you take his $32,000 car out for a joy ride?"

"Well, I was in Vietnam with him."

He still wasn't convinced. "So what's his name?"

"Joe Cline."

"What's his phone number?"

I gave him Joe's number and they went back to their car. I didn't know it then, but they were calling him. And, of course, Joe told them we were going to deliver the car up to San Francisco and he was going to come up in a few days to pick it up.

After they spoke to Joe they got the Packer out in front of the car and they start running him through the drunk driving tests. You know, touching his nose, walking the line, and making him basically tap dance out in front of the Benz. I was surprised that they didn't have him take off his sunglasses. If they had seen how bloodshot his eyes were they probably would have run him through more tests, but he passed the ones they gave him.

About the time that the officers finished their tests, one of the detectives came back to the car and said to me, "You know, this guy was going 90-something miles an hour while you were sleeping."

I had to bite my tongue not to laugh, but I kept a straight face and said, "Well listen, I'm going to have a stern talking with him, because that's just bullshit. You know, I just fell asleep; I didn't know anything about this until you pulled us over."

He paused for a moment and then said, "Well, do you have a driver's license?"

"Sure." I showed him my driver's license; of course, it was from Florida. And Packer's driver's license was from New Jersey.

After he looked at my license he handed it back to me and said, "Well, I want you to drive the car."

"Oh, okay." I said, "no problem."

He turned to the officer who had conducted the drunk driving tests and said, "Write him up."

The officer only wrote the Packer a ticket for speeding. Cost him $100, which was quite a bit of money back then, but they didn't get him for drunk driving. We couldn't believe it.

The Packer walked around the car and got in on the passenger's side while I switched to the driver's seat.

After we switched seats, the detective said, "Okay, you can go."

"What the fuck?" I said as we drove away. "Did that really just happen?"

The Packer looked at me and said, "Well, lucky they didn't know I just took a hit of LSD a few minutes before they pulled us over."

"Have you lost your fucking mind?" I asked. "Where'd you get that?"

"Joe gave it to me while we were in Los Angeles."

" Jesus Christ, how do you feel?" I asked.

"I don't feel bad."

I just shook my head, smiled and said, "Listen, I told him I was going to give you a stern talking to, so I'll just act mean here for a few minutes, but goddamn good job. We got away. We're driving away. Everything's good."

So we headed to San Francisco.

As we drove up the road I couldn't help but think how the luck of the devil had saved me again.

Chapter 30: Chasing the Dragon

1977

Still living in California, I drove down to Los Angeles from my house in San Francisco to see a friend. And there was this girl—an Italian with long, black hair. She was just gorgeous. Her name was Vanessa.

We all started snorting cocaine and drinking. My new Mercedes convertible was such a beautiful automobile, and I wanted to show it off to this girl. I asked if she wanted to go for a ride. She smiled and followed me to the car. I helped her into her seat and we went for a ride. As one might imagine, it led to something nice.

I spent the next couple of days with this girl. It was amazing; so amazing, in fact, that I asked her to move to San Francisco with me. She didn't even hesitate when she said yes. So we went from Los Angeles up to San Francisco, some 400 miles or more, and she moved in.

Life was good. I really liked the girl. She was Italian, but from Dallas, Texas, and had the Texas accent. We were having a hell of a good time together.

I guess about a year went by, and then one Friday afternoon, Vanessa comes home. She walked toward the room and stopped just inside the door. "I've got a present for you."

"Well, that's good. What is it?" I asked.

"It's her," she said, as she stepped to the side, so I could see the door.

And in through the door came this Italian girl. She was probably 24 or 25 years old. She had dark olive skin and black hair that was kind of curly, falling all the way to her ass. She had it braided around her head. But, her body, Wow! She had a number ten body. I mean, she was the hottest woman I had ever seen.

All I could say was, "Damn. What's this? Is this my birthday present?"

And my girlfriend said, "Yeah, this is a present for you."

Now having two girls at once had been on my mind a few times, and I quickly realized that I couldn't resist this girl. But I also knew that an attitude like that had gotten many a man killed before. In the last few years I had made a number of enemies, so I was always cautious. I tore my eyes away from the Italian girl, looked at my girlfriend and asked, "Is this some setup? I'm going to get hurt and snatched—whacked? Some shit's going to happen."

But, she just laughed as she walked across the room and reached out her hand.

"No. This is no set up. I told you. This is a gift. Her name is Tahani. C'mon, let's go have some fun."

What's a guy supposed to do, upset his girl?

What an amazing weekend. It was just me and these two incredibly beautiful women. We snorted blow, drank and fucked like rabbits for the entire weekend—in every room of the house and in every position you could imagine.

The Italian girl left early Monday morning and I thanked my girl.

"Jesus, baby." I told her, "That was something. That was nice."

"Yes, it was," she said.

About a week later, Vanessa came home from shopping. She said, "Let's go meet Tahani and have a drink. She told me she's got someone with her, a guy that you might want to meet."

Now the hairs on the back of my head stood up. "No. No. No. No. I don't want to meet anybody."

"For Christ's sake, Jack, it's three in the afternoon. We'll go to the Old Mill over in Mill Valley."

I still wasn't convinced that this wasn't a setup of some kind.

She looked at me for a minute and then said, "If you're that worried about it, call your boys."

"Yeah," I said, "I'm not going to meet no one, unless I got a couple of guys with me."

So I called my boys and said, "Listen. I'm going in with my baby here and we're going to meet Tahani. You know, the Italian girl I told you about that spent the weekend. But she's with some guy she wants me to meet. I don't know if he's with the police and their trying to set me up. I don't have a clue who this guy is, but I'm going to go over and find out. Just back me up."

Of course, they agreed and said they would meet me at the Old Mill.

So, Vanessa and I go over to Mill Valley. We didn't get there till later in the afternoon – nothing too weird, like 5 or 6 pm. We parked the car and walked in. Sure as shit, there was Tahani sitting at a table. Sitting next to her was Omar Sharif. I mean, this guy looked just like Omar Sharif.

And I said to myself, "Oh, God. Who is this?"

I couldn't figure out what nationality he was. He was real dark. Swarthy.

Tahani saw us and gave a small wave. We started to walk over to the table. As we walked I glanced around the club. I was relieved to see my boy, the Packer, sitting at the far end of the bar, watching us. So, Vanessa and I got to the table and sat down. As best as I can remember, there were two other guys at the table with us and our girls.

As soon as we sat down, Tahani introduced the guy sitting next to her. "Hey, this is my friend, Al-Taneen."

As I shook his hand, I said, "Hey, buddy. How you doing?"

"Good. Good. Good. Good." And I could hear a real strong accent. "No disrespect," I said, "but what nationality are you?"

"I'm Persian."

"Persian? Yeah. You're Iranian."

"Yes," he replied. "But you know there's a lot of trouble. Many Americans don't like Iranians and I don't know what kind of guy you are."

"Hey, hey, hey. I do not give a fuck where you're from. I honestly don't. You go to school here in the United States?"

"Yes, I've got a degree from Berkeley."

To a newcomer, the Bay Area is a little different. It's more advanced than a lot of places. The guy working in the gas station or the convenience store can have a PhD in chemistry, for Christ's sake. And being an East Coast boy, the intellectual level back home wasn't as high or anywhere close to what it was in the Bay Area. But we had other things going for us, being East Coast boys. We knew more about the business we were in, which was basically smuggling and selling dope.

So we ordered drinks and started talking. In the smuggling business it helps to talk the small talk. It helps break the ice. So, we're drinking and shooting the shit. Eventually things begin to really relax and we get to laughing.

Before I know it, three or four hours go by. And I realized that I still didn't know anything about this guy. So, I nodded towards Tahani and asked, "Is this your girlfriend?"

He shook his head and said, "No. She's not. She's a friend of mine."

"Really?" Now I wasn't thinking of any kinky sex with any men involved. But I saw that Italian, and I liked her, and she'd already spent a weekend at the house. I wanted her to come back.

We talked for a few more minutes and I told them I had to go to the restroom.

About 30 seconds after I entered the restroom, the Packer came in.

"What do you think?" he asked.

"Well, listen. I don't feel anything bad from this guy. I'm going to take these two up to the house."

He looked at me questionably. "I don't like that motherfucker."

"Well, yeah. But you don't like anyone."

"No. No. There's something wrong with this motherfucker. I don't like him."

"Well, why don't you like him?"

"Where the fuck is he from?"

"He's Persian."

"Persian, my fucking ass. He's one of those Arabs. I don't like Arabs."

I said, "What the fuck? How many Arabs do you know?"

He thought about it for a moment. "None."

"Come on, man," I said, "let me take them back to the house."

He shook his head. "You just want that Italian pussy."

"Yeah, but let me take the guy back to the house and see what's up.

Because I don't have a clue what this guy wants. Maybe we can make some money."

I could tell he didn't like it, but he finally said okay.

I went back to the table and invited them to my house. He graciously accepted and we all left. I invited them into the main living room where we all sat down.

Of course, at the time, I was making pills. I was involved in smuggling. I was flipping kilos of blow and stepping on 'em. I was doing everything. I was a drug dealer, smuggler, the whole thing. And things were going really well. I told you about the brand new Benz. I also had a really, really nice house. It was just beautiful.

So, we all sit down and started shooting the shit. This Persian had impeccable manners. I don't think I have met a man even to this day who had as impeccable manners as this Persian.

After we had talked for 30 minutes or so, the Persian looked at me. You're a little bit different, Jack. You're not like a regular American."

"Well, I'm not a regular American. I'm a Vietnam veteran, and I've been in the game for a long time. I'm in the business."

He smiled. "Well, you got a little taste?"

"Well, yeah. Sure I have a taste." So I brought out some blow and I laid it out.

I think we freebased this blow. Freebasing was a pain in the ass. Once you get the freebase out of the Petri dishes you had to use high-intensity lamps to make it powder. Then, once she crystallized, it was real smooth. It tasted good to freebase. But, we discovered early on that it was much easier making crack, with just baking soda and ammonia added. We would put half a gram in a bong and hit it with a blowtorch. Much easier.

So the Persian, Tahani, and Vanessa and I started doing dope. Another benefit of using crack is that it doesn't take much dope when you do it that way. Half a gram; hit it with a blow torch. The best part is that you get high immediately.

So we are all doing this dope. Al-Teneen sits back. "Well, you know I've got a little something. I've got this dragon."

"Dragon?" I said. "What the fuck is that?"

"It's heroin."

"Yeah. Well, how do you do it?"

"In my country, they do it on gum wrappers. And they keep a low flame with a match. You make a straw out of tinfoil. And the reason you make the straw is because after you smoke it for an hour or so, the residue builds up in the straw. You open the straw up and you can get a massive hit. It's really, really good dope."

"Can you show me how?"

So, he showed me how to make it; the way you wrap the straw up around a pencil and wrap it back. While I was looking at what we had made, he broke out about a gram of these brown looking crystals. I'd never seen anything like it. He ripped off a strip of tinfoil, hit it with a Bic lighter, and it melted into a glob.

He handed the strip to me and said, "Why don't you run this?"

I wasn't sure how to do it because I had never seen anything like this. So he explained. "Run this down the tinfoil, and it'll take the edge off of the coke."

So I did. It tasted just like shit. In fact, we nicknamed it eck-eck, that's how disgusting it tasted.

But it sure did work. It got you high as a motherfucker.

After we had all taken a hit, I asked him, "Isn't this shit expensive?"

"Yeah. This goes for $500 a gram."

"What?" I was amazed. "Five hundred a gram? No shit?"

That was as much as China White heroin at the time at around $600 a gram. But, I never shot that. I snorted it. Everyone has heard numerous times that all you need is a match head, and most of the time, that is bullshit. All you need is a match head of cocaine—that was always bullshit. I always needed a line at least a half a foot long.

But with China White, that's really all you needed, was a little, little bit. And it got you high as a bitch. So we kept talking, and next thing I know, it's the next day. You know? The sun is coming up.

Everyone was completely wasted, so I said, "Well, why don't you two just kick back and crash out here?"

Al-Teneen just laid back on the couch and said, "If it's okay with you, I'll just sleep here on the couch."

"Fine by me," I said, as my girl and the Italian got up and went to the bedroom. We were all fucked up on cocaine, but that didn't stop us from having a great morning.

We all slept and laid around the house until 2 or 3 pm.

After everyone was up, I said, "Well, let's go downtown and get something to eat. I need coffee and some food."

We drove down to the local café to order some food. I ordered coffee, bacon and eggs, but Al-Teneen, he ordered a strawberry shortcake. Yeah. A great, big piece of strawberry shortcake with this big pile of whipped cream on top. And he ate it like it was the Last Supper.

As he was finishing his shortcake, I said, "Hey, buddy. I don't know if I've ever seen anybody eat strawberry shortcake in the morning."

"It's that fucking dope. You need something sweet."

"Well, I'm going to eat my bacon and eggs."

As we were eating, he said, "You know, we got a little fucked up last night, and we talked all night. Why don't just you and I get together and have a chat?"

"Great." I said.

I gave the Benz to my old lady and she took the Italian. Away they went. I got into Al-Teneen's car and we went down to the docks of Sausalito. We got out and started to walk down the docks.

And as we were walking on the docks, he said, "I can get this merchandise for $12 a gram."

"What? Jesus Christ! And you can flip it for how much?"

"I can flip it for $500 a gram."

"Well, that doesn't put me into the flipping end of it. What do you need from me, because I don't know how to sell heroin? It's basically just for my own consumption and my guys."

"I need someone to smuggle it. I've been looking for someone with experience in the smuggling business for some time now. Tahani told me that she thought you did some smuggling and suggested that we meet. After hearing about your operation last night, I think you're a guy I can trust to get the job done. Can you help me?"

"Yeah, I can help you. Where do we get it?"

"Iran."

"Oh, come on, bro." I said. "You mean Iran, as in Persia, as in over in the Middle East? I can't go to the Middle East."

"Well, maybe we can work something out. Let me get a hold of my brothers, and let's have a chat. One of my brothers is a big-time guy. He owns grocery stores and gas stations in London. Why don't we fly over to London? You can bring one of your guys and we'll check it out. We'll shoot the shit with my brother and see what we can do."

He could see that I still wasn't convinced. "Maybe we can get it up from Tehran to London. And then from London you could get it down to that mansion in the islands."

Now, first of all, I'd never been to London. But, I figured, what the hell. I said, "Well, that sounds good. Yeah. Sure. In the meantime, let's do some business here."

He just smiled and said, "Good."

So we started working with Al-Teneen. It was easy. We were making a killing from only bringing up three or four kilos at a time from Miami to San Francisco and then breaking it up. He could move merchandise as fast as we were bringing it in. That man could sell coke. We were making maximum dollars.

We never had any trouble. There was no tripping in the mud puddle and losing. The guy was right on the money every time. Everything was good.

Everyone liked his dope. After a couple of runs, my boys were curious how good this guy's merchandise was because of how fast he was selling it. So I bought a gram, you know, in good faith. It was good, and highly addictive. Both Luco and the Packer caught the habit real quick. It wasn't the worst habit in the world, but they did that heroin on a regular basis. Of course, they did cocaine as well.

After working with Al-Teneen for a couple of months, I pulled Luco and Bobby aside and asked them whether we should we do serious business with this motherfucker. They both agreed that he had good dope.

Now I was worried about him being from Iran. So I asked Luco what he thought, and he said, “Fuck it. He’s from Iran, but he’s not a regular Iranian either. You know? He’s smart. Let’s go to London and check it out.”

So I took the big guy with me and we flew over to London to meet Al-Teneen’s brother. He looked like Omar Sharif, too. Only his brother was very rich. He was all suit and tie. He smoked cigars and had several Mercedes Benz cars. I knew he wasn’t rich from pumping gasoline or selling shit out of convenience stores. He was rich in the heroin business.

We all sat down and after some friendly talk, I said, “Listen. It’s very difficult to get the merchandise if you’re in Iran. If we get three kilos, which isn’t very much money (about $36,000), we’d be lucky. But if you’re here in London, well then you might be talking about like $26 a gram.”

He just puffed on his cigar and said, “Maybe I can talk you guys into going to Iran and picking the merchandise up. I’m all hooked up. I’ve got all my guys. There’s nothing to worry about. Everything’s fine in Iran.”

Well, we were in negotiations with this guy for the better part of a year before we went to Iran.

I actually didn’t go to Iran. Luco and Bobby went instead. When they got there the entire country was a mess because the Shah had just left. The Shah had his boys, called the Savak. They were like the Shah’s secret police and the Savak were bad motherfuckers. They hurt and tortured the people, and no one liked them. I didn’t really know all the politics of the Shah. I’ve heard seven or eight different versions.

Now there was trouble in the street. For Christ's sake, I thought, a revolution's beginning and my boys are right in the middle of Tehran. If they got caught with three kilos of heroin, the Iranians would have put my boys up against the wall and shot 'em.

Well, communications had broken down because of the revolution. I started to get worried about 'em because we were hearing the news on BBC. There was trouble. Oh, shit. There's a revolution going on in Iran and my two best friends are there.

Finally, they called us from London. "Hey, we'll be in tomorrow afternoon. Get our friend ready."

"Well, what the fuck happened?" I asked.

"We'll tell you when we land."

So, I had to wait until they landed to hear what happened.

It turned out that we made a plan to stay at my mansion in the islands. There we would figure out how to get the dope into the U.S. But, first we had to get the Packer and Luco past customs on the island.

When I bought the mansion, the Packer had traveled back and forth with me to help put it all together. He helped with hiring the carpenters and construction guys.

During the time he befriended a guy at the airport. He would act just like a porter for Bobby. He had it all worked out with customs and immigration. He would wait for Bobby's plane and once Bobby was in line for customs, he would slip the guy a U.S. $10 bill. Then the guy would go in and get the bags. When he came back out he would walk to the head of the line and nod to the customs official who would then wave him through. Of course, he would give $5 on the backside to the customs official. When Bobby would get to the same official, he didn't have anything to worry about. They'd let him walk through without any questions.

Bobby's friend would do that all day long. I imagine he made a good deal of money doing it, too.

So, while we're talking on the phone about our plan, how to get everyone through customs, the Packer said, "I'll just use the guy I've always used at the airport."

In the past we had used the guy at the airport to also bring in television sets. We brought in guns. We brought in handcuffs. We brought everything in that way.

We had taken care of the police as well. We brought them all kinds of new guns. So the police were hooked up. We had them in our pocket, but I certainly didn't want to tell them about bringing in heroin.

"Jesus Christ," I said. "Are you sure? How much should we give him, a couple grand?"

"No. No." replied Bobby, the Packer. "It would look suspicious. Just give him the $10 like usual."

So, a friend and I went to the airport to find the porter.

I handed him $10 and said, "Hey, we've got some guys coming in."

"Oh, good, good, good. Who are they?"

"Well, you know, the guy that usually brings the big TVs in."

He smiled and said, "Oh, okay. I'll just stay up here on top of the airport."

There was no terminal in those days, just a tarmac.

The next day, in came British Air with Luco and Bobby getting off the plane. Our porter just walked up, grabbed their bags and walked 'em right through customs.

A short drive later, we were at the mansion. Once we got back to the mansion Luco told me what happened to them in Tehran.

Luco and Bobby were staying in the Sheraton in Tehran, where every night the power would shut off at 9 o'clock. My guys couldn't leave the hotel. So what did they do? They spent the majority of their time chasing the dragon.

But they weren't worried about it. They just stayed in their hotel chasing that damn dragon. This went on for about a week. Then one day they decided to go to the hotel bar and get a whiskey. But the bartender told them the bar was closed because there was no more whiskey to be sold.

For some reason that woke the two motherfuckers up to the reality of the situation they were in. And they started talking about what they were going to do to get out of all that shit.

It was the Packer who came up with the idea. The Iranians are known for a number of things and one of them is pistachios. He had seen that they sold these great big, one and two-kilo containers of pistachios. So, he went down to the local market and bought a one-kilo and a two-kilo container of pistachios.

I didn't realize how good a nickname the Packer was for Bobby until we had worked together for a few years; that man knows how to pack dope. He is gifted. He can pack anything—or unpack it for that matter. So, he packed the three kilos of pure heroin in with the pistachio nuts. That wasn't planned, and looking back, it was some damn smart, hippie-shit flying. It worked. You couldn't tell that the cans had anything but pistachios in them.

They thought everything was going good until they went to the airport. When they went to buy tickets to leave the country, they were told that all the seats were sold. Frustrated, they went back to their hotel and waited until the next morning. But, when they went back the next morning, they were told the same thing, all the seats were sold. They just kept going back to the airport and kept being told that all the seats were sold.

Finally, on the fourth or fifth day, Luco asked the attendant, "Well, wait a minute. Don't you have anything in first class?"

"Yes. We have first-class tickets."

"Well, give me two of those." He said.

Luco later told me that he felt very foolish for not asking sooner because they could have been out of the country a couple days earlier.

So they bought the first-class tickets, flew to Kuwait and then onto London. Once they made it to London, they stayed in transit, so there wouldn't be any customs. From there they took a flight to the islands.

After Luco told us what happened, I said, "Listen, boys. You got to be smart here."

They just nodded their approval.

Then Luco said, "You got any blow?"

And I said, "Yeah. I do." So we ended up snorting.

After we had done the cocaine I looked at both of them and said, "Now we've got the plan from Iran really worked out well here, but how the fuck are we going to get it into the United States?"

Luco is a world traveler. He's traveled more than anyone I know, and I've got about 40 countries under my belt. But this guy, he dwarfs me. He's been everywhere. He's traveled the world over and over again.

So, Luco said, "I noticed a little something the last time I flew back to Miami. I flew in through St. Croix. I cleared customs in St. Croix."

In those days, passengers exited the plane from the front and the back, right onto the tarmac; half would go out the front and the other half out the back. Then they have a customs official walk through the plane.

St. Croix was a pre-clearing for U.S. customs. So if you cleared in St. Croix, you wouldn't have to clear once you landed in Miami.

"Well, listen." Luco continued, "I looked at 'em. They clear customs, but they do it very quick. That might be our opportunity. Let's fly to St. Croix and just check it out."

We all agreed and flew to St. Croix the next day. Luco was right. Everything was outside, including immigrations and customs.

After we reviewed the main customs, Luco said, "Let's take a look at how they clear the plane."

Now we're in line with our bags to go through immigration and customs. Because it is outside, we have a full view of the airplane. At the back of the plane were three or four customs officials getting ready to enter the plane.

"Okay." I said, "Let's time them."

I looked at my watch when they went up the rear stairs and entered the plane, then again when they exited out the front. It only took 57 seconds. In other words, they walked straight through the plane and walked off.

I looked at the boys and said, "That's it. That's it right there."

When we got back to the islands I told the boys what I had in mind.

"We can hire those two girls from Key West. Those girls are good. They can stay down here, have a decent time with us, and then we'll fly 'em to St. Croix."

"They'll stick four or five ounces of heroin down in their panties. Nobody's going to touch their asses."

I continued, “We’ll get ‘em right through in the islands, and get ‘em on the airplane. But once they take off from the islands we’ll have ‘em duct tape the heroin in the bathroom, underneath the sink, up around the pipes. We’ll set it all up and show ‘em how to do it.”

‘They’ll clear customs like it’s nothing. They’ll get back on the airplane, go to the bathroom right away, and stick it back into their panties. Then in Miami they’ll walk off the plane like they flew from Davenport, Iowa to Chicago. You know? No customs.”

“If we go as well,” Bobby added, “we can each get ten ounces at a time. At $500 a gram, this shit is worth a fortune. We can start rolling in the money, and everything will start working good.”

We decided to give it a shot. We hired the girls from Key West and showed them what to do. We then bought tickets and went to the airport. Well it worked slick as shit. No problem whatsoever. Not one problem.

We got rid of a kilo, worth about five-hundred grand, fairly quick. And things were going really good.

As usual, it was all just business. It might be considered dirty business, but the way I looked at it, I figured it was just a little piss-ass, three-kilo heroin job. There are runners who smuggle in 500 kilos of heroin every month. So that is how I justified it.

Then one day, Al-Teneen said, “Hey. You know? Being a chemist, I know this chemical that will let us double our merchandise.”

“No shit?” I said, “What’s that?”

“It’s called antiprine. It’s the only substance that will melt and take the form of the heroin. If you hit it with a Bic lighter, it melts and then you can chase it. It’s going to take away the potency, of course. But, we can cut it and double the merchandise.”

"Well," I said, "we've got about a kilo left."

He then smiled. "Well, now it's two kilos. We'll give 'em a little discount, and we'll sell it at $375 a gram. See if we can wholesale it out and dump this shit off."

Man, it worked just like it shipped. We got the antiprine. We whacked it and made a little extra money.

Looking back, Berkeley was one wild place at the time. It was something. Some of the smartest chemists in the world lived there. They were making everything, including cocaine. I know guys who were actually making cocaine. It looked like re-rock. It was a solid, solid rock. You had to hit it with a screwdriver and a hammer. But it was still unbelievable blow. It was great dope.

Chapter 31: Misplacing $150K

1978

Sometimes everyone has to laugh at themselves. In 1978 my wife rented a small house in Tiburon. It was up on the side of the mountain, overlooking San Francisco.

The mountainside was so steep that the house was on stilts. You walked right in from where you could park two cars. The kitchen was on the right. Straight ahead was a combination living/dining room area. There was a staircase that went down to the bathroom and a small bedroom. It was a little, tiny house with a deck overlooking San Francisco and Tiburon.

Things were going okay. And, of course, I was snorting cocaine, chasing the dragon and doing dope all the time, plus I was working. One evening I came home around midnight and I had about $60,000 in cash with me. I saw that my wife was still up. I said, "Hey, baby. I'm just gonna get fucked up and watch cable."

Having cable in California was just great, especially since I had none in Miami. There was this guy on TV named Jay Brown. He ran a big car dealership down in San Jose, and he played the old movies. So when my wife asked what I was going to watch, I said, "Well, I'm just gonna sit down in the living room, smoke a little coke, chase the dragon and see what movie Jay Brown has on tonight."

But instead of sitting down and watching TV, I broke out all my guns. I had a 12-gauge shotgun, like a riot gun from the Roaring '20s, the one with a pump and an 18-inch barrel. It was in mint condition. It was a beautiful gun. I also had a Walther PPKS 380, a .38 caliber, hammerless revolver, and, of course, the old reliable Browning 9mm.

I was smoking dope, chasing the dragon and bonging cocaine, and the next thing I knew it was daylight.

For no real reason I decided that I would count my money. I had the $60,000 I'd brought home and I thought I had another $90,000 in the house. I got up and put all the money on the living room table.

I then started putting the hundreds together with rubber bands. In those days, we put it all together in $5,000 stacks. I was fucked up. I had spent the entire night snorting cocaine and chasing the dragon, and now it was 8 or 9 in the morning. Somehow I made it down the stairs and went to bed.

I finally woke up about 3 or 4 in the afternoon. I went upstairs and the wife was up. I looked at her and said, "Can I get something to eat?"

She smiled at me. "Sure. Would you like breakfast?"

"Sure."

My regular breakfast was eggs, bacon, toast and grits. Being from the South, though born in Syria, Vanessa knew how to make a big breakfast.

As I was eating I suddenly realized that all the money I had left on the coffee table was missing.

I looked around the room to see if my wife had moved it to the counter or something. When I didn't see it, I said, "Where the hell's my money?"

She looked at me and said, "What money?"

"I had all the money out last night on the coffee table. I counted it and put it into bundles and left it on the coffee table."

She shrugged her shoulders and said, "Well, I don't know where it is."

"What?"

I immediately got up and went downstairs and started going through the closet. I had several pairs of cowboy boots and she had all kinds of high-end clothes. I went through the whole closet but didn't find anything. I then went through the bed and then the rest of the bedroom, which took about ten minutes. Nothing.

In frustration, I went upstairs and looked through the living room but didn't find anything either. I thought I was losing my mind; I couldn't find $150,000.

"What the fuck?" I said in frustration.

I turned to my wife and asked, "You been out?"

"No, I haven't left the house."

"Well, wait a minute. Did you steal that fucking money?"

"What?" she said in a very upset tone. "Have you lost your goddamn mind? You've been up all night doing dope, you fucking moron."

She looked around the room before she continued, "You've got the money somewhere here in the house."

"Well, look at this house. It's a little dinky house. Where the fuck could I have hid the money?"

So we started tearing the house apart. We looked in the kitchen. We looked behind the refrigerator, the stove, and underneath the sink. We went through all the cupboards, all the drawers, we looked through the whole goddamn entire house and could not find the money.

We went downstairs and went through all our clothes again. Then we went through the rest of bedroom. We had one of those beds that was up off the ground. It had six drawers on each side. The Packer had bought it for me. It was perfect for the house because you could cram a lot of shit into it. But there wasn't any money in the drawers.

So, we went through the entire house again, nothing. It didn't take that long but it was the better part of an hour scouring, looking for that goddamn money.

Finally, my wife stopped and said, "I bet you I know where that money is."

"Where, baby?"

She smiled and said, "In the couch."

"Well, who would put the fucking money in the couch?" I asked.

So, we went into the living room and tipped the couch upside down. On the bottom was a zipper that held the cover on. We unzipped it and found $150,000 stacked inside of it.

I was so fucked up I didn't even know where I hid my own money. Of course, I had to grease down my old lady for helping me find it.

Chapter 32:
Shot in the Head by a Mummy

1978

Still 1978 and still living in California.

Luco, the Big Guy, was a real prick, but he always came across as a friendly fellow and he knew 40 or 50 people, a lot of them girls. Many of the girls we called coke whores. But after the dragon came into their lives, we called a few of them smack whores.

Well, there was this one little girl from Buffalo. She was a gorgeous little girl, about five feet tall and smart, well-educated, sharp as shit. But, she had a couple of weaknesses. One was cocaine. She also had a real bad one for the dragon. The little bitch loved to chase the dragon.

On occasion we'd use her to stash coke or to stash heroin. One time, we ended up with 500 pounds of cheap weed. It was a lower commercial Colombian weed that we got in Miami on the front because our guys couldn't sell it. We told them that as a favor we'd work it out. So, we took it to California and we stashed it with her.

Well, we were moving it, but it was very difficult. It was at a cheap price, but California, even back in those days, was a touchy market. It was hard as a motherfucker to sell anything if you didn't have the Santa Marta Gold or Thai sticks or some high-end Jamaican coolie. But we were moving it, slowly but surely, just in small amounts.

One morning Luco and I went to the girl's place to get a tally on the merchandise. She had a little shed adjacent to her apartment where we stashed the dope. We had left 500 pounds, but when we opened up the shed there was only 400 pounds inside.

I was really pissed off.

"Well, what the fuck?" I said. "That little bitch stole 100 pounds of weed."

Luco shook his head. "No, she couldn't have done that."

So we went into her apartment to find out what happened to the missing hundred pounds.

When I asked her about the missing weed she acted dumb and said, "Well, why are you saying that to me?"

"The lock on the door is broke and 100 pounds is gone. Any good thief would have taken it all. It sounds like a little cunt's involved and that would be you. You took our merchandise."

"No, no, no. I didn't take it," she started whining.

I looked at the Big Guy and said, "This bitch is guilty. She stole the merchandise."

Luco didn't speak. He just reached into his pocket and pulled out a hammerless .38 pistol.

The minute he took that .38 out of his pocket she went pale and told us where the weed went. "Shithead took it. It's my fault. He took it. He didn't take it all. He took 100 pounds."

"Where is this motherfucker?" I asked.

"I don't know, but he's gonna bring the money back. He's splitting the deal with me. I worked it all out with him. I'm sorry. Please don't hurt me."

I let her sweat for a couple of minutes and then said, "We're not gonna hurt you, but you better be here when we get back." I turned and walked out the door.

"What are we going to do?" Luco asked as we walked to the shed in back.

"We're gonna set this cocksucker up."

We immediately moved the merchandise to another place and then went back to the bitch's apartment.

When we walked back into the house she was sitting at a small table looking scared.

I looked at her and said, "Now we own your ass. Either you're gonna have to move or you're gonna work with us."

She looked a bit relieved and said, "No, no, no. I don't like this motherfucker anyway."

Now I knew she wouldn't leave and that she'd be more than willing to help us because she was a junkie, and she didn't have any money.

If a junkie doesn't have any money, they become the worst piece of shit slime in the world. A junkie would dig up his or her dead mother and melt down her wedding ring for money. They're terrible. They're disgusting. But if a junkie has money, he or she is able to work. I've seen them both ways.

She was a junkie without money. So, we told her that if she helped us set him up and get our merchandise back we would give her $5,000. That was all that it took to get her to go to work for us.

It took us about a month before we were finally able to set him up. Through the girl, we offered him $60,000 worth of smack at a reduced rate. The plan was that she was going to lure her man to the Big Guy, because her man thought it was my weed when he conspired with her. He didn't know the Big Guy was involved.

They had just built a new resort marina hotel over in Berkeley, right down on the water. It was at the end of Telegraph near the Bay Bridge.

When we were ready, we came up with a sample that hadn't been cut and had the girl deliver it to our target. When he was satisfied, we had the girl tell him we would deliver in two days.

In order for our plan to work we needed some additional help. So I went up to Fairfax. At that time Fairfax was kind of like Key West. Key West was a union hall for smugglers and sailors. Fairfax was a union hall for armed robbers, degenerates, druggies and dope dealers.

I had four or five guys up there that I knew very well. One of them was ex-Army and a bad motherfucker who I'll call Vance. He was a Vietnam veteran and a monster. He stood 6' 4" and was 250 pounds of solid muscle. His wife had recently died of cancer of the cervix, a terrible death. She'd lingered for the better part of a year. Her death really destroyed this young man and he had caught a real bad smack habit. Overall he was a good guy, roughly the same age as us.

I found Vance in Fairfax and told him that the guy had taken our weed.

"Well, listen." I said, "We'll give you $5,000 to help us out."

"Okay." He said, "What's your plan?"

"We're going to lure him into this hotel over in Berkeley, and when he comes in, the Big Guy and you will greet him. I'm going to stand in the bathroom. It's your job to swing on him, take him down, handcuff him and duct tape him. We'll just take whatever money he has on him. I'll walk out of the hotel room, down to the end of the hall, out the back door and get in my wife's brand new car, a Lancia. I'll drive around, and you and Luco come out the sliding glass doors, get into the car and everything will be good. We'll drive off. Kind of a simple plan, there shouldn't be any problems."

Two days later, we went to the hotel at the arranged time. Sure as shit, the guy comes to the door and Luco brings him in. They walked into the room and Vince swings on him and he hits him right in the stomach. The guy goes right down. He went down and Luco and Vance started working on him. They put their boots to him, then punched him; they really fucked him up.

As they were beating on him, I picked up the saddle bags and walked out the door, down to the end of the hall, out the back door and got into my old lady's car just like we had discussed. As I started the car I could see Vance and Luco coming out of the back door so I didn't have to go all the way to where the sliding glass door was. They just jumped in. Vance jumped into the passenger seat in the front and Luco got in the back seat.

As soon as they were in, I slammed it into first gear and took off. Well, it was foggy, rainy and nasty, making it hard to see through the front window. Before I got to second gear, something horrid stepped out of the back door of the hotel. It was torn all to pieces. Tattered cloth hung from each of its limbs. I didn't recognize what the fuck the deal was. When the wiper blades cleared the rain from the window I looked closer and recognized that it was the fuckhead that we had just taken down. Luco and Vance had just done a piss-poor job on duct taping him. They hadn't handcuffed his hands behind his back. They had only duct taped his hands and feet. Now, here he was, an ancient monster ready to kill. I could see all the tape hanging in ribbons from his wrist, arms and ankles. He raised his hand and pointed at the car.

As I drove by the passenger-side window exploded, and something smashed into the steering column between my hands.

Vance jerked sideways and screamed, "I'm hit!"

I glanced over at Vance. He had his hand over a big gash on the side of his head and blood was streaming down his face. I put it to the floor and sped off.

Now the Mummy could have killed us. There's no question. He had it. But the gun jumped him. He didn't fire any more shots and we got away before he figured it out.

I'll never forget what Vance said as we were driving away. He pulled his hand away from his head, looked at the blood, and then said, "Hey, listen. I'm gonna need another five grand."

I laugh about it today, but at the time it wasn't funny at all. We took him back to my house and looked at his wound. Luckily it was only superficial and got him patched up pretty quickly. My old lady was pretty pissed off that her car had a bullet hole in it and needed the window replaced. We didn't know exactly where the bullet went until we got back to the house. It hit dead center into the windshield, came back and landed right between my hands on the steering column. Once again, the luck of the devil got me through it.

Chapter 33:

Watch Your Mouth

1980

You know, when smuggling and selling dope, one has a tendency to tell the good stories, the ones with no trouble. Sort of like a gambler going to Las Vegas. No one likes to dwell on the times they lost, you know, that pain in your guts for losing. Jesus, I hate that. This particular story, it's about winning, but there was some trouble.

We moved back to Miami in 1980 and established our abilities to sell tons and tons of marijuana.

One day I got a call from the Brooklyn Boy. He asked us to come over to his house.

So, we went, and the first thing he says is, "Hey, we got a little situation."

"What type of situation?" I asked.

"I know this Italian guy that will only work with gringos."

"That's a bit odd." I said.

"Well, they're not from a family, but they have a little crew and they smuggle small loads. But, they've managed to get their hands on a shrimp boat and they have some serious merchandise."

"What do you mean by serious merchandise?" I asked.

"They've got 15,000 pounds of weed."

"15,000 pounds?"

"Yeah, and it's a little more than what they're used to flipping. They can take care of 1,000 or 2,000 pounds, but this is a little much for them and since they're my friends, I don't even want my standard partners to know about this."

"Okay," I said, "what do you want us to do?"

"I'd like to just kinda go behind their backs and have you guys sell it for me. We can make a little deal, and cut 'em out."

The Brooklyn Boy and I go way back, so I said, "No, problem." (He was my dear, dear friend. He passed away in '89. I loved the guy.)

We went to see the guys who had the weed. It was an Italian boy that was born and raised in South Miami. Seriously, he weighed over 400 pounds. But, he was the nicest guy you could ever meet. The guys that worked for him were all rednecks from the South. I never particularly cared for those racist, redneck cocksuckers. Still don't.

The Italian trusted the Brooklyn Boy and from what we were told, he was a pretty good smuggler for small boats. You know, little 36-, 38-foot sailboats that could take 1,000-2,000 pounds a trip.

So we agreed to pick up a truck with 4,000 pounds of weed at the McDonald's in Perine.

Prior to this time we had met a group of Cubans who were really good about moving merchandise. We called them the good Cubans because of how fast they could flip weed. So, we gave the weed to the good Cubans and they went to work on it immediately.

The Italian was so impressed with how quickly we moved the truckload of weed that he fronted us the rest of the 15,000 pounds.

Well, we were probably a week into the deal, and we had sold about $700,000-$800,000 worth, and we got a call from the Italian's wife telling us that he had tipped over dead in the kitchen. The guy was 31 years old and just dropped dead. It was a complete mind fuck for all of us. Of course our first thoughts went to him and his family. But our next thoughts were, "Wait a minute. We've got 15,000 pounds of that crew's weed."

Well, one of the little redneck cocksuckers called the Brooklyn Boy and said he wanted the weed back. The Brooklyn Boy was a real diplomat. He knew how to talk to people. He was kinda like a union organizer. He worked out deals between the Colombians and the Cubans, who really hated each other. In fact, he taught me how to interface, be a liaison between enemies.

So, the Brooklyn Boy was on the phone and said, "You know, you're gonna cause a lot of trouble. We've already got the merchandise fronted out."

But, the redneck interrupted him and said, "Hey, you don't give the merchandise back, you've got the fucking problem."

The Brooklyn Boy just hung up on him right on the spot and said, "Hey, let's go."

There were about six of us at his house at the time, and when he hung up the phone, we asked him what happened.

"I got a problem with the rednecks," He said, "and they don't live more than ten minutes away."

In 1980 I had a townhouse up in Kendale Lakes, about 15 minutes north. I looked at the Brooklyn Boy and said, "Listen, you just come with us."

He nodded, looked at the other guys, and said, "The rest of you get into the wind."

Everyone immediately left his house and Luco and I took the Brooklyn Boy to my Kendale Lakes townhouse.

Once we were secure, I said, "Okay, listen, let's think this through. We don't wanna be driven from our own homes and we don't want any other problem. What are our options?"

As we talked we realized that the rednecks didn't really know me or the Big Guy very well, but they did know what we looked like and that gave me an idea.

"Well, maybe I can bluff them," I said.

The Brooklyn Boy looked at me and said, "Let's try it."

So about midnight, we went out into the street to the nearest pay phone. The first call I made was to the big Italian's wife.

"Hey, listen sweetie," I said, "we're terribly sorry. I mean, this is terrible what's happened. We wanna let you know that you're not going to lose any money. We're going to take care of you, but we're not, and I repeat, we're not going to give that merchandise back. All right?"

"Yes," she replied, "that sounds good to me."

"Good. Is there any way that you can cool off the rednecks and tell them that everything's all right?"

"Not really." She said. "I have no control over them and quite frankly, they've been extremely rude to me. They never would've talked like that when the old man was alive. He hasn't been dead a day and here they are talking all kinds of shit to me."

Now this really pissed me off. I learned early on that in this business having impeccable manners was the only way you did things.

"Okay," I said, "we're going to try to bluff these guys. If manners don't work, we can always go to Plan B. What's that redneck's phone number?"

She thanked me and gave me the number, and we went back to the condo in Kendale Lakes and we formulated a game plan.

After some conversation I looked at Luco and The Brooklyn Boy. "I'm gonna see if I can bluff these guys."

We waited 'til late the next afternoon before we walked down to the pay phone and called them.

When the redneck answered, I said, "Hey, how are you?"

"Who's this?" He asked.

"I'm with the Brooklyn Boy."

"And which one are you?"

"I'm the little guy and I've got the Big Guy here with me as well."

"Yeah, I want you to tell the Brooklyn Boy..."

"Whoa, whoa, whoa, hold on." I said cutting him off. "Here's the deal. You've sassed and disrespected the Brooklyn Boy and the Italian's wife. Right now, you got a fucking problem. First off, The Brooklyn Boy is not giving back one pound of that fucking herb. Secondly, we're prepared to go to war with your fucking ass in the next 24 hours if you do not change your tone and your story. And if you don't start showing the proper respect to us and the Italian's old lady, consider yourself at war with us. We'll move on you right fucking now. Nobody's living at the house anymore, you have nowhere to go. You're like a fish out of water. You're just a stupid, fucking redneck shithead and I'm not gonna put up with your shit! Now, when we move on your guys, we're gonna move on *you* first. We're gonna concentrate all of our action on your fucking ass. We're not gonna be sassing and threating. This isn't about fist-fighting, this is about moving on your fucking ass. You have fucked up."

After a few seconds he said, "I'm sorry."

"What?" I asked. I was shocked. I figured the guy would talk some shit, and there was gonna be a big fucking problem. But he repeated himself.

"I apologize." He said. "I was out of line. I apologize all the way around. I don't want any trouble from you guys."

"Good, good." I said. "Listen, we never wanna see you again. We're never gonna talk to you again. We don't wanna see any of your boys. Don't come by any of our houses. Don't go by the Brooklyn Boy's house. If the Brooklyn Boy ends up with so much as a key scrape on his car, you're at war. This fucking ends right now. We'll pay the monies owed to the Italian's wife. We're gonna take our time, and we're gonna maximize the dollar. For you fucking up, we're gonna have to take some of this merchandise out of state, and it may be a few weeks before we get all the money. So right now, this is over."

"I'm sorry." He said. "I apologize to you and the Brooklyn Boy."

I paused a few seconds and said, "Good. You're a lot smarter than I thought. I Appreciate it." And I hung up the phone.

I couldn't believe that it worked as well as it did, but looking back we had developed quite a reputation in the business. People knew not to mess with us.

And, we took care of the business. I think it took about two months to sell all that merchandise. We paid the Italian's wife what we owed. And as for the Rednecks, the case was closed. We never saw them or heard from them or had any trouble with them again.

In the dope game, sometimes it pays to be the devil.

Chapter 34:

Jack's Way of Rehabbing

1980

Just before I moved back to Miami, I was living in San Anselmo, California, between San Rafael and Fairfax.

We were doing business with this Egyptian that looked like Rudolph Valentino. In fact, he had a picture on the wall over in Berkeley where he was dressed up like an Argentinian cowboy with a picture of Rudolph Valentino right next to him, and you couldn't tell the difference.

He was a nice guy, but he had a little problem. He chased the dragon. He wasn't my connection for the dragon but he had been chasing the dragon for years. He had a degree in chemistry from Berkeley. We started doing business with him in the pill business.

Eventually we ended up giving him one of our pill machines, sort of fronting it to him so that he could bang out a load of pills. But he stole the pill machine and ran off into the wind owing us $20,000. We didn't see him again for a couple of years. Then all of a sudden he shows up.

Luco was sitting at a bar called Nave's, which is in downtown Fairfax, where the Egyptian walks in and goes to the cigarette machine. He liked to smoke Camels.

Luco got up and walked over to the cigarette machine. "Hey."

The Egyptian got his cigarette pack out of the machine, turned to Luco and said, "Hey, I've been looking for you guys. I still have your machine. I'd like to give it back to you. There was a little discrepancy, I think around $20,000. I have your money, as well. I want to pay you back. Everything's good."

So they switched numbers and Luco came over to my San Anselmo house which sat on a hill. It had eight picture windows. It was beautiful. I was paying $1,400 a month in rent in 1980, which was a fortune at that time.

Luco stepped into the house. "You're not going to believe who I just saw."

I said, "Who's that?"

"The Egyptian."

I started laughing. "Well, what's the deal with him?"

"We're supposed to call him. He has a beeper number and the whole shit. He said he's living over in Berkeley. He says he wants to give us back our pill machine and pay us back the money he owes us. We're supposed to call him tonight."

"Fuck yeah." I said, "I'll believe that when I see it."

"No, no, no. I believe him."

Now, Luco and I had been working together for years and he had a way of knowing what was up. So, if he believed the Egyptian, I did too.

So that night we called him and we hooked up at a bar about halfway between both our houses.

We sat down and started shooting the shit. During the conversation he pulled out a wad of cash and paid us half the money he owed us and he told us he had the pill machine in his car.

After we moved the pill machine to our car he turned to us and said, "I need you guys to please help me out. I need to move some blow."

In 1980 cocaine was a wicked expense. I think it was $45,000 or $50,000 a kilo. So, I asked him how much he had. He said he had a kilo of Peruvian flake. When he brought it out it was like little scales of rose-pink colored blow. When you snorted it, it was like candy. It was just smooth and the head was no jack, no peeking out the window, no tweaking shit. You only had to do a three or four-inch rail to get a real good high. It was beautiful, very nice blow. We nicknamed it rosebud.

After we tried it he asked us, "Can you move this blow?"

"Of course we can." I replied.

It was easy as shit to move. We started flipping it for $1,800 an ounce and we're smiling. But there was just one problem. This guy had stolen our stuff and disappeared for two years. So, we started talking about what we should do to this guy.

It was Luco who came up with the idea. "Let's move a few more kilos for him and then set the piece of shit up for stealing our pill machine and running off with the 20-Gs."

But my old lady didn't think that was right. "Well, he's coming back and he's paying you."

"No, no, no, no." I said. "This motherfucker never would have paid us if he hadn't run into Luco at that bar."

So we started moving one or two kilos and were getting ready to set this guy up. Now, he had us take off the money that he owed us, and that was one quality I liked about this guy. He was born and raised in Egypt, but he was not Muslim. He was a Coptic Christian and his family had power and wealth. That's how they afforded him the luxury of going to UC Berkeley.

One day he asked me where had come from and I told him that I was from Maine.

As soon as he found out I was from Maine, he asked me an odd question, "Do you know how to get your hands on a granite saw?"

"I'm sure if I went to New Hampshire I can get a granite saw, but why the fuck do you want a granite saw?"

"Because I have friends that travel in and out of Luxor. I'd like to go down to some of the tombs to cut some of the antiquities off and smuggle them back in to the U.S. We could make a fortune."

I had never heard anyone say anything like that before, and quite frankly, I didn't even know where Luxor was, but it amused me. It was something that I had never heard, and I liked it.

But, I didn't like it enough to forget about how he had skipped out on us with our pill machine and $20K. Luco and I continued to talk about what we should do to this guy to teach him a lesson for fucking with us.

After we had moved a few kilos for him, I just decided we couldn't let what he did slide. I turned to Luco and said, "Well, fuck it. Let's make him pay. Let's set him up."

"How do you want to do it?" Luco asked.

"He said he had 20 kilos of the rosebud left. Let's set him up for 10 kilos."

"That sounds good to me."

The deal would be that the Egyptian would bring another guy, a gringo, a white boy, to my house. But, what they didn't know was that we had moved everything out of the house except for the furniture in the living room and the kitchen.

Luco waited for the Egyptian upstairs while Vance, the guy that got shot in the head, and I waited in the basement with a 12-gauge shotgun and a Browning 9 mm. I had the 12 gauge.

When the Egyptian and the white boy finally arrived and came into the house, Luco greeted them, led them into the living room and had them sit on the couch.

"Is everything good?" Luco asked once everyone was seated.

"Yeah, it's in the car." The Egyptian replied.

Now we had set it up so that once Luco knew where the rosebud was, he would give us the code. So, Luco said, "Hey, everything's good. We're real happy to see you."

It worked just beautiful. They didn't know what to do when Vance led the way up the stairs and jumped right out in front of both of them and I pulled up to the side. We had them cornered with the 12 gauge and 9mm. We put them on the floor, handcuffed and duct taped them. I made sure that we did a real good job this time, because I wasn't about to face another mummy.

After I knew they were secure, we took their keys and went out to the car to get the ten kilos of rosebud out of the trunk.

Now we didn't want to fuck these guys up. We didn't want to hurt these guys. We just wanted to make them pay the tax.

When we came back in I walked over to the white boy laying on the floor and said, "Hey, listen. There's nothing personal about you, but this mother-fucking Egyptian he caused us a lot of pain and agony when he took that pill machine and 20 grand from us. His disrespect really bothered us. You have the misfortune of being caught up with this motherfucker, so if you guys want us to leave, basically you can go fuck yourself. We're not going anywhere."

We all turned and walked out the door, leaving them in the house.

We had moved all of our stuff to a house in Lake Tahoe because it was only about four-and-a-half hours from the Bay Area. We had already set it up with our connections that we were going to start moving the merchandise.

Of course, once we got to Tahoe, we went right back into smoking cocaine. We didn't cook the rosebud into freebase. We cooked it into crack instead, because it was much easier to use and because it was so beautiful. We also had eight or nine grams of the dragon with us as well.

I actually quit chasing the dragon and doing cocaine while I was living in Lake Tahoe, just gorgeous country. Luco, my old lady and I had rented a cabin.

One time we were up all night, and I was smoking blow in crack form in a bong. It was just becoming daylight. I had four or five strips of aluminum foil laid out on the table. The tinfoil had great big globs of the dragon on it and I had a straw all ready to take a hit of the crack, then run the dragon right after it. What you would do is you'd hit the crack and you'd get high. That would last somewhere between one and four seconds, then it's gone. So, you then run down and chase the dragon for five or six runs.

I did this all the time, but for some reason this time, it flipped me the fuck out. As daylight was just arriving, my wife came walking across the living room floor. I will never be able to forget the image. She had one of those high-end negligee gowns on that had real big sleeves, kind of like a Japanese kimono, but not tied off. She was coming across the living room with a blow torch in her hands. The flame looked like it was three-feet long in the predawn light.

As she was walking towards me she kept saying, "Don't worry, baby. I won't burn you. Don't worry, baby. I won't burn you." It was more horrifying than the Mummy with the gun in the alley. But it got much worse. As she was getting ready to light the bong with the torch I noticed that her hands were shaking, causing the flames to bounce.

She finally put that torch on the bong and I took that hit which lasted three or four seconds. Then I ran the dragon probably eight or nine times while my wife just sat back and watched with the blow torch still running. As I finished my hit she turned the blow torch off.

Just before my last hit, I looked at my wife and said, "You know what? The minute this blow is gone, I'm done with this shit. We're moving. I'm going back to Maine."

And she said, "I'm not leaving the Bay Area."

"Oh, but you are." I said. "You're either leaving the Bay Area or you're staying in the Bay Area. Looking at you coming across the floor with a three-fucking-feet long flame coming out of that goddamn thing was horrifying. I'm fucking done."

It took about a week to smoke the rest of it, but when that was gone, I was done.

I moved all the merchandise to guys in the Bay Area. It only took two, maybe three weeks to sell all 10 kilos. I took the money and moved back to Maine.

Before we left I asked my wife, "Baby, are you coming or not?"

She said, "Yes, I'm coming with you."

When I left, I took a couple of ounces of rosebud back to Maine with me. Between my brother and all my cousins, we just drank whiskey and beer, smoked cigarettes, and snorted the rest of the coke. That was it. I never did any coke or heroin again for four or five years.

For me, it was fuck rehab. It was Charlie Sheen time. Charlie said, "All you motherfuckers don't have an idea what you're talking about. I can quit doing dope any time I want to." That's what I did. I quit right then. I never had an urge for it. At least three or four years went by before I took a couple of little bumps of coke, but heroin and crack, never again.

Am I saying don't try to get clean? Don't try to get straight? Absolutely not. If you've got a problem, well, deal with it. But certainly don't let any of those quack rehab cocksuckers get into your life and go through some 12-step program. You're gonna have to quit on your own.

My only suggestion is do what I did. I moved to where there was no heroin or cocaine and that's how I quit. If you want to quit you have to do the same, move somewhere where there isn't any.

Does that make me some big fucking deal? That I know more than some psychiatrist? No, but I don't like people getting scammed into thinking you can walk into some rehab center and drop down on one knee and suddenly quit doing dope. Fuck that. It's bullshit. Move somewhere where there's no dope, if you can. Other than that, best of luck to you.

Chapter 35: The Deranged Colombian

1981-82

I knew of a young Colombian who was only 24 to 25 years old, and he belonged to a good-sized crew. They were with the Medellin Cartel, and he had worked his way up from the street just like Pablo and a number of the boys, by stealing cars and moving dope—just little nickel-and-dime shit to move his way up the ladder.

He had finally found himself in a position to get close to one of the high level cartel members. He had gained his trust by doing numerous deeds. I didn't see them personally, but I understand he wasn't afraid to go all the way. So they sent him on a mission. They had 8,000 kilos of blow that they had smuggled up to Mexico and then across the border into Downey, California. And they sent this kid to look after the distribution of the merchandise. That was his job.

He was all hooked up. He was sitting on top of 8,000 kilos of blow that he had stashed across three apartments in Downey. They were townhouses with an attached garage. He would assign a working man to a townhouse, usually with his wife and children.

The working man would pick up the dope and take it home in the trunk of his car. When he got home he would drive into the garage and close the door. Once the door was closed, he would take the merchandise out of the car and into the house without anyone seeing what he was doing.

The next morning, the man would dress in a suit and would load the merchandise into the car, usually a gray

Toyota. When he left it looked as if he was going to work like everyone else. Once he got to his location, he would change into shorts and a t-shirt and move the merchandise. Before he went home he changed back into his suit. Through this setup they were able to move merchandise in and out without anybody really knowing it.

Well, he had been kicking out the blow for the better part of two weeks, and then, bam, everyone in Colombia from top to bottom got whacked. The whole crew got killed. There was no one left.

And there he was, 23-24 years old with 8,000 kilos of blow. But, this kid had been trained. He knew the network in the United States and knew all of the mechanisms for distributing the merchandise.

So, he said, "Fuck it!" He worked all that merchandise by himself and blow was very, very pricey in the early to mid-'80s; you could get $25-30,000 on the dump. He flipped it all. He was getting money back from all over—California, Nevada and Seattle. And, of course, he kept all of that money and went back to Colombia a very wealthy young man.

Right after that, he started his own blow business, but he was cautious. He stepped right into construction and started building. His first loan was for an apartment building. And it didn't take long for him to have one of the largest construction companies in Cartagena. It was great for laundering all the money he was making in the blow business. But then he discovered the love of his life: beauty pageants.

For those who haven't been to Colombia or are not familiar with Colombians, they love beauty pageants. And there's a good reason for that: They have some of the most gorgeous, beautiful women in the entire world.

He liked to solicit contestants from up in the mountains—girls that came from poor families and who were not slick, not born into money. Girls he could manipulate.

He would go to these beauty contests all over Colombia; whether there was a contest in Bucaramanga, Buena Ventura, Cali, Medellin, Bogota, Cartagena or Santa Marta. At these beauty contests he would pick out the girl he liked the best and say to her, "You're gonna win."

Of course, she'd get all excited and say, "Oh, really?"

He knew he had her then, and would sweeten the deal by saying, "Oh, yeah. You're gonna win, and there's a prize that goes with that: $25,000 and a tour all over Colombia. You'll be heralded as the queen. You'll get a chance to travel and you can live in my apartment."

Of course, what poor girl wouldn't want all of that? Twenty-five grand in Colombia is a fortune. He would then start banging these girls. He would captivate these girls and take them to back his apartments. He would shower them with gifts and money and let them use his fancy cars. He would even have the girl's family, her mother, father and sometimes siblings move into the apartments with them.

He wasn't doing this with just one girl at a time. He had many apartments like this. Of course he had each girl feeling like she was something special.

After the girl's family would move in, he'd keep them for about a month. Then one day he would pick a vantage point to watch what was to happen. Once he had a vantage point he'd send in his men, who would go to the apartment and clean everything out of it.

Then they would take the family down the street and say, "Hey, fuck you! You're done. You get nothing. You cause any trouble, we'll murder you, you pieces of shit." And they'd throw the entire family into the street. And he would be masturbating the entire time. That's how he got his jollies off.

Then he'd move on to the next girl in the next apartment.

He was just one deranged Colombian.

Chapter 36:
Brass Balls

1981-1982

In the days, the early '80s, the weed business went from early October right through April of the next year; summertime was the dead time.

Everything was going good. The Brooklyn Boy had made some new contacts and we had walked into his house in the middle of one of his meetings. He introduced us to a Cuban and a Chinese-Jamaican. The Cuban was very right-wing, so we started calling him the Right-Wing Cuban. We talked for a bit and they said liked what we brought to the table. They wanted to do business with us. They fronted us 10,000 pounds to see what we could do.

We flipped the 10,000 pounds in just over three weeks. Luco and I had kept the money at my place and when we sold the last of the weed we pulled it out and counted it. We had over $2 million for the Brooklyn Boy. To say we were excited was an understatement. We put the money into a couple of bags and went to the Brooklyn Boy's house. When we showed him the money he was elated. It was quite exciting to walk into a situation like that. Within a few weeks I actually made $500,000. It was very, very nice for everyone.

Of course we were now in good graces with everyone. We all became really close after that. So it was no more than three or four weeks later and they had another load for us, but this time it was for 25,000 pounds.

We were getting ready for the next run when the Brooklyn Boy came over to my house and said, "Hey, the Chinaman is talking shit."

Luco and I were both surprised and I asked, "Why? How come he's talking shit? We brought $2,750,000 to the house. We didn't steal any money. We're back."

"I don't know." The Brooklyn Boy said, "I think there's some little game he's running. I thought you'd want to know."

I thought about it for a few seconds and said, "I think he needs to go."

"No, No, Jack. We can't do that," he replied.

We talked about what to do and decided to just focus on the next shipment, doing business with the Right-Wing Cuban. The Right-Wing Cuban was a nice guy and I liked working with him. We set up the time for the next load and made arrangements with the Cuban. He would sell half, 12,500 pounds, and we would turn the other 12,500 pounds.

It took about two weeks to move the merchandise and get paid off. So, then we were really in good graces. The next time we took $3,437,000 to the Brooklyn Boy's house. All of this took place in a little over a month. Things were going well and, of course, another 25,000 pounds were planned for the beginning of the year.

The Colombians had a policy where they would go on vacation from December 20 to January 20. During that time we couldn't get work out of them. Not only would they take a month off, they would also take off any major Colombian holidays, and they had what seemed like 50 holidays a year. We were planning on the next load in late January.

Just before the next load was due to come, I met the Cuban and his whole crew. They were all hot-blooded and all wound up.

He walked into the house and before I could say anything, he said, "Hey, I've got a big problem."

"What's the matter?" we asked.

"Some business has taken place with some friends of mine and one of the Colombians accused me of stealing 10,000 pounds of Santa Marta Gold."

We didn't say anything, we just looked at him.

"Tomorrow at 12 noon," he continued, "I'm going to have a meeting with the Colombians. If that fucking Colombian says that I took 10,000 pounds of weed from them or accuses me of taking the 10,000 pounds, I'm going to shoot the motherfucker immediately. I don't' give a fuck who's there, I'm going to shoot him in the face."

He paused and looked at each one of us. "Who will go with me?"

"I'll go with you," Luco, The Brooklyn Boy and I said, almost in unison.

So automatically there were nine of us. We told him that we also needed to get the Chinese-Jamaican.

The Right-Wing Cuban told us that he would have his guys ready, but when we talked to the Chinese-Jamaican, he said didn't like the sound of it, and that he didn't want any part of it.

Aha. I knew it right there. We hadn't been working with this little chicken-shit cocksucker for two months and he is showing his true colors.

So here was the plan. We were all armed to the teeth. We were going to a shopping mall over on Flagler because it was public. We were going to have the meeting right in the open. The Colombians were going to come and talk with us about the missing 10,000 pounds of weed that the Right-Wing Cuban had been accused of stealing.

A couple of the Right-Wing Cuban's men sat at a table on one side of the court and Luco and I sat maybe six or seven tables away on the other side. The Brooklyn Boy and a couple of the Cuban's men sat at the table next to The Cuban.

Well, as we're sitting there waiting for the meeting, the Colombians finally came in. All three looked relatively young, like in their early 30s. They came in and sat down across from the Brooklyn Boy, the Right-Wing Cuban and his crew. I didn't think the Colombians would only come with three people, so I looked around the room. Sure enough, there were at least 10 other Colombians scattered throughout the food court, but none of them looked over 21 years old. They all looked like kids, like a little gangbanging organization. But I knew that these were big-time Colombian Cartel guys.

Luco and I talked about what we should do if all shit broke loose. We decided that the best thing to do was to pull out the Brownie and shoot off 13 or so rounds into the air and get the fuck out of there. We didn't want to hurt any civilians. We didn't want any civilians to get caught up in the middle of this shit, but we had to show them that we had balls.

For some reason I suddenly thought how that chicken-shit motherfucking Chinese-Jamaican was not there for this meeting. It was just us.

Well, I kept looking around the food court, watching the Colombians. They kept coming by and they were smiling. They knew who we were and we knew who they were. You could feel the tension in the air. It wouldn't take much for the situation to explode.

Then all of a sudden the Cuban got up and shook hands with the Colombians. Then the Brooklyn Boy shook hands with them. The meeting was over. We all stood up, walked outside, and waited for the Cuban.

The Cuban came out and said, “Hey. You fucking gringos got brass balls. Let’s go to my house right now and have a little party.”

The Brooklyn Boy got in the van with us and the Cubans left in their car. We all met over at the Cuban’s house and had a great party.

This was the beginning of a beautiful relationship that lasted quite a long time.

Chapter 37:

Two Mako Boats Make a Ton

1983

After the Right-Wing Cuban talked with the Colombians, things really started to rock and roll. The Cuban had a big crew, bigger than I realized. It was huge.

They were smuggling weed day and night, all the time. Sometimes it would just show up out of the blue. There would be 6,000 pounds here, 4,000 pounds there. We'd get 2,000 pounds one day and another 5,000 pounds the next day. Every now and then they would bring in 20,000 pounds or more.

We were just flipping weed constantly as it came in. There just weren't any schedules set up. The Cuban had connections all over the world. He worked with several other groups of Cubans and a couple groups of Colombians. Meanwhile he was also working with us. So we just kept flipping weed.

We had it set up where we would move the weed to the good Cubans, who had multiple houses set up for distribution. It was understood that we were not the only game in town. The good Cubans had multiple smugglers besides us bringing them weed as well. Even though we had made several million dollars in a few weeks, we were not even a drop in the bucket compared to the amount of weed that was being brought into the United States. It was all just business to us.

The good Cubans were moving the merchandise so quickly that we gave them all of our merchandise on the arm. They took the majority of it to New York City, where they got maximum dollar. So everyone was getting rich. We were doing very well, not as well as the big boys, but we were happy.

We had worked our way in, so we no longer had the Packer picking the merchandise up each time from the Right-Wing Cubans and delivering it to the good Cubans. We actually used the Right-Wing Cuban's connections and the guy's sailors to deliver merchandise.

They would bring in a load to one particular house out in the Redlands, where the good Cubans owned multiple houses. And we'd work the merchandise out of there for a week or so. We were also taking care of business up the Panhandle of Florida using another boat.

Luco and I were at one of the houses in Panama City, which is in the Panhandle, and I got a call at about 7 or 8 p.m. from the Brooklyn Boy.

"Hey, listen," he said. "We've got some more weed. We've got a few thousand pounds coming into Redlands tomorrow afternoon. Can you get back here and flip it?"

"No problem." I said. "We'll leave first thing in the morning."

So, the following morning we got up at 6, left Panama City and drove straight through to Miami. When we got to Brooklyn Boy's house, the Cuban and his crew were there.

After some pleasantries, the Cuban said, "I have 2,000 pounds. It's beautiful."

"Better than Santa Marta Gold?" I asked.

"Well, it's not from Santa Marta, but it is beautiful, beautiful merchandise. It's the same price as the previous shipments. Can you have your boys flip it?"

"No problem whatsoever," I said, "but we need to prearrange a meeting. Where are you bringing it up to?"

"You just name the spot and I'll have my boys be there."

"All right."

So I went out and talked with the good Cubans.

"We've got a ton coming," I said. "Where would you like to have us bring it?"

"The same house you brought it to last time,"

I returned and told the crew. "It's going to be easy. We're going to bring it to the same house as last time. But hey, don't do it until I give you the go-ahead. We don't want any trouble with anyone. We just want to give them a heads-up that it's coming to the same house as last time."

Things rarely go just right with any of these deals. Something usually goes wrong. This one turned out being a case of lost in translation.

The next day I got a call from the Right-Wing Cuban.

"Hey, I can't get a hold of them," he said. "I told the crew that it was the same house as last time. They're bringing it straight to the guy's house right now."

"Holy fuck!" I said. "You can't do that. He's not prepared for it."

I called the good Cuban to explain the situation so that he'd have a heads up.

"Hey, listen." I said. "There's been a fuck-up. They're bringing the merchandise to the same house as we worked the big load last time."

"Well, you can't do that," he said. "I have another load in that house right now."

I hung up the phone and got Luco and the Packer. We drove over to the house.

As I pulled up to the house there were two huge dually pickups with MAKO boats on trailers behind them, parked on the street in front of the gates.

Now I don't remember exactly what was said, but the good Cuban later told me that this is the only time he ever had a harsh word for me.

As I walked up to him he looked at me and said, "Jack, this shit better be good merchandise."

"I'm sorry." I apologized. "It got lost in translation. It's my fault."

"It just better be good merchandise."

We walked to the gates and he had his men pull both of the MAKOs into the yard. Once the gates were secured, we climbed onboard the boats, lifted up the center cockpits and there was 2,000 pounds of the best weed I had ever seen.

He smiled and said, "Hey, it's good. Same price?"

"Same price," I said.

"Good. No problem," he said. "I'll cash you out tonight."

Later that night he paid me in $100 bills.

Chapter 38:

50,000 Pounds of Weed

November 1983

I was up in Maine deer hunting. I always took as much time as I could in September, October, and the end of November to hunt deer, bear and moose, but deer in particular. We had quite a crew up near a little town called Rangeley, Maine. It was a small town of only about 140-150 people, but they were all outlaws. Even native Mainers were afraid to go there. It's still pretty cool today.

It was a November deer hunt and it was snowing. I had rented a little camp close to my cousin's house. He lived in the middle of nowhere. He came over to my camp and told me that my wife had been calling all day, sort of an emergency situation.

So we went back to his house and I called my wife.

"Hey, baby." She said, "Listen. The Brooklyn Boy has been calling every half-hour all day. I told him I probably wouldn't be able to get a hold of you until this evening because you were hunting. He said please call him right away."

I called the Brooklyn Boy and as soon as he heard my voice he said, "Oh, shit. We've got a situation."

"What's going on?" I asked.

He responded in a code that we used to make sure that no one but us knew what we were talking about. "In a couple of days our friend is going to have a lot of work."

"Oh, well shit. That's good. When's this supposed to take place?"

"Well, not tonight," he said, "but tomorrow night can you come down?"

Well, I was in Maine and the Brooklyn Boy was in Miami. The Packer was in Toms River, New Jersey, and Luco, the Big Guy, was in San Francisco. So I called the Packer and told him the story. "I need you in Miami ASAP," I told him.

"Okay. No problem. I'll get the first flight out."

I had trouble reaching Luco. He just didn't answer his phone. When I finally reached him, he said, "Don't worry. I'll get the red-eye."

Finally I called my wife and said, "Listen, I'll be home as soon as I can, but it's snowing like a bitch and I'm up in the mountains."

Now, I was a couple of hundred miles from my house and normally it would only take about four hours to get home. But it was snowing and even with my four-wheel drive it took me the better part of eight hours.

The following morning, at 6 o'clock, I was on a bird to Miami.

I arrived in Miami the night they did the job. The Right-Wing Cuban had 50,000 pounds coming in on a freighter and he was going to give us 25,000 pounds of it.

Everything went according to plan. They had filled up every room in a little small motel in Grassy Key. Looking back I have to laugh because the manager had a "No Vacancy" sign up. The motel had 12 rooms and everything was full of weed.

The Packer went down and started working with the Right-Wing Cuban. The Right-wing Cuban would only do business in the daylight hours. They used one-ton dually pickup trucks to move 1,000 pounds at a time. They started caravanning back and forth, moving all the merchandise up into the Redlands in South Florida, directly adjacent to the homestead. They took merchandise to the stash houses that the good Cubans used. They had three or four stash houses and we made arrangements with them to move the 25,000 pounds into them.

By this time we had done a lot of business with the good Cubans and they were the best, the very best, so we put it all on the arm to them. They started paying and over the better part of two weeks we dumped 25,000 pounds. At $50 a pound profit for Santa Marta Gold, everyone did very well.

The Packer actually made extra money because he ended up driving merchandise back and forth from the Keys, plus we greased him down real solid from our end.

I thought those days would never end, but they were certainly about to do just that.

Chapter 39: Cocaine Paratrooper

1983

I don't know why, but people seem fascinated with how we smuggled dope. I'm often asked how creative we got when we were smuggling dope into the United States. This question is almost always followed up by people wanting to know what the craziest thing we did was. Well, the craziest thing I saw done wasn't something I did personally, but I did pay a guy to do it.

It was 1983 and we had just done four or five thousand pounds of weed with the good Cubans. Weed was coming from all different angles. I had different guys selling and smuggling for me as well.

But I always tried to flip my merchandise to the good Cubans. I felt that they were the best. They always paid without any stories. One day I got a call from them asking me if I could come down that afternoon at 4 or 5 o'clock, so we could square up the rest of our business.

At the time I was living in an apartment at Coconut Grove. So, I drove down to Homestead where the good Cuban lived. He had 10 acres, which he had turned into a very big nursery. He had all kinds of tropical plants and trees. It was a perfect cover to bring in merchandise, because trucks were always coming and going. Most of the guys doing big-time business had some type of legal operation that they operated and used for smuggling.

I walked in and everything was normal. I shook hands with the good Cuban. He had a briefcase next to his chair. He reached down and placed it on the table in front of us. "Here's the rest of the money," he said. "Nice doing business. When do you expect another one?"

"They're working on it right now. We should have another one within a month."

He nodded and said, "I'd like to introduce you to my cousin. He's a Vietnam veteran. He's one hell of a nice guy. I think you'll like him. He said he has a business proposal for us, and I thought that maybe you'd be interested in listening to it. It's something different."

I said, ""Sure," because if I have one weakness, it's Vietnam veterans. They gave so much and got shit on when they came home.

Well, anyway, in comes this guy, definitely a Cuban. He stood about 5' 10" and weighed about 180 pounds. He was a stocky guy. He had on an army t-shirt, real faded Levi Strauss jeans, and combat boots that had been buffed, but not spit-shined. He was immaculate.

As the guy walked over to where we were sitting the good Cuban stood up and said, "This is my cousin and he's got a business proposal for us."

I stood and shook hands with him, and we all sat down. I said, "Hey, how are you doing? Your cousin tells me you're a Vietnam veteran?"

"Yeah."

"With who?"

"173rd Airborne."

"Oh. No shit?" I said. "Me too, USS Intrepid"

"You all right?"

"Yeah, I'm fine," he answered. "I got shot up a little. I caught some shrapnel that left me with a problem in my kidneys and bowels."

"Jesus Christ. How's the VA treating you?" I asked.

"The VA's not worth a shit. They're not doing their job. They're not taking care of me, and they're giving me a hard time about getting my disability. I'd like 100 percent out, but there's no chance of it. Anyway, I've got my regular doctors I'm going to, but I'm not getting any help from the VA."

I didn't know what to say, so I just said, "Oh, man."

He asked me about my military experience, so I told him about being in the Navy on board the Intrepid and serving in Vietnam. It didn't take very long for the camaraderie to build. There was a bond there. He did have a "don't fuck with me" look and he had an "I'm one bad motherfucker, stay away from me, leave me alone" edge about him. Most people would know it was best to leave this guy alone. But he was very friendly to me. Very nice.

After we had talked about various stuff for a while, he said, "I've got a business proposal. So let me lay it out. I can score kilos of blow over in the Bahamas for $7,000 a kilo."

"Seven thousand a kilo?"

"Yep."

"Yeah. That's a great price. That's good," I said.

"I can get 10 kilos for $70,000 and I'll need $5,000 in expenses. So, I need $75,000 total."

"What's your plan?"

"I'm going to have my friend fly me over and we'll pick up the merchandise. Then on the way back, as we're making our approach to Tamiami airport, I'm going to parachute out of the plane right down the street."

‘What kind of plane is it?” I asked.

“Well, it’s a Cessna 150. I’m trained to make low and high jumps. I’ve been trained to jump into enemy fire, so this is a piece of cake.”

“Are you shitting me?” I asked.

“Well, I was in the 173rd Airborne. I might as well make use of all that training, specialties, all that blood that was left, and I might as well make it pay.”

So I looked at my friend, the good Cuban, and said, “Well, I’ve never really heard anything like this.”

He just smiled and said, “Thirty-seven thousand, five-hundred dollars each. Are you in?”

“What’s my end?” I asked.

”Three kilos for you, three kilos for me, and four for my cousin and the pilot.”

I did a quick calculation in my head and realized that I could at least triple my money.

“I’m in,” I said, and turned to his cousin. “When are you going to make this move?”

“Next weekend. In about five or six days.”

“That sounds good.” I said.

I bent over and opened the briefcase he had just given me, counted out $37,500 and gave it back to him.

I left and drove over to Luco’s house to tell him the story. He couldn’t believe it either.

He just shook his head. “Holy fucking shit! The guy’s going to jump out of a plane? That’s pretty crazy.” He thought about it for a few seconds and then continued, “Well, the timing is right. The guy’s just paid off the load.

Everything's good. We got the money and it's good for politics. I like it. Good job!"

Six days later the good Cuban called and said, "Hey, my cousin's home. Would you like to come down and have dinner?"

I left immediately. When I arrived at his house he laughed and said, "You should have seen it. He jumped out and landed right down the street at 248th and 197th Avenue, just like he planned.

He handed me a Publix shopping bag with three kilos of blow in it. I took it out to my car and put it into the trunk. We shook hands when I left, still laughing and shaking our heads.

Chapter 40:

Square Grouper

1984

I got a call from the Brooklyn Boy. He asked, "Could you come over?"

I said yeah, and I went down to his house.

"What's going on?"

"I got a call from the fisherman in Marathon. He said he had some merchandise and wanted us to come down and take a look at it. Will you drive down with me?"

So, we lit up a joint and headed to Marathon.

We arrived at the fisherman's house a couple of hours later. It was a huge house that was built on stilts and there was a big garage attached.

As we were walking up to the house he came out and greeted us.

After some pleasantries, the Brooklyn Boy asked, "So, what's going on?"

"A few days ago I went out to pull up traps and when I got there, as far as I could see, there was nothing but square grouper."

"No shit?"

"Yeah." He said, "It was on the West Coast. I fish all the way up towards Marco Island. We were just off the Everglades when we ran into it. So the crew and I started loading it."

He took us to his garage. When he opened it up there were crocus sacks stacked from floor to ceiling. A crocus sack is basically a burlap bag that weighs 60-90 pounds, depending on what's in it. When they are filled, and tied tightly full of marijuana, they are called square groupers. He had several fans blowing across the sacks.

We started cutting open the sacks and saw that some of the weed was wet from the saltwater and was no good. But inside those 60-90 pound bundles of square grouper, the weed looked like it had never been touched or damaged. And the best part was that it was Santa Marta Gold.

After we looked at the merchandise, the fisherman said, "Listen. I can sell a few hundred pounds but I can't sell all this. There's just too much."

The Brooklyn Boy just smiled and said, "Well, don't worry. We can sell all the weed that's not wet or moldy.

So we started to talk about how we were going to dry it and he said, "Would you help me get it out of here? The wife and kids are getting to bitch. I've got them over to my mother's house. Would you help me out?"

"Sure," we said.

We looked it over again and discovered that a lot of it was all fucked up, but we didn't really have the time to go through it all.

We told him we would get our boys in Miami and come back as fast as we could.

Later on that day we returned with two pickups and a van. The pickups had camper tops with smoked windows. The van had a ladder on top with a stick-on electrical company name. We packed up the trucks and headed north.

As soon as we got to our stash house we started breaking it down and airing it out. We used dehumidifiers and fans to dry it. We started off with 7,000 pounds of wet crap and got 2,350 pounds of Santa Marta Gold.

It was really easy to flip. We just repackaged it nice and neat, and took it over to the good Cuban. I gave it to him on the arm.

Three or four days later we got paid the normal price of $325 a pound, which amounted to $763,750. We gave the fisherman $350,000 and that made him very happy.

Chapter 41:

The Colombian Mafioso's Sister

1985

My Colombian friend had gotten himself into some serious trouble and he had to go back to Colombia.

Our arrangement had worked like this. When he was in Colombia, I called and tried to speak to him every day, or at least I made the attempt. The Colombian telephone system in 1985 was terrible. It was very, very hard to call Cartagena, Barranquilla or Santa Marta. Sometimes it would take hours, and sometimes it would take days.

But I would always attempt to call him at least once a day. If I couldn't get through, I'd wait 'til the next day. Of course, the Colombians ... well the Colombians are "mañana, mañana, mañana." They loved to travel and it seemed that they were all over the place.

One time it took me three days to get through on the phone. When I finally reached him, he was out of his mind.

"Jack, please, please, you need to help me, Jack." He said. "I can't believe what happened. My sister's boyfriend was arrested by the DEA in Los Angeles and now they are looking for her."

"Where is she?" I asked.

"She is at a friend of mine's house in San Francisco. But I'm nervous because he's connected to her boyfriend. Jack, I'm scared they are going to get my sister."

"How can I help"?

"Well, let's get her out of San Francisco as soon as possible. And would you please take her to your house in Miami? You are the only one I trust."

"No problem, how do I get in touch with her?" I asked.

"Let me give you the phone numbers. And let me know how much money you'll need."

I said, "Don't worry about the money until I get her to my house."

"Don't worry; I'll go get her, I'll bring her back to Miami, and we'll figure out how to get her home. And, of course, I won't touch her." I made sure to emphasize that last part because Colombians are infamously protective of their sisters. Oh, Jesus, they won't have any gringos touching their sisters.

"I know you won't, my friend."

"What does she have for papers?" I asked.

"She has a visa, but she overstayed."

"Don't worry. Don't worry. We'll get her home safe."

"Thank you, my brother. Please keep in touch with me and let me know how things are going."

I flew out to San Francisco the next day and rented a car. I got a hold of his friend and found out that she was staying at the Howard Johnson's over in Corte Madera. I went over to pick her up. Now I had never seen her before, but I had heard about her. When I first saw her I thought she was a Movie star. She was drop dead gorgeous, just beautiful, but as timid as a deer.

She was dressed to the nines and looked like she stepped out of a Paris fashion magazine, which I knew would be a problem, because it would draw way too much attention to us.

"Listen, honey. Your brother sent me here to help you. This is no joke, so do exactly as I say and we'll have no problems. You have to trust me. First, we've got to change the way you look. You need low-cut boots, jeans, not the ones that look like they're painted on, sweatshirt; no makeup and we need to do something with your hair. We've got a long ride ahead and we don't want to draw any attention to ourselves."

"Okay," she said in broken English. "Where are you taking me?"

"I'm going to drive you to Miami. Don't worry. You stay with me and absolutely nothing is going to happen to you."

She was sweet but I could see that she was terrified.

"Relax," I said. "I'm not going to touch you. I'm not going to hurt you. I love your brother and your family. I'm going to get you to Miami and I'm going to help you get back home to Colombia. There's nothing to worry about. I've got it all worked out. You just hang tough. We're going to have to take a little detour because I don't want to drive you down the southern route from San Francisco to Miami; too many Border Patrol checkpoints on I-10. I'm going to drive you through Reno and take I-80 to St. Louis, then work our way south to Miami."

She relaxed after I told her my plan. We only drove during daylight hours, stopping at motels near the exits. Our first stop was Winnemucca, Nevada. She said, "Jack, I want to stay with you, please don't leave me alone."

"Are you out of your fucking mind? You get your room, I get my room, and then there won't be any trouble. Let's be smart."

She gave me a strange look; no one had ever rejected this woman before.

Her brother was the only solid Colombian that I had ever met and I wasn't going to fuck up business over a piece of ass.

That's how we traveled until we got to Miami.

I took her right to my apartment.

Once she was comfortable I explained that there were rules. "You cannot go out. You cannot make any phone calls. You stay in the house. We don't want to be responsible for something bad happening to you. If you listen to me and trust me, we'll get you home."

"Okay," she said.

I had a travel agent in Fort Pierce who I went to see after we had rested a day or so.

"Listen." I explained. "We have a Colombian girl and she's got a problem. I want you to charter a plane and get her to Curaçao."

"I know a charter company that has Lear jets," he said.

"Great, find out how much a one-way charter is to Curaçao."

"No problem," he replied, "I'll find out right now."

He made the call and said the charter would cost $6,500. He asked if he could put a thousand on top for himself.

"I'll call you back later tonight and let you know," I said.

So I checked with the Colombians and they said there would be no problem with the money or her going to Curaçao. They could just go there and pick her up.

We paid the travel agent with cash, then he chartered the plane though his company. He went to the leasing company, cut the check and set it up for a couple days later. She was with me until all the arrangements were made.

Two days later, I drove her to the Melbourne airport at eight o'clock in the morning. In those days you could drive up on the tarmac next to the plane. No customs or immigration when leaving the country. I told the travel agent I needed a few minutes with the girl.

We stepped out behind my car. It was not a Bogey-Ingrid moment. We both started laughing, hugged, and I said, "I'll see you in Santa Marta."

I stopped at the first pay phone I saw and called her brother. Maybe it was luck of the devil; he picked up on the second ring.

"Your sister will be on the island in three hours."

"Jack, please come visit me as soon as you can." That was all he said in reply.

Chapter 42:

Bruno Friend of Pablo Escobar

1985

I'd like to talk about another friend of mine. His name is Bruno and he was a friend of Pablo Escobar. Now, to set the record straight, I never met Pablo the Doctor. I never met him. He had three 727s that he used for flying in tens of thousands of kilos of cocaine from Colombia into Mexico. I had heard about Bruno for a couple of years before I met him. He was dating the sister of a friend of mine from Colombia.

One day I was down on Brickell Avenue at my Colombia friend's apartment.

"Listen," he said, "would you like to meet my future brother-in-law, Bruno?"

"Of course," I said.

"I've talked to him about you over the last couple of years and he would like to meet you as well."

I had heard rumors that Bruno was a guy that you can't fuck with. It was rumored that he was one of the only men in the world that Pablo said to "leave alone" and that Pablo did not even want to fuck with him. So, I was very interested meeting him.

"Does he have a crew?" I asked.

"Oh, yeah. He's got a huge crew. He is huge. He's worth millions and millions of dollars."

"Jesus Christ! Let me meet this motherfucker. Is he as fucking bad as the rumors portray?"

"Oh, yeah. He's one mean motherfucker. If he has the slightest inclination, the slightest bad feeling, the slightest twitch, he'll blow your brains out."

"Holy shit!" Then I asked, "I've heard he's into witchcraft. Is that right?"

"Oh, fuck yeah. He's got a *brujah*."

"Donde esta es brujah?"

"Actually, he goes to a witch in Haiti."

"Wait a minute," I said. "He goes to Haiti and sees a fucking witch?"

"Yeah. He really, really believes in that shit."

"Oh, man. Well, why the fuck does he want to meet me?"

"I'm not sure, but it's going to be easy. He's staying with my sister. We'll just go in and talk to him."

"Okay," I said. "Is there anything I need to know before we talk to him?"

"Just tell him the truth and just tell him exactly what you can do."

"Okay."

So we went over to the condos on Brickell around 7 p.m. I later learned that he lived all over the place. He had condos all over the city.

We walk in and I say, "Hi," to his brother and his sister who were at the condo. His sister went upstairs to the bedroom and left my friend, his brother, and I standing in the kitchen.

A few minutes later a guy about 5' 10" came around the counter. He weighed about 165 pounds and looked like he worked out. He had a wine colored, tailored shirt, black dress slacks, black boots and a Cartier watch. And he carried himself like a king, but not overly pretentious.

As he walked across the room towards us, he said, "Hey, my friend. How are you?"

"Great, great."

"And your name is Jack?"

"Yes, and you're Bruno?" I raised my hand in greeting.

Colombians don't grab and shake hands like Americans. Every time an American shakes someone's hand it's like we want to arm-wrestle. We grab and we shake like we have something to prove, especially if you're in the military. Actually, all Americans seem to do it.

Colombians are a more, well, they call it civilized. They don't shake hands with a big grab. You open your hand and you touch in a soft shake, not a hard squeeze. I knew that. I'd been learning their customs and I'd been working with the Colombians for a couple of years before this meeting. So that is how I shook his hand. He didn't grab mine, I didn't grab his.

After the shake, he said, "Would you mind a shot of *aguardiente*?"

"Yes, I'd love one."

So he broke out the *aguardiente*, we smoked a bazooka, and we started talking.

After we had each taken a couple of hits, Bruno said, "You know, I don't mean to be rude, but I don't have much time. Is it okay to start talking a little business?"

"Certainly. I'd love to talk business."

"I understand that you have marijuana connections here in Miami and that you can sell large quantities of marijuana."

"I can sell all the marijuana you can put your hands on," I said confidently.

He looked at me questionably. "Really? Can you sell 30,000 pounds of marijuana?"

I smiled and answered, "Absolutely."

"Okay. I have 30,000 pounds of marijuana in Arizona. I'll transport it here to Miami and I'll actually front it to you."

"No shit?" I said. "I love it."

"May I ask who you'll be selling this merchandise to?"

"Certainly," I said, "I'll be selling it to the Cubans."

"Oh, no," he said, "I don't like fucking Cubans."

"Well, that's strange," I said, "Cubans don't like Colombians either."

He looked at me for about a second and then he started laughing.

I just smiled and said, "No, no, no. These Cubans are not like right-wing Cubans. They're not. They came over when they were young boys. They were raised here in Miami. They listen to Bob Dylan and Led Zeppelin and they're not right-wing Cubans. They don't hate Fidel. They don't hate anyone. They just like to do business,"

"Oh, I see," he said. "Well, they're fucking Americans then."

"Yeah, they're just as gringo as I am."

"Okay. I can handle that. Thirty-thousand pounds, four-and-a-quarter."

I looked him straight in the eye and said, "Bruno, sir, that's not going to work."

"What do you mean that's not going to work?"

"That's too high." I said.

"You haven't even seen the merchandise."

"It doesn't matter," I said. "If you give me the highest quality Colombian weed, that's not going to work. And while we're discussing it, I would expect the highest quality Colombian weed, high-end commercial, correct?"

"Yeah. It's Santa Marta Gold, high end."

"Yes, exactly. That weed has to come to me for $270 a pound."

"Jesus Christ, really?" What are you going to flip it for?"

"I will flip it for $320, a $50 bill. But, I'm sure you understand that I've got people to take care of."

He nodded and said, "Okay. Do I need to bring the merchandise here and stash it myself?"

"No. These Cubans have multiple stash houses. You front me the 30,000 pounds, you put it on the arm, we'll start paying."

"Well, get to the paying part."

"Well, right off the bat," I continued, "if it is a high-end commercial Santa Marta Gold, we'll probably see on day one between $600,000 and $700,000. The next day will probably be another $600,000 to $800,000. Maybe two days with no money. The third day will be a million dollars and the next day $250,000. It's always going to be over $250,000 a pop. You're going to get a few million. It may take as long as a month."

"A month?" he said and looked at me. "You actually are in the wholesale marijuana business."

"Yes, sir."

"I'll tell you what. I've got 30,000 pounds for you right now. It's Friday. On Monday, Tuesday, or Wednesday at the latest, I'll put 30,000 on you. You come to me, you bring your men, I'll put you together with my men, and you tell me where to deliver the merchandise. It may take a few vehicles. I'll put it to you on the arm, $270 a pound."

"Yes, sir," I said. "These guys are good, but I haven't heard anything bad about you, bro. I've heard that if you get twitched once in a while you can be a very evil person. No disrespect."

He looked at me and smiled a very wicked smile. "Jack, I'm the sweetest guy in the world. I heard a rumor or two about you."

"Well, that's bullshit," I said. "I'm the sweetest man in the world."

He looked at me for a minute and said, "Okay, 30,000 pounds on the arm."

"Thank you very much."

The meeting was over and we left.

That was on Friday. On Saturday I talked to the Cubans, I talked to my boys, and we got it all set up.

Then, late Sunday afternoon, the phone rings. I answered and it was my Colombian friend.

"Jack. We've got a problem." He said this a little hysterically.

"Calm down," I said. "What's the matter?"

"The DEA just shot Bruno."

"What? What do you mean, shot him?"

"They knocked on his door. When he opened the door, they shot him right in the chest with a .357 Magnum. It hit his rib and went out his back."

"Did it kill him?"

"No. He's still alive. He's up in Broward, in the hospital, but we're not going to see him for a while because he's wanted in at least 20 countries."

"No shit?" I said. "Listen, don't worry. I'll send up my attorneys right away."

"Really? Thanks, Jack."

So I called my attorney and he went to the hospital.

When the attorney came back he said, "Can you believe that Bruno isn't even under heavy guard? All they have is just one fucking piss-ass deputy from Broward County."

Ultimately, they shipped him away and he ended up doing eight years in a federal penitentiary. That was my first meeting with Bruno.

Chapter 43:

Colombian Mafia Part 1

1985

Let's fast forward to the second half of the eighties. I had already been in the dope game damn close to 20 years and even though I was considered family, I had played fuck the dog and sell the pups with the Colombians for years and years. It was just all part of the business.

Now were they all bad? No, they were not. In fact, the majority of the Colombians, I really, really liked. But, were they pieces of shit when it came to paying and cheating me? Yes. So did I get even with 'em? Yes, a number of times.

But this particular time, I had the regular Colombian from Santa Marta. He was one of the Colombians that I really did like. He was a nice guy, but a cheap motherfucker when it came to laying out the money. Well, he introduced me to the Bogota boys.

Now for those of you who are not familiar with the Colombians, the Bogota boys are severely and fiercely nationalistic. They are also racist motherfuckers, just like everywhere else in the world. The Colombian boys who live on the coast look down upon Medellin, Bogota and Cali as uppity guys. And, of course, Bogota, Medellin and Cali look down on the coast boys as basically lazy fucking Colombians that like to hang around on the beach and wear shorts and smoke pot.

There's always a little argument about this. They were all in the weed business, but the Bogota Boys were mainly in the cocaine business up in the mountains.

My Colombian from Santa Marta was one of those guys who did wear shorts. He was worth millions and millions of dollars, and always carried himself like he was the king of Spain. But he was always a little tight on the dollar bill because he lavished monies all over the place. So he always spent his money relatively fast and usually didn't have very much money on hand.

He introduced me to the Bogota boys and we did two or three runs for them.

But the entire time I kept saying to myself, "Well, wait a minute. I'm doing all of this fine work and I'm not getting paid." But, I decided to wait it out and see what happened.

Then, one day the head Bogota boy came to me and said, "Hey, we're having trouble with that Colombian. We don't want to do any more business with that Santa Marta boy."

"What do you mean?" I said, "What are you talking about?"

"We got to cut him out."

"Cut him out? Isn't that going to cause problems?"

"No, because we'll cut his fucking head off."

"What? You don't want to do that."

"Yes I do," he said. "Look at the way he carries himself. Let's get rid of that motherfucker. We don't need him in the business. No one at the top likes him because he carries himself like he's something, and he's fucking nothing. He doesn't wear a suit. He doesn't wear a tie. He doesn't say the right shit. He's always late. He's a lazy motherfucker. He never kicks back. Fuck him."

"Listen," I said, "I don't want to hurt him. I like that kid."

"Yeah, we know you like him. We know it and we kind of had a hunch you would say that. But here's the deal. He's out. You want to do business with us? He's gone. You're in. Say it right now. In or out?"

I really liked the Santa Marta Boy. He was always a nice guy to me. I wondered if I was making a big mistake, but I chose to work with the Bogota boys and cut him out. In the dope business, this is called "jumping his head." I jumped his head.

The way it all ended up, you could also say I saved his life. But that's a later story.

Anyway, as soon as I told the Bogota boy I was in, he said, "We want to build another boat."

"Well, what do you want?" I asked.

"We want a 65-foot boat, but we want it to be our boat. We don't want that motherfucker included."

"Are you shitting me?" I said. "That's going to be pricey."

"You come up with the numbers and we'll buy it. Of course, try to get it as cheap as you can."

So I returned to the states and went to a boat builder I knew in Panama City. Now this guy didn't use a computer, he didn't even use a calculator. He didn't even have a high school diploma and he used a slide rule. But he was a damn good boat builder.

I told him, "Listen. I'm going to need a 65."

"Schooner-rigged?"

"No. Catch-rigged. We don't need to go with a schooner and the sails and all that traditional sailor shit. Because whatever sail we have up, we will always have the motor running full bore anyway. We want it as fast as we can get. We don't want five-and-a-half to six knots. We want seven-

and-a-half, eight, eight-and-a-half knots, where we can crank the whore, fly everything, and run the motor."

"What do you want for an engine in it?" he asked.

"I don't know exactly. I'm not a mechanic. What makes it go the fastest? Is it necessary to have a great big diesel?"

"No, not really. I don't think we're going to have to go with a great, big monster. Let me do the numbers. Are you going to hang around for a few days?"

"Yeah. I'm not going anywhere. Just figure the numbers. Get that slide rule out and go over it with your sons. I'll be staying down on Panama City Beach."

I figured I would be in the area for about a month doing business, so I went down and rented a condo right on the beach. It was nice because it was in the winter and there was no one there. Panama City just runs in the summer.

About 10 days later he called me. "I came up with a number. It will cost you $675,000."

"Hey, you know who you're dealing with?" I said, "The Colombians have the reputation of ... oh, God. They'll kill women and children and whole families."

At the time, I understood that to be true with Colombians down in Colombia. But as far as I saw how the Colombians did business in the U.S., they really were not that brutal. Maybe with one another in Colombia, but not with me or my crew, and I never saw any of that. But, I heard multiple stories of how they killed, and all kinds of trouble down there.

In fact, I thought the guys we were working with, the good Cubans and the bad Cubans, were much more brutal than the Colombians. We had no fear of them, none whatsoever.

But I kept hammering the guy building the boat. "Hey, they're Colombians. Oh, wow. They're so bad. You don't want to run over that number. So is that the number? Have you built in plenty of money for yourself? Is everything good?"

"Yes, I've built in enough money for myself and even added a bit in case we decide to upgrade during the construction. So, we're fine."

"Okay," I said.

So I made the arrangements with the Colombian.

I would meet with this group of Colombians the same way we always met. We would travel to places all over the world so that no one would know what we were doing. They were generally one to two-hour meetings. Back and forth I would go. An hour in Rio de Janeiro, a month later an hour in Amsterdam and in another month, St. Martin or Costa Rica.

I would go to Germany, Rome, Madrid, St. Kitts, Nassau. Sometimes we would meet in Barbados or in St. Lucia. One time we met in Port of Spain, Trinidad. I've been from one end of Venezuela to the other. I met them in Aruba numerous times.

The meeting to discuss the final number for the boat was in Rio. It took me 10 hours to fly from Miami to Rio. I was down there at Copacabana and the Colombians came at night for our meeting. Now this meeting was just to get the cost of the boat and to set up the next time I was to call them.

I did not forget how they fucked with me. I did not forget how they cheated my fucking ass. So, I put 'em on a $40,000 a month expense account. I said the boat would cost $950,000.

When they questioned the cost I told them how I had to take care of my friends, and keep myself alive as well. They decided that it was a reasonable cost and told me to order the boat.

Finally, I was able to say to these guys, at least in my head, "Fuck you, you crooked cocksuckers." Because they had played that game for so long, for so much fucking money, and had cheated me out of my fucking money. So that was the ticket. That was the meeting.

At the end of every meeting we would set up the next one. So, I set up the next one for Amsterdam. That meeting was a bit longer. I think we spent three or four days there because Amsterdam is quite a town.

Chapter 44: Colombian Mafia Part II

1985

Hey, excuse me for the last chapter. I didn't really get all the details out to you. I guess I got kind of worked up about those motherfuckers not paying me. Yes, they did order the boat for $675,000. But I didn't really explain why they would pay so much money. And, of course, me tacking on an extra few dollars for myself making the total cost $950,000.

Well, the reason they were willing to pay all that money, and eventually did pay all that money, was because that boat was built to hold 1,000 kilos of blow, which is quite a little chunk. So $675,000.00 was the agreement we came to for a boat that would hold 1,000 kilos.

Now as I mentioned at the end of the last chapter our first meeting to confirm the purchase of the boat and the next meeting was in Amsterdam. Now we always talked in a made up code.

For instance I might ask, "Are we going to the place where the big cross is?"

And the reply would be, "Yes, we'll meet under the big cross."

It was a bunch of convoluted code. No one knew what we were talking but us. But we all knew that the big cross wasn't a Christian cross in front of a church, it was a small café that sat at the crossroads of two main streets, near the Hilton Hotel at the center of town.

So, anyway, I flew to Amsterdam and checked into the Hilton Hotel. The Colombians would pick me up in a cab and we would make a little tour of the town, so that it appeared that we were tourists. We visited places like Anne Frank's house and of course we visited the Red-light district.

Well, on this particular trip I was riding around with three of the Colombians, and we were going down a backstreet with a cab driver. There was a van in front of us, and the van stopped in the middle of the street. Out of the van stepped a bunch of musicians. And they started unloading their instruments, and taking them into this little bar or club.

And the cab driver put the car in park and shut his lights off and just stayed there.

Now this really irritated me and I said, "Hey, buddy. In the United States, someone would blow the horn or say, 'Hey, what the fuck?'"

He just chuckled and said, "When we're all five years old here in Holland, we're all taken down to the waterworks company and we're told that 66% of our country is three meters below sea level. So we have much more important things to worry about than heroin, cocaine, marijuana, whoring, or musicians unloading their van while we're right behind them. We're a very patient people."

That struck the Colombians and me very, very strange, but as we talked about it, it seemed to make sense.

"Those people are smart." I said.

Now I love the people of Holland. I hope that I am saying the right things about these people. You guys have a leg up on most of the world.

So, we wait for the musicians to unload and then continue on our way. Well the Colombians took me to the Yab Yum Club. That's an infamous whorehouse in Amsterdam. It's probably one of the best in the whole world. So, it was an incredible experience. We went in and we talked and chatted with the girls. It was a lot like the whorehouses in Colombia; it was more about the experience, than just banging some whore and we had a great time.

After the proper greetings we started talking business and of course the boat came up.

"How's the boat?" They asked, "What's the deal? How's it look is everything good?"

"Yes. Everything does look good. But I'm going to need one follow-up meeting with you. Let's give it another 30 days and then make sure we're on the same page. Why don't we pick someplace nice and warm for out next meeting?"

"Let's make it San Jose, Costa Rica." They said, "Easier on you and easier on us as well. You can jump down to Costa Rica real simple."

"Okay." I said with a smile.

"You look kind of happy, Jack. What's going on?"

"Well, I don't want to stick my dick out in the wind here. But you offered to pay that money for a ship that would hold 1,000 kilos. I think I have a surprise for you. But I'm not sure."

"What kind of surprise?"

"I'm going to bring the builder of the boat with me the next time we meet."

"Why do you want to bring the boat builder to our next meeting?"

"I think he made a mistake."

"What kind of mistake?" they asked.

"On how many kilos she'll hold."

"Jack, are you saying that we've given the initial down payment, and monies have been paid, and corporations set up, and all of the machinations of running phony papers in Venezuela, and attorney? ... And you're saying what?"

I waited a few seconds before I answered. "I'm saying that the motherfucker will not hold 1,000 kilos of blow. She'll hold 1,500."

"Oh, you got to be shitting me?" They said in disbelief.

"Sometimes mistakes are made and this is a nice little mistake. But," I said, "I don't really want to guarantee that until I bring all of the diagrams and the boat builder himself to meet with you."

"Ok. What do you want from us?"

"When we bring him to San Jose, then you have everything set up at the Key West Club. And I want the best fucking whores known to man for this guy. You treat him like a king. You treat him like one of those big, fat kings over in the Polynesian islands were they carry him around in that big basket, using five, six guys carry him around. You know? That's how he needs to be treated."

Now, before I went to Amsterdam to meet these guys the boat builder told me it was a guarantee that it would hold 1,500 kilos. But I wanted to keep 'em in suspense so I could get him down to Costa Rica. I wanted him to look the Colombian right in the eye and say "Here it is in cubic inches and meters – and the metric system, of course – 1,500 kilos."

A month and a half later I took the boat builder to Costa Rica. And you'll see in the next chapter the Colombians kept their word and treated him like a king.

Chapter 45:

Colombian Mafia Part III

1985

In Amsterdam, I promised the Colombians to bring the builder down to Costa Rica. And now it was time to go to Costa Rica. I was always excited to go there because of the Hotel Del Rey and the Key Largo whorehouse. Besides all that, the people of Costa Rica were just friendly. It was just a nice place to go, full of tourists and it was good for us. It just felt good there.

There was just one hitch, the boat builder was scared. He'd heard so many rumors that the Colombians were these horrible, terrible people, and that if he made any mistakes, they would kill him, that he started to believe them. So, I sat down with him and we talked.

"Come on, man." I said, "Are you out of your mind? They're going to treat you like a king. You're doing a big, big favor for them. So just relax. Take it easy. Just don't say anything. When it comes time to lay out the boat, give the measurements, etc., just lay out the plans and let me talk. You don't say a word; I'll take care of the rest."

This didn't work. He was still scared. It was still weighing on his mind. So, I decided to take him to Miami, which gave me three or four days to sort of coddle him and get him ready for the trip. Once I got him to Miami I brought in the rest of my boys, The Packer and the Big Guy. We all kept talking to him and telling him everything was going to be fine.

Well, the big day came and we boarded the plane. All the arrangements had been made with the Colombians. We were going to meet at the Hotel Del Rey in San Jose. The flight went well and we got checked in to the Hotel Del Rey. A short while later the Colombians arrived. There were two of them this time. They were all friendly. Everybody was happy.

We took the boat builder to the room they had rented and we started going over the details. And the boat builder performed beautifully. He told them that he had miscalculated at first, but confirmed that she would hold 1,500 kilos of cocaine, as long as each kilo was 2 x 6 x 8 inches. As long as they were all uniformly put together in these exact dimensions, they would slip in very easily and would fit very nice.

The Colombians were all excited and we talked all the numbers. And, of course, I'd gone over it with 'em that it would cost $950,000, still tacking on a few extra bucks for myself. The Colombians agreed and the deal was done.

After we concluded business we took the boat builder to the Key Largo whorehouse. And, of course, the Hotel Del Rey was always full of girls and fine food. So we just wined and dined him all that day and the next.

I started talking with the Colombians about putting together the first 1,500 kilos. We had to work out the logistics like how long it was going to take to get the boat finished and where we were going to do this. Where are we going to unload it? We just had to work out all the arrangements that needed to be done.

Now we didn't want to sell any shit commercial blow. No, we wanted something special because there was so much money involved. So, we went to get a special cook that the Colombians knew and asked him to make 1,500 of pure, pure blow. It's kind of like the weed business; you could get the high-end weed, or you could just get the commercial pick. We wanted to cook out 1,500 beautiful kilos of a top-notch blow that we could flip easily.

And, the way we wanted to flip this merchandise was without any Americans being involved. I made it clear from the beginning. "Never introduce me to an American." I said, "Never show me a fucking gringo. Any time you show me a gringo, there's the DEA. I never want to see a gringo. The only people that I want to do business with are Colombians. And all I want to do is hand off merchandise. My job is transportation only."

So we started cutting the details. We had about four months to go before the boat was completed. We were all salivating at the money we were going to make. At that time pure blow was going for $20,000 wholesale in the United States. We were going to flip 1,500 kilos, bringing the total to $30 million dollars U.S. The deal was that the cartel would keep half, $15 million. The other $15 million would be split in two for us to divvy up with the crew and to cover all of our expenses and properties; where to bring it in, how to do that. Everything all added up, and we were just going over the details.

But, of course, the biggest issue was when the boat was to be completed. Since it was going to be about four months from that date, we laughed, we joked, and we just had a really good time. It was one of those meetings that felt really good, because there was nothing pending. It was just in the early stages and we didn't have to do any work. We all just wanted to do this nice big load and then we would go from there.

Chapter 46:

Cali Cartel to the Italian Mafia with Love Part I

1985

Business had exploded for us up until the mid '80s. We were smuggling 25,000 pounds of marijuana every 75 days. We worked multiple connections in South America and were bringing the merchandise up to Dog Rocks off the coast of Cuba. From there the Cubans would bring it into Grassy Key.

These guys were great. When I say, "Cubans," these were the Right-Wing Cubans. They were all 10-12 years older than me and they really hated Fidel Castro. The real right-wing Cubans of Miami were a special breed. They were also some of the best smugglers in the world. They smuggled everything: people, guns, whatever—for various administrations—back and forth to Cuba. They just naturally expanded into the marijuana business.

Business for us especially boomed from 1980 to 1983. I was getting a piece of the action on all kinds of loads. I was involved in the smuggling part of it. Acting as broker, I was flipping them for a finder's fee. But, by the middle of the decade things had changed a lot.

Ronald Reagan, credited with ending communism by bankrupting the Russians, was president at the time. And I have to give him the credit. But what Reagan was especially credited for, at least relative to my business, is shutting down big-time marijuana operations. Essentially, by the end of 1983, the game was over. There were no more big freighters coming up. There was no more open-ended smuggling of marijuana. It was just done.

When I say Ronald Reagan really ended the marijuana business, I mean he really did. We lost ten 25,000-pound loads in a row. We lost 250,000 pounds over two-and-a-half to three years. Not only that, but we had 16 guys that got locked up. It was a scary time. No one talked. Everyone kept their goddamn mouths shut.

Now the dope smuggling business is like any other business, when one avenue for income dries up, people look for another. We were no different. We realized that we had to change what we were doing if we wanted to survive and continue making money. That's the effect that Reagan had on the entire dope smuggling business.

In response, the entire dope smuggling industry moved from marijuana to cocaine. Reagan stopped the marijuana business, but as a result, the cocaine business really started to boom.

At the time I worked with an organized-crime family that was really more like a disorganized-crime family. They were a mix of Italians; I was the only non-Italian in the group. Luco, the Big Guy, introduced me to the head guy of the local crew.

Let me make something clear: We never worked for anyone but ourselves. We worked *with* this guy, never *for* him. Of course, being in the weed business, he had the Cubans that he had befriended and they would do the unloading. He also worked with the Colombians because he met a special connection in the late '70s.

He had met the governor of Magdalena Province, which includes Santa Marta, Colombia. Now you know why it was such a special connection. That's where the Santa Marta Gold came from.

So, we were really well connected at that time and things were really booming. Of course, we wanted to get in on all the best action and make more money, so we were investing pretty heavily in smuggling marijuana. But, as I said, we lost ten loads in a row when Mr. Reagan shut down the big-time marijuana smuggling business.

However, I was raised on the cocaine business in Miami from as early as the late '70s. We just needed to shift back to selling cocaine. So, I had started building the boat up in the Panhandle of Florida. It had four compartments. I had the boat partially built when we lost the ten loads in a row, and I was running out of money. I was down to my last $100,000.

Looking back now, I have to say to myself, "Damn. All of that money down the drain." But, I hadn't completely wasted all that money. I owned a few houses and a mansion down in the Caribbean islands that was beautiful. I bought the island mansion for a song and dance, but I had put a lot of money into it. I also had a couple of houses and two hunting camps in Maine.

So, I owned a lot of property, but I didn't have any cash. I only had $100,000, which in those days was just shit money. A couple of bottles of Chateau Lafite Rothchild, two whores and a picnic, and you were broke. I may have lost everything, but I survived.

Losing the 10 loads of marijuana in a row, essentially 250,000 pounds, left all of us virtually broke. The money was gone. We kept chasing and kept trying to work it out, but the Coast Guard kept knocking off the Colombian freighters before they could deliver the merchandise. I attribute all of it to Reagan's war on drugs.

I guess I could say that I did more than survive, because looking back, I always held the luck of the devil and this time proved no different. It was at this time that I met a Colombian who reintroduced us to the cocaine business. I'll never forget the first night I met him.

Long before we met, I had smuggled into the U.S. a young Colombian boy who was the bastard son of the governor of Santa Marta, Magdalena Province. We brought him up on a boat with the German.

The kid was at the house and heard us kind of bitchin' and moaning about the losses. He said, "Hey, I've got somebody that you guys would like to meet."

Of course we were all seasoned dope boys at the time, and had been in the business 14 or 15 years. In fact, the Brooklyn Boy had been in the business longer than the rest of us. He started back in the '60s.

"Well, who is this guy?" we asked.

"He's a friend of mine from Santa Marta"

"Santa Marta?" That got my attention. "Well, what kind of business is he in?"

"He's in the smuggling business, but I think you'd really like him. Why don't I bring him over?"

I looked the kid in the eyes and asked, "Is this guy serious?"

He smiled and said, "Oh, he's very serious."

We laughed when he said that, because we were questioning him thoroughly on who this guy was.

So we thought about it a little bit and said, "Well, hey. What the hell?"

We suffered all kinds of trouble from losing all that weed business and all that money. So, we decided to set up a meeting at the Brooklyn Boy's house with the young Colombian we brought into America and his friend, who was another young Colombian boy, only 23 years old.

When I answered the Brooklyn Boy's door I was shocked. Though this Colombian was only 23, five guys came with him.

I opened the door and said, "*Hola, como estas? Mi casa es su casa.*"

He smiled and said, "I speak a little bit of English."

We invited him and his bodyguards in. We walked him through the living room into the kitchen. Once he sat down we started making café cubano, espresso. We had also rolled marijuana and placed a bottle of our aguaniente on the table. Aguaniente, to the Colombians, is like Sambuca liqueur is to the Italians, Uzo to the Greeks, or Arac is to the Egyptians or the Middle Eastern Arabs. It's a liquor that has a liquorish taste. There's no way I can describe what aguaniente does to you or how it tastes going down. It's almost an acquired taste. A lot of people do not like it. It's a very, very powerful liquor and some Colombians love it.

We started smoking pot and with the bottle of aguaniente on the table and then began to basically make small talk like, "You're from Colombia. We've been there." Of course, we had been all over the world.

The Brooklyn Boy, Luco and I were the only three attending this meeting. Talk soon strayed to girls and his town of Santa Marta. He asked us about Cartegeña and we had told him war stories of how we knew Cartegeña. We talked about how we knew Barranquilla, Colombia, how we smuggled ourselves in and out of Maicao, how we had been to Cucuta, how we had run from the police and how we had smuggled tons after tons of weed out of his country in the '70s. He seemed to find all the war stories most amusing.

While we were talking he nodded, grinned, laughed and interjected always at the right time. He was just very personable, and he seemed like a very nice young man.

The conversation went on and on. Then he dropped it on us.

"Listen, my friends. I don't want to be in the marijuana business. I want to be in the cocaine business with you."

When hearing this, the Brooklyn Boy sort of got up on his high horse because he had made millions and millions from marijuana and he managed to save a little bit of money. When I say a little bit of money, I mean he owned houses, apartment buildings, cars and all kinds of things. He made a lot of money in the game and he was smart with it. Luco and I had saved a little bit of money, but things were terribly bad for us all the way around and we were very interested in changing the game.

The Brooklyn Boy said he didn't want anything to do with cocaine. He said he'd pass on going into this deal. The Colombian said okay.

We continued to drink and socialize, and agreed to exchange phone and beeper numbers. After this exchange, away he went. The meeting probably took a couple of hours.

One night, about a week later, I got a beep and it's the young Colombian. Though he was just a young boy in my mind, he had already made close to $20 million. He was very, very smart. Much smarter than the rest of us nitwits, because he bought land and businesses in his native country, Colombia.

Among the common traits of Colombians, some of which I have already mentioned, is their fierce nationalism. They worship their country. They love it. But, they also love the United States because of all of its opportunities. They made sure that all of their children were born here so that they'd have U.S. passports. They also bought condos for places to stay when they came to the U.S. When the money really started rolling their way they just started grabbing properties over on the beach. It's a fact that Miami was actually built on the cocaine trade.

"I'd like to sit down and run something by you," the young Colombian told me on the phone.

"Okay," I replied, "where would you like to meet?"

"Is Coconut Grove okay?"

"I live in Coconut Grove," I said, "just come to my house."

So, he comes over to the apartment that I kept in the Grove, and once he sits down, he asks me, "Can we smoke a bazooka?"

I laughed and said, "Oh, sure. Hell, yeah. Let's smoke it."

So I pulled out a bottle of *aguardiente* and we started drinking and smoking. He mixed the liquor in with tobacco and marijuana, which gave it a real distinct smell.

And as we're getting high he asked, "Can you help me out? Because the marijuana business, well, it's over. I don't like marijuana anyway. It's a pain in the ass. It's too big. It's too bulky and it's just not enough money. We're hooked up in the cocaine business. Let's smuggle cocaine."

He paused for a minute, looked at me and continued, "Do you have any problem with that?"

"None whatsoever," I said, "I'd love to. Shit, I don't have any money because of the feds stopping the marijuana business."

"Did you mention something about how you were building a boat?"

"Yeah."

"Well, you got any pictures?"

"Well, sure." I said as I got up to get the photos.

This young Colombian is the man who really has to take credit for building the secret compartments into smuggling boats. In Spanish it's called *caleta.* I brought out the pictures and when he saw the compartments for ballast, fuel and water, he said, "Well, wait a minute. Can't we fill those compartments with cocaine?"

"Well, shit. I think so." For some reason I hadn't really thought about smuggling dope in them before because we had such a great setup already.

"Well, how about we make a deal?" he asked. "I will pay for the rest of the boat to be built. Let's work something out."

"Well, let's go show you the boat." I said.

"Where is it?"

"In Panama City, in the panhandle of Florida."

"How far is that?"

"It's quite a yank from Miami, like 750 miles."

"I'll charter a plane and we'll just fly up there in a couple of days. Let me check it out. Let's see if it'll work. You guys talk to him. We'll cut him in on a piece of the action."

"Oh, okay."

So a couple of days later we went over to the Tamiami Airport, which is off of Kendall Drive. You make a left and go down 137th Avenue. It's still there today. We rented an airplane there that I think had seven or eight seats, all of red leather. There were five of us. We flew up to Panama City, rented a car and drove to the boat builder's yard.

The boat builder had never gone to school. But, he was a complete genius. He was a Southern boy from Georgia, as sweet and kind a man as you've ever seen. He was in his mid-50s, a regular country boy, just a nice guy. He had four boys and they all were machinists. They wore jeans, cowboy boots, denim shirts, leather jackets and watch caps. They were sailors and they built boats out of steel. They were incredible boats. This particular boat was fairly cheap. It cost about $275,000 to build. But, we had been unable to pay the guy because we were all out of money from the loss of ten shipments in a row.

We talked to the boat builder and told him that we didn't want the ballasts. We didn't want the lead pigs put into the four compartments either. What we wanted was to keep the compartments so that they were accessible and so that we could fill them up with merchandise. So, we asked the boat builder if we could put merchandise into the compartments instead putting the lead pigs in.

He thought about it a minute, pulled out his slide rule, which was always at his side, and said, "Oh, all right. Well, let me do the figuring." He never went to school and he had no formal education. The guy was just one of those natural geniuses.

He finished his slide rule figuring and said, "Yep, we can make it work."

"Okay." I said, "How many kilos can she hold?"

He did some more calculating with the slide rule. "If the packages are 2 x 6 x 8 inches, it will hold 300."

I just smiled and said, "Finish building the boat and we'll start paying."

"Really? I thought this was a dead soldier."

"No, no, no," I said, pointing to the Colombian. "My friend and I have worked it out."

The Colombian and I had made a deal before we reached the boat builder. I told him I had put about $100,000 into the boat already, but he would need to pay the rest. He said he would, but he didn't want to lay out all the remaining money for the boat right up front. After some negotiation he agreed to give the boat builder $50,000 up front.

"That will get him going," he said, "and we can pay him the rest after we move some merchandise."

He then looked at me. "Would you please help me out? Would you start flipping some kilos to help get the money for this boat?"

"Sure, I can flip some kilos out in Los Angeles."

I don't really remember how much kilos were going for in those days, but cocaine fluctuated. In 1970 they didn't sell kilos, they sold pounds. You could get a pound of pure blow for $7,200 in 1971. By the mid '80s it was up to about $28,000 a pound wholesale.

I had to get a deal so that I could make six or seven thousand a kilo to help pay on the boat and survive.

"If you can sell 50 kilos over the next couple of months," the young Colombian said, "then no problem. I'll kick up all the money. But, I also want to be a partner in the ownership of the boat."

"Okay." I agreed.

So we paid the boat builder $50,000 to get started. Once this deal was done we all flew back to Miami.

It took about eight months to complete the boat. When we saw that boat we loved it. It was made of steel and it was beautiful, just beautiful.

Chapter 47:

Cali Cartel to the Italian Mafia with Love Part II

1985

We started flipping kilos to pay for the boat. It was a real pain in the ass to get cash from California to Miami. I'd fly out of Ontario, California to Las Vegas with the money packed neatly into one of my bags. Once I got to Las Vegas I'd check into one of the major hotels. Then the next day I would just check in the bag with the money in it and it would go right through to Miami. The boys would then pick me up in Miami.

We never lost a dime, never lost a kilo. There was no cheating. There was no stepping on anyone. Everything was on the up and up. And slowly but surely, over a six month period, we paid for the boat.

We got the boat all up and running, then one day the boat builder pulled out his slide rule and said, "Hey, wait a minute. If these kilos can be made to be two inches wide, six inches deep and eight inches long, each one of these compartments will hold 75 kilos. You've got four compartments, so you can put 300 kilos in this little boat."

Of course we were excited. When the Colombians found out, they were thrilled and immediately wanted to have the big maiden voyage. We had the boat taken to St. Martin and another crew took the boat from St. Martin to Grenada. We were going to fly to Grenada and take it from there.

As we discussed the trip with the Colombians, they said, "Hey, listen. We want you to get this merchandise to Italy. These are Romans, the *Mafiosos* from Rome."

"Oh, Jesus Christ." I said. "Al Pacino and Robert De Niro guys?"

"Well, not exactly," He said.

"What do you mean?"

"Well, they don't look like Al and De Niro. This guy's got blond hair and, no disrespect to him, but he looks a little bit like *Maricõn.*"

"Wait a minute. Wait a minute." I said, "We can't be going and dealing with gay—you know. Hey, listen, we're gangsters. Now, what? Faggots in our kind of work? That doesn't make any sense."

He chuckled and said, "Well, he isn't gay."

"Okay," I said, "just tell me what he is."

In a serious tone he said, "He's a bad motherfucker. They've been in a war with the Calabrese and the Sicilians and the Napolitano's. There's been a war going on. This guy's still alive. He's done business with the big boys up in Medellin. We trust him. Everything's good."

After some discussion we agreed to meet this guy before we went to Grenada. The Roman said he wanted to meet in Aruba, so we flew to Aruba. We set up a place to meet and arrived a few minutes early.

It was easy to know who it was we were going to do business with there because you couldn't miss him in a crowd. He had blond hair, blue eyes and he was immaculately dressed; he had dress pants, English handmade shoes and he was tailored, spit and polished. The guy looked like a movie star. He also had unbelievable manners, even though his English was broken. But, he spoke fluent Spanish to the Colombians.

As he walked across the room towards us, Luco said he looked like he was of Sicilian descent.

The guy was just close enough to hear us and said, "Oh, no. Sicilian? They're the most terrible people in the world. They are horrible."

Luco got a bit defensive and said, "Well, my family's all Sicilian."

The Roman stopped, looked at Luco, then smiled and said, "Oh, you're no fucking Sicilian. You're an American. You're no Sicilian, but please never go to Sicily. They're no good. They fucking rob you and steal and cheat. They're no good."

That broke the ice and we all started to laugh. We had a hell of a meeting with the Roman in Aruba.

On our way home we decided that before we got the deal locked up we were going to take the boat down to Grenada. But, before we took the boat down we needed to meet with the Roman one more time. So the Colombians brought him through Maracaibo, Venezuela to Maicao. They brought us in the same way but had different guys take us in. So, my guys from Colombia show up in four or five Toyota Land Cruisers. And I got in with my friend—my really good friend, the younger boy from Miami. He had a couple of bodyguards in the back and he, the driver and I sat in the front seat.

Now Maicao is arguably the biggest shithole in the world. I mean, it is terrible. It's right in the middle of the desert and it's hot as hell all of the time. The whole town is run by Palestinians. As we drove down the main street I didn't see a Colombian anywhere.

I looked at my friend and asked, "Who are these guys? These guys are all Arabs."

"Yeah." He said, "The Palestinians live here."

"Well, you gotta be shitting me."

He just smiled and said, "No, no, no. They work for us."

I nodded my approval. "Great. I know some Arabs back in San Francisco, the nicest guys I ever met."

"Oh, these guys are sweethearts. They control all these shops. All the swag that comes out of Venezuela, all the stolen cars, the TV sets, radios, all the merchandise they sell in Colombia comes through here. Everyone's bought and paid for. The whole fucking town is corrupt. Everyone's corrupt. All the stores are owned by the Medellin boys, but they're in a partnership with the Palestinians."

"Well that is quite an operation." I said. "Real nice."

The town only had one hotel and for some reason I remember they made grilled chicken. So anyway, we get to the hotel and we started cooking and eating and everybody was happy.

We started snorting dope and I said, "What time does the Italian come? What time does the Roman come?"

"He should be here in a couple of hours and we're going to go pick him up."

So a couple of hours later we're driving around looking for this Roman. We turn a corner and there's this guy. He's wearing tan slacks, a light beige shirt, brown custom-made English shoes and he has a yellow sweater tied in a knot around his neck.

Well, it was 110 degrees outside and as soon as I saw him I said, "Jesus Christ, my bro. Is that our man? Is that our Roman?"

My Colombian friend looked alarmed and said, "Oh, we'd better get him quickly. They're going to kill him. They're going to rape him."

"Holy shit!" I exclaimed. "Get him in the vehicle."

So we pulled over and got him into the vehicle as quickly as possible and the first thing he says is, "This is the biggest shithole I've ever been to and I've been all over Africa and smuggled hash with the Arabs."

As we drove back to the hotel I learned that he had been all over the Sahara and spoke five different languages. This guy was sharp as shit and a real gangster. He just didn't look like it.

Well, the idea was that we had to get a little up-front money to get back to Grenada, do the pick-up and then cross the ocean to Italy. So, we worked out the details; he was going to front us $20,000. Once we had a deal the Roman flew back to Italy.

It was weird because at the time you could fly into Grenada from the United States without needing a visa, but if you flew from Grenada into Venezuela you needed a visa.

Well, there we were in Maicao and we had eaten the Colombians out of house and home, but we needed to get across the border in order to get back to the boat and then go on to the pick-up location. The Colombians said they would help us. There was just one problem. A few hours before we were supposed to leave Maracaibo for Maicao, they had told us we couldn't bring any clothes because we were only going to be over there for a few hours and then come back."

I then told them, "Okay, but listen, I need clothes. I've got to stay clean."

"No problem," they said. "We've got everything right here. Go to the store at the end of the street; the Palestinians run it. Get anything you want, tell them it's on us."

So we went to the store and were greeted by one of the Palestinians, who said, "Come on in. Let's drink some tea."

Anyone who has met a Palestinian knows there are no sweeter people on the planet.

So, we're drinking tea and the Palestinian breaks out a bunch of guns. We start talking as we are looking at the guns. He then said, "You know, would you guys mind if my brother came up? He's a schoolteacher. He teaches English and he'd like to practice his English."

"Wait a minute." I said, "Your brother is Palestinian, and he's here in Maicao teaching English to the La Guajira Indians and what few Spanish guys—Colombians—live here?"

"Yeah."

I found that rather strange, but said, "Okay. Have your brother come up."

So his brother came up and we all started talking. They were amazed that we did not hate Palestinians.

"Come on, boys," I said, "don't be ridiculous. This is business. We don't hate anyone. There's no racism here. You know, you guys are good. This is kind of fun."

He smiled and said, "Would you like to smoke some hash?"

"Jesus, you guys got hash down here in the middle of the desert?"

"Sure," he said, "they bring it to us from the Middle East."

So we smoked hash and we hung out.

When we returned to the hotel early in the evening, the Colombians told us, "We're sorry. You're going to have to wait another day."

"Well, Jesus Christ." I said, "Can't we leave at night?"

They looked alarmed and said, “Oh, no, no, no. You can’t leave at night. The La Guajira Indians.”

“What about the Indians?”

“They’re like cannibals and they love to eat white people.”

I thought they were joking, so I said, “What? Have you lost your fucking minds? Fuck you!”

“No, no, no,” my friend protested, “I’m not shitting you. They might not like to eat white people and they might not be cannibals, but they’re bad motherfuckers and you can’t be running around in the middle of the desert in the middle of the night. It’s over 100 miles from Maicao to Maracaibo.”

I looked at my friend questioningly for a few seconds. I still didn’t believe what I was hearing. But I could tell from the look on his face that he was not trying to pull one over on me.

Finally I said, “Well, Goddamn. Okay, okay. You guys are afraid to do that?”

“Yeah.”

I thought about what he had just said for a few seconds more and said, “Well, if the Colombians are afraid to drive across the desert, I sure as hell don’t want to.”

So, the $20,000 came the next day. We split it up between Luco and I. I had seven or eight thousand in the front pocket of my shorts and it is hot as a bitch.

The Colombians got a cab for us and they told the cab driver, “You drive these boys straight to Maracaibo to a real nice hotel, drop them off and don’t charge them any money. There’s no bullshitting. You don’t even need to talk to them.” Now, I don’t speak Spanish, but I could see the

Colombians giving this stern lecture to this guy, and they told me what they said when they were finished.

When they were done the driver took us out to his cab, a nice cab. I think it was a Chevy Classic Caprice, probably eight or nine years old and it was air-conditioned.

"Thank God," I said when we got in the vehicle and I felt the air blowing.

It was about 3 o'clock in the afternoon when we got started, and we only had a few hours to go to get to Maracaibo. The ride went real smooth until just about 4 p.m. That's when the car started overheating and broke down in the middle of the desert.

I could only think of one thing to say, "God damn. Colombia."

Colombia sits near the equator, so it's daylight from 6 o'clock in the morning until 6 at night. It's dark from 6 at night until 6 in the morning. You get these real nice 12 hour days. But, our day is about to end and I started thinking about what my Colombian friend had said the night before.

So I tapped the driver on his shoulder and said, "Oh, shit, bro. What about these fucking Indians coming in the middle of the night?"

He didn't say anything, just shrugged his shoulders.

Another problem with being at the equator is that the sun is very intense; it will burn the skin right off of you if you're not used to it. My skin is white as milk and here it is 4 in the afternoon. I knew that I might be in trouble if we didn't find a solution soon.

Each day I was with my Colombian friend I had purchased new clothes. And it just happened that on this day I had on a red t-shirt and some new shorts. So, I took my t-shirt, wrapped it around my head and stepped out in the middle of the road to flag down the first cab that came by.

I don't speak a lot of Spanish, just very little. So, when the cab stopped, I said, "Oh, *por favor, mi hermano. Es necessito vamos va Americi rapido. Mucho, mucho trabajo en Miami. Puerto ese noche. Por favor. Por favor.* Help me."

He looked at me for a few seconds and said, "Okay, okay, okay. Get in the cab."

As we tried to get into the second cab the driver of the cab that broke down tried to give us the money back that the Colombians had paid him.

I just put my hand up to refuse the money and said, "No, no, no. Keep that. Keep that."

But he got very persistent saying, "No, no, no. No, no, no. No, no, no." Finally he walked over to me, took my hand and he gave the money back. It was in pesos. I forget how much it was—$100, some shit like that. I took the money and put it in my pocket.

Well, Luco got into the back and I got into the front passenger seat. As soon as I got in I noticed that this cab had no air conditioning, but Jesus, it was getting dark and I was afraid of those fucking Indians.

Well, the rest of the ride to Maracaibo went really smooth until we got to the outskirts of town. And, of course, it's South America, so there were roadblocks all over the place. It looked like they had the entire army on patrol.

So we got to the roadblock and there was the army. There were eight or nine soldiers and they had this little bunker. They even had a machine gun on the bunker pointed right at the cars. The soldiers were kind of walking around looking at the different cars and the captain came up to the window.

As soon as he saw me he asked, "*Tu hablas Espanol*?"

"*Lo siento, no. No hablo.*" I said and I played like I didn't know a word. Well, I didn't know too many, but I certainly knew more and I could have talked to him a little bit.

He looked at me for a few seconds and said, "*Tu tiene papeles passeportes, por favor.*"

So I handed him my passport. Then all of a sudden I noticed a loud noise from the back seat. I looked in the back to see and hear the big buy snoring. Luco didn't go 400 pounds then, but Jesus Christ, he was probably close to 340, 350 pounds. It was hard to get new shorts for him because he's so big. They had to keep washing his clothes. Now his shorts had rode up and his nuts were showing, and his pocket was sticking out, which was full of money, probably $12,000 or $13,000. And he had his mouth wide open, snoring really loud.

I was about to start laughing at how hilarious he looked when the *capitano* said, "Hey, *droga? Droga?*"

I looked around and said, "No, no, no, no. *Plata.*"

"Oh, *plata*?"

"*Si.*" I said.

The captain leaned forward and asked the cab driver, "These two *pendejos* come from Maicao?"

"No. I picked them up in the middle of the desert."

The captain looked at me and said, "Ah." He looked at my passport and saw that I had a Venezuelan stamp, and a visa from Grenada. That did it. That did the whole deal. He handed me my passport and waived us through. He never woke my friend up. He was just snoring in the back seat, out like a light.

We went on to Maracaibo. From there we went up to Grenada and prepared our boat to pick up the merchandise.

Chapter 48:

Cali Cartel to the Italian Mafia with Love Part III

1985

Once we got to Grenada we prepped the boat and called our contact on the radio to set up the drop. We always spoke code over the radio so that no one would know what we were talking about. We didn't discuss where we were going or what we were planning to do because we had made all of the arrangements in our previous meetings.

When we were in Maicao we agreed to do an airplane drop about 150 miles southwest of Isla de Avis, that's an island south of Puerto Rico. Now I had sworn after I left the Navy that I would never go to sea again, especially on a smaller boat, but that is how we planned to get to the island.

In 1968 I had to ride on the *USS Camden* (AOE-2) to get to my assignment on the *Intrepid*. The *Camden* was a smaller naval ship and, of course, we had to go right through the middle of a typhoon. I got very sick. I puked for five of the six days. The fucking sailors called me "Sea Pussy" because I couldn't work. I just puked and puked and puked. It was a terrible experience.

We met the *Intrepid* in the Gulf of Tonkin. An aircraft carrier, the *Intrepid* was huge compared to the *Camden*. I was flown to the *Intrepid* on a chopper and when I stepped onto its deck it was like stepping into a shopping mall. The ship didn't move at all. I was never seasick again. Over time I fell in love with that ship, but that's another story.

Being out of money at the time our smuggling boat was made, I couldn't pay any sailors and I couldn't pay any up-front money. So, I had to go on the mission aboard this small boat with the boys.

As the trip approached I just kept thinking about my time on the *Camden*. The *Camden* was a small naval ship, but that's only because I was comparing it to the *Intrepid*, which was huge. The *Camden* was actually a pretty good sized ship and it got tossed around during that storm.

For this trip we were about to get on a little, dinky, 44-foot schooner. I just didn't want to go. I was sure that I'd be sick the entire trip. I wasn't interested in seeing an airplane drop out at sea because there was a real risk of running into the Navy or the Coast Guard. After all, President Reagan had really cracked down on the drug smuggling business as sea, especially marijuana smuggling. So there was a real risk that we would run into them.

But, I was more worried about getting seasick than 20-30 years in prison for the mission.

The day of reckoning came, the time to go to sea. To save money, Luco, the Big Guy, served as our captain. I chose him because of his experience in the Merchant Marines. I also took Bobby, The Packer. So, it was just us three. Just imagine the three stooges and you'll get a feeling for the situation.

As mentioned, we had the boat taken to St. Martin and another crew took the boat from St. Martin to

Grenada. After our meeting with the Colombians and the Roman in Maicao, we flew to Grenada and got onboard the boat.

The plan was to head for some islands called the Los Roques off the coast of Venezuela. Los Roques is a pretty famous resort destinatoin now, but at that time it was a great place to do a drop. Once we got there, we would use call signs to communicate with the Colombians and again use code when talking on the radio.

For this particular trip the call signs were, "Attila, Attila, Attila, Conan." We would call out, "Attila, Attila, Attila, Conan."

And the Colombians would reply, "Conan. Attila, Attila, Attila."

To which we would reply, "Copia, Copia, Copia."

Even though the Colombians are some of the nicest people I've ever met, it's always *mañana, mañana, mañana*. For most of the Colombians, *mañana* is a big word—Spanish for "tomorrow." So, when we got to Los Roques it was *mañana, mañana, mañana*. They kept stalling. We were out there fucking around for five or six days. By the end of the week we were heating cans of ravioli on the manifold for lunch and dinner. As our food and water started to run low I finally had enough.

I got the Colombians on the radio and said, "Listen. We can't take any more of this shit. It's not, 'tomorrow, tomorrow, tomorrow.' So, we're going up the islands."

For anyone who has not been to St. Kitts, it's a little, dinky island. But what a sweet island it is. They are really nice people.

We pulled into St. Kitts and it was like a remake of *Das Boot*. We were starving because we hadn't had the right food in about three days. We had a Zodiac that we used to go ashore. Once the boat was squared away and we were on shore I hired a cab driver.

The driver asked us where he could take us.

"Hey. listen buddy," I said. "I'll give you $100 a day. You just take care of us. Take us where we can get the best food, whisky and beer. We just want to eat and drink."

He agreed to show us around the town. So we spent our time eating and drinking, and enjoying the town. We had a single-sideband radio that we used to talk to the Colombians each day. And of course it was *mañana*, *mañana*, *mañana*. Finally, after another five or six days they called us and said they were ready.

But, I kept asking, "Is this for sure? For sure? Because we don't fuck around. We don't want to go all the way down to Los Roques again and then be told *mañana* again. We just don't want to do it."

"No, no, no." They said, "Hey, go back to where you started," which was Grenada.

So we took off and we headed back to Grenada. When we got to Grenada we called them on the radio and asked if they were ready to go.

"Okay," they said, "we're ready. We'll be at the spot at 1500 hours in two days."

Now the deal was that they were going to dump 300 kilos out of the sky in a little twin-engine Beech at the coordinates. Those coordinates were obtained by Satellite Navigator. This was before GPS. We had to use the satellites that went overhead every 12 hours, but at the time it was real high tech.

Once the drop was made we would pull it out of the water and stash it in the boat.

The entire time we were heading back to Grenada I was actually thinking "Oh, God. When we go to sea in that schooner I hope I don't get sick and fall into the Sea Pussy category again." But I didn't. We took off and the sea was beautiful, three- and four-foot swells, just beautiful. Well, we got to the Satellite Navigator coordinates and we started tacking back and forth, waiting for the drop.

All of a sudden I hear over the radio, "*Guardia, guardia, guardia, guardia, la bomba, la bomba,*" and over the top of the mast, about 50 feet, comes a twin-engine Beech.

He looked like Sky King. He flew past us and then did a 180. He came back and they started dumping 10-30 kilo bundles out of the back of the plane. They were so close I could see the faces of the pilot, co-pilot and the guy who was dumping the merchandise out of the plane. They made several passes, unloading the merchandise just off the bow of the boat. It was very exciting.

When they were done we fished it all out of the water and stowed it away on the boat. Once we had picked up all the merchandise we took it back to the island of St. Martin because there were no customs. Once there we prepared to move it to Italy. I have to admit that to get the merchandise to Italy we came up with something very slick.

Chapter 49:

Cali Cartel to the Italian Mafia with Love Part IV

1985

We were finally ready to execute this slick plan to get our merchandise to Italy.

There was this good-looking couple. They both had blond hair and blue eyes. But, the man was one of those guys who you just don't immediately like. He couldn't drink either. If he drank three beers, he was drunk and he'd run his fucking mouth.

Now, his wife, she was a very good-looking girl, but kind of snotty. She grew up with a little bit of money. She thought she was hot shit and she was not thinking far from the truth. But, as I've maintained throughout my career of smuggling drugs, this was a business, and you did business with whoever you needed to in order to make the money.

It turns out that we'd had a little problem with the guy about a year before our trip to Grenada. He was over in Naples and got drunk; he sassed the shit out of me because he thought I didn't like his wife.

This really pissed me off, but I didn't want to burn any bridges because we were going to need this guy to take care of our boat. So, I just said, "Hey, watch your mouth. Watch your fucking mouth."

But, he continued to sass me. Because we needed him later, I just walked away, but the Big Guy did not. Luco walked over to him and read him the riot act. But he just blew the Big Guy off.

Often, with drunks and drug addicts, mistakes are made. Usually the next day they apologize. Well, the next morning, sure as shit, he apologized to the Big Guy and he wanted to apologize to me, but I was nowhere to be found. I never forgot what he said because in the dope game you can't have people running their fucking mouths. I don't care how big you are or how tough you think you are. If you run your fucking mouth you will have a problem, unless we absolutely need you to do something. Well, this was the perfect opportunity.

So, here it is a year later and we have the perfect opportunity to get on this guy. I said to Luco, "Hey, I'm thinking we need this motherfucker and that blond bitch to do something. We need them to pick the boat up in St. Martin and deliver it to Italy."

"What do you suggest they do?" he asked.

"They make the great circle route," I said. "They can go up to Bermuda, then around the big circle to the Azores. Finally they can come into Cadiz, Spain, and then go to the drop-off point in Porto Cervo, Sardinia."

For those who have never been to Porto Cervo, it's a beautiful, beautiful place.

Luco was a little concerned because it was getting a little late in the year. It would be October before we could get the boat across the Atlantic and you don't want to be doing the great circle route in the winter because of the terrible seas. We would be skirting the hurricane season. But after we talked about it he agreed that we should call the Blondie Twins and have them do it.

So I called them over to Miami Beach. As soon as they sat down, the guy started to apologize. "I'm sorry about what happened last year."

I shook my head and said, "Forget all that. It's nothing. You were just drinking a little bit. Forget that. I want you to deliver this boat from St. Martin to Bermuda, to the Azores, to Cadiz, Spain, and then to Porto Cervo, Sardinia."

"Why are you taking this boat to Sardinia?" the guy asked.

"Because I've got it sold to an Italian guy over there."

His wife was a lot sharper than he was and asked, "What's the money look like?"

"The fee for doing that is $25,000. I'll give you $5,000 up front to get the boat from St. Martin to Bermuda. Once you get to Bermuda I'll give you another $5,000. Once you get to Cadiz, Spain, I'll give you another $5,000 and when you come into Porto Cervo, I'll cash you out another $10,000."

His wife was about to say something, but I cut her off. "Don't tell me the fucking story that my mother's sister's brother stole this and somebody needs a goddamn liver transplant. Oh, no. Her fucking pancreas. I don't need any fucking shit. All I'm going to tell you is I've got $25,000. You run out of fucking money, that's on you. And if you fuck up and don't deliver my boat, you'll have a problem. I'll be upset."

I hadn't even finished the last sentence when the guy blurts out, "Well, what's on this boat?"

"What do you mean, what's on the boat?"

"Are you taking something over on the boat?"

I said, "Why the fuck would you ask that?" surprised at his stupidity.

"Well, because you guys always have all kinds of money and none of you have a job."

I couldn't believe this dumbass would say something like that. "What? What do you mean, none of us have a job? You don't know my fucking business."

Of course, this shit-bag motherfucker didn't know I was broke then. I was down to my last $100,000. I needed this to go off without a hitch.

I looked at both of them in turn and as seriously as I could, said, "Listen. There's no dope on it. Get a goddamn dog. Search the boat. But I'll tell you something. If you smoke marijuana on my boat, if I find out that you were doing drugs on my boat, if you get nailed for pot or coke—and I don't give a fuck if it's a gram—I'll be upset."

Everyone in the business knows that when a man's upset, that means he's upset. These two were not in the business, but they knew what I meant.

So, the Blondie Twins agreed. They went out and hired a guy to take them across—a South African who said he had always wanted to cross the pond. They paid him a wage. I think it was like $3,000.

Sure as shit, everything went well. They flew down to St. Martin and took the boat to Bermuda. We gave them another $5,000 and they took the boat to the Azores and then on to Cadiz, Spain.

In the meantime, the Big Guy flew into Cadiz to meet them and I flew over to meet the Roman.

I said to myself, "Holy shit!" as the Roman's guys picked me up with a real crew—seven or eight with a couple BMWs and a Benz. The Roman was spit and polished. These guys were hardcore *Mafiosos*, but they were sweet and kind to me because I was bringing in the merchandise.

"Is everything good?" the Roman asked.

"Everything's good." I replied.

"And how long before you'll be in Porto Cervo?"

"The boat will be into Porto Cervo in two days."

"Okay. Why don't we run you around Rome and give you the guided tour? You need some girls?"

"Well, of course." I said enthusiastically.

We picked up some girls, but we didn't do any drugs. They didn't smoke pot. They didn't snort cocaine. Only the girls were on our agenda.

The Roman would change his clothes five times a day. He'd go from breakfast wear, to lunch wear, to mid-afternoon wear, to the goddamn early-evening wear, and then he'd eat his main meal around 10 at night. Even though he'd eat like a horse, he only weighed about 140 pounds, and he was about 5'10" tall. I don't know, maybe he was bulimic, but he was a nice guy to me.

The next day, the Roman tells me, "Well, here's the deal. Here's what we're going to do. We're going to take a Mercedes-Benz and we're going to drive it down to the shore. Then we're going to put it on a ferry boat and we're going to take the ferry over to Sardinia."

"Jesus." I said, "How long is that boat ride?"

"It's about 12-16 hours depending on the weather."

"Shit!" I thought to myself, "Just what I need, another small boat to get sick on."

"We'll leave tonight," the Roman continued, "and we'll get into Olbia, where Porto Cervo is, early tomorrow morning. When we get there, you check in at the hotel because there will be no one there and we'll get a deal on the rooms."

"What do you mean there will be no one there?" I asked.

"This is where the rich and the elite Europeans come for vacation, but the fuckers are all gone for the season and all the hotels are going to have a minimum staff. We'll have the whole place to ourselves."

I couldn't believe our luck. Here we thought that we were leaving too late because of the bad weather the schooner might run into on the way across the Atlantic, and it was that same bad weather that kept all the tourists away.

The Roman smiled at me. "I've got it all hooked up. I've got some grease laid out. We'll get a hotel room and food. Everything's good."

I nodded my head. "Okay."

That night we went to the ferry. It took us all night to get to Olbia, a port city on the north side of Sardinia. As the sun started to rise we went from Olbia to Porto Cervo.

Porto Cervo was a beautiful marina. There was a little knoll that came out into the port area and on top of it was a great big station. The Roman told me that the Carbonari had built it and still used it for their secret meetings. I didn't ask him how he knew about their secret meetings.

I'd learned that in this game you could meet people from many different secret organizations. I really didn't care who they were or what organizations they belonged to. If I could make some money working with them I would. It was just business to me.

We found that the marina was still not completely full, but probably 70 percent full, I'd say. So as the ferry pulled into the dock, sure as shit, there's the boat floating out in the marina. The Big Guy was on it with the Blondies and the South African.

When they got close enough for us to hear, I said, "Hey, how are you? Everything good?"

They said they were good and that the trip had been uneventful. We helped them tie off and then I said, "Go get a room. We'll grease you down in a couple of days. Enjoy yourself. See the sights. Go to the Coliseum, Spanish Steps, the Vatican, you know, the regular tourist shit."

They seemed more than eager to get off the boat and left in a cab. Luco and I made sure the boat was secure and then we went to the hotel to wait for the Roman to tell us when he wanted to unload the merchandise off from the boat.

So a couple days go by and one afternoon, Luco and I are sitting on the boat, where we are talking about the station at the top of the knoll. And as we are talking a group of men left the station, came down to the docks and walked right out to our boat. I knew immediately how the Roman knew about the Carbonari and the station.

As they approached the boat I smiled and said, "Hey, how are you?"

One of the men at the front of the group responded, "Good. Are you Americans?"

"Yeah."

"Oh, we like Americans," he said.

He then asked if we liked movies and, of course, we said yes. Now, Italians worship Al Pacino and Robert De Niro—I mean worship them. So we talked about movies; from *Mean Streets* to of course the big one, *The Godfather*. After a few minutes of conversation the leader of the group looked at Luco and said, "Ah, *Italiano*."

"*Si*," Luco responded. "My mother and father came over on the boat from Sicily."

"Oh, I see," he said. Then he spoke a little louder for all of his men to hear. "We'd better be careful, he might be part of the mafia."

There was a brief moment of silence and then he and his men all started to laugh.

"Well, Jesus Christ." I said as Luco and I laughed along with them. Everything was good.

We went back to the hotel and ordered some drinks. While we were waiting for our drinks I looked at the Roman and asked, "What are we going to do here, buddy?"

"Why don't you just jerk that merchandise out on Sunday morning? Make like you're getting everything stowed away and cleaning up your boat. Like you're making everything nice, and putting everything out for laundering. Just put it all in sea bags and put it out on the dock with everything else."

"Okay, then what?" I asked.

"One of you will need to rent a car. Drive it out onto the peer and out to the boat. Load the merchandise into the trunk and drive it to the top of the knoll and park it."

"You just want him to leave the car there?" I asked.

"Yes. At around 5 in the afternoon we're going to bring two cars to the parking lot. One of the cars will have a broken headlight. The other will be a Mercedes. We'll split the merchandise between your car and the Mercedes. Once everything is loaded we'll send the car with the broken light ahead. If there are any police in the area, they'll pull over the car with the broken light and we'll proceed on into Rome."

He looked at us for a few seconds and asked, "Any questions?"

I just shook my head. "No."

He nodded his head in understanding. We spent the rest of the afternoon drinking and shootin' the shit with our new business partners.

There were 300 kilos in the boat and it was worth $60,000 a kilo to the Italians, so this trip was worth $18 million to us. Now the $18 million had to be cut right in two to the boys in the Cali Cartel. So, there was going to be $9 million going to us, not directly to me. I had to cut that in two—so $4.5 million—and then that had to be cut as well.

In the end it was still going to be a very, very nice payday. Luco and I were both going to get $1.25 million each. Of course, we were going to have to grease our man and throw our grease around to make everything nice and neat. But, that was just nickel and dime stuff to keep everyone happy.

I was really looking forward to payday. I only wish I would have known what was going to happen next.

Chapter 50:

Cali Cartel to the Italian Mafia with Love Part V

1985

We did our job. Sunday morning we went down to the boat and started to clean it up. We took everything, including the 300 kilos of cocaine, and put it on the dock.

The Packer rented a Fiat and drove it out onto the peer. We unloaded the boat and the Packer drove the rental car to the turnout at the top of the hill. He parked the car, and as he stepped out, another Benz pulled up and he sat in its back seat. They brought him back down to the dock and we finished cleaning the boat.

That evening we returned to the parking lot with the Roman in a Mercedes and a car with a broken headlight. We split the merchandise between the Fiat and the Mercedes, then started for Rome. We sent the car with the broken headlight out ahead so that if there were any police, they would pull over the car with the broken headlight and the Mercedes and Fiat would just pass by. Everything went smoothly; no problems whatsoever.

The Colombians were going to use their money launderers in Italy, New York and Miami to move the money around. We would pick up our cut in the United States. We got on the plane and we all felt great. Everything was great, or so we thought.

We waited for our money for about two weeks, but nothing. Luco and the Packer asked me what we were going to do.

"Well," I said, "the rules are that no matter what happens, if a Colombian gives you five kilos of blow and you trip and fall in a fucking mud puddle, and lose it all, you owe for the five keys. So, I will call them and get our money."

I got the Colombians on the phone and I said, "*Yo soy, Colombiano.* You owe me some money."

Colombians would rather sell their fucking children than give up their money, and they started to whine. Meanwhile, I am not talking disrespectfully to the Colombians. I'm not. That's just the deal. That's the way they are, but I was hot.

"Come on man, I need that money. What about my men?" I said.

"All we can kick up right now is $600,000."

"Six hundred thousand dollars?" I raised my voice in disbelief. "What's that? Two whores, a bottle of wine and dinner?"

Then I paused for a moment and thought about what he had just said. How come he can only pay me $600,000? We should be getting $18 million for that job, I thought to myself.

"Where is my money?" I asked.

"He stole it," he said calmly.

"What do you mean he stole it?" I asked.

"That fucking Italian stole every bit of the merchandise from us! He came up with a story, said he got busted. We checked into it and found out that he didn't get busted."

"And now there's nothing you can do?" I stated more than asked.

"Well, wait. Now don't panic. Of course there's something we're going to do. We're going to try to work this out. We're going to go after him."

"Well, get him for Christ's sake. I want my goddamn money."

Well, time went on. One story led to another. A couple of months go by and they finally call me, but the news wasn't good.

"Hey, the money is gone," they said.

"What do you mean the money is gone?"

"The money's gone. We're sorry. We can give you another $100,000."

"You know, we do all that fucking work, we go all the way across the pond and now I'm losing millions of dollars here. You guys are supposed to be the greatest, the biggest and the baddest motherfuckers in the world. You all have millions and millions of dollars and this is how you treat us."

"Listen Jack, listen. We've got another job for you."

I couldn't believe what they just said. We just lost several million dollars and they wanted us to do another job. "Another job my fucking ass. This is terrible. You're not doing the right thing."

"Will you please, please continue to work?"

I was done with this bullshit, but the fact that we were completely broke, that we needed the money, made me consider what he said. I had to come up with something that would guarantee we got paid. So, I said, "Okay, but you're going to have to pay all up-front cash this time to take care of my men. I want $40,000 a month for expenses."

"Well, you know, the boat is half mine," he said.

"Great," I said. "You can take it."

Of course, he and I both knew that couldn't happen. So he agreed to the deal and we started to work out the details of our next trip. It was a business to me and I had to do what was right for the business.

The Italians stealing all of the merchandise—that was something that really pissed everyone off.

To finish this story, about a year went by and I'd heard all the scuttlebutt about how the Colombians were looking for him. They were trying to find him, but couldn't. The people saying that were out of their fucking minds, because the Colombians had a crew that worked out of Spain and Italy.

Finally, more than a year went by and, of course, we had moved on. We were working and doing other things. The Colombians and I set up a meeting in Panama and I flew down there.

We started talking, eating, drinking, shooting the shit like we always did at these things, and the Colombian said, "Well, you know, we have a little news."

"What? What happened?" I asked.

"Well, you know the Roman?"

"Oh, that piece of shit." I said in disgust.

"Yeah. His father-in-law showed up in Barranquilla."

"What? For what?"

"He wanted to buy 400 kilos of blow, but one of my men recognized him from being with that piece of shit, the Roman, at a deal we did three or four years before he did business with you."

"Well, where is he now?"

"My men instantly snatched him and they took him up into the mountains in Santa Marta, and that's where he is right now."

"Well, what's the deal?" I asked.

"We want all our money, so I've hired a guy who is trying to broker a deal with the Roman. They're negotiating with the Roman right now, back and forth, to pay for what he stole when you took the merchandise over to him from the airplane drop."

"Am I going to get anything out of that?"

"I don't know because the guy, this broker in the deal, is a prick."

"Oh, Jesus Christ," I said as I shook my head in disbelief. It was always some story or another with these guys.

Well, they kept the Roman's father-in-law for over a year and they didn't settle. Of course, this is the story that I got from the fucking Colombians. I know they cheated me. I'm sure they didn't settle on the whole amount owed, but they did settle on a substantial amount. Not only did the Roman end up paying, he had to go through the nightmare of having his father-in-law down in the jungles of Colombia for over a year. That's not pleasant.

In the end we got nothing out of that deal.

Chapter 51:

Cocaine on Miami Beach

1987

Well, the Italians stealing 300 kilos of merchandise upset everyone. We were talking to the Colombians every day, and the bottom line was the boat was in Sardinia.

The biggest question now was how we were going to get that boat back down into the islands or to the next spot to load it up. Meanwhile, the Colombians wanted to work right away because they had lost a ton of money. So it was that the Colombians came up with the solution.

They asked us if we could have the boat shipped down on a freighter. We thought that was an interesting idea. They told us that if we could get it shipped down to La Guairá, Venezuela (that's off the Caribbean, down on the ocean near the mountain of Caracas), they could get it loaded at the marina in La Guairá.

I told them that we'd look around. We went up to Livorno and checked out numerous shipping agencies, finally finding a guy in Livorno who said he could do it. He was a nice guy. If we took the mast down and the bowsprit, he could put it on a freighter and ship it to Venezuela for $25,000. He said it would be 10 days before they left and it would take another 10 days to get it to La Guairá, Venezuela. So we made all the arrangements.

The Colombians had these secret police from the army. They were the army intelligence, but the Cartel had them all paid and hooked up. The Colombians said that the army intelligence would bring the merchandise right down to La

Guairá, and we could load it right there in the marina. This would be easy as hell because we wouldn't be at sea, juggling and bustling around in a rocking boat.

When the Colombians were first presented to us, they presented themselves as gods. They couldn't do anything wrong. And I think we bought into it a bit. But we kept seeing, time and time again, that the Colombians were just a bunch of fuck-ups, just like everyone else. And since we got screwed out of all of that money, we did not have a great big love for the Colombians anymore. It just put a bad taste in our mouths.

Since they were now paying us a monthly sum of $40,000, that made it a bit easier to want to work with them. So, the big guy went up and did all the arrangements, including sailing the boat from Porto Cervo, Sardinia, up to Livorno and paying the shipping company.

Then we set up a meeting. I think I flew to the Dominican Republic and talked it all out with the Colombians; we set up some creative financing.

Luco, the Packer and I all flew down to La Guairá and met the captain who brought the boat in from Italy. We unloaded it and got it up on the weighs right away.

We had to wait for three or four days before the secret-army police arrived. They were thc intelligence division of the army and they were some bad motherfuckers. All of them were 6-4", 6-5" tall and very muscular. They were just monstrous. They did not look anything like your regular Venezuelan.

These were all professionally trained military personnel and they looked polished. They were all dressed in high-end jeans, boots, and really nice t-shirts. They looked like good American gangsters, and they all spoke English very well.

The cartel didn't trust anyone; no one working the deal was from the outside. Everyone was paid by the cartel and this was a perfect example. They brought the merchandise down in four cars that were painted to look like taxicabs. The cartel owned the cars and the drivers. It actually looked really weird because they had two guys per cab and they pulled in at about 1 in the morning. Though the marina had security at the gate, everybody was all greased down and taken care of by the cartel.

The drivers pulled the cabs in, right up to the boat. We unloaded the merchandise and packed it all up. We sealed the hatch with a corking substance called 5200, which hardens up underwater; rock hard and waterproof. Once that was done, we took care of the painting. We had four compartments, so this took most of the night. Once the compartments were sealed and painted, we would fill them with water. This made it nearly impossible to find the dope.

The next morning we launched the boat in the water. Then the Packer, the Big Guy and I took the boat up to St. Martin. We dropped the hook in St. Martin, which we had done time and time again because of no customs there.

I had made the arrangements with the Colombians and told them that we could get it unloaded in the Keys for $200,000 at an unloading house. An unloading house is a house that sits right on the water where we could unload the boat and get the merchandise ready for transport by vehicle to a stash house in Miami. This was done as soon as possible. That is how we would work the merchandise, how we would distribute the dope.

But the money kept getting fucked around. And since we didn't get paid for the Italy job, we really felt we had to start making up for that.

So, we took a gamble. We brought the merchandise right into the Miami Beach marina. For anyone who doesn't know Miami Beach very well, right across from the Miami Beach Marina is the Coast Guard. It sounded really cool because we knew that no one could find that merchandise.

Still, we had giant balls. We didn't give a fuck. We just needed an extra couple hundred thousand that we were going to stick in our pockets. And if we got popped and knocked off, well, what the fuck. If not, we were going to go away for 15 or 20 years anyway. So it didn't really make any difference to us.

Sure as shit, we got a crew to take the boat right into the Miami Beach marina. We hired a crew that did not know the merchandise was onboard because we didn't want to pay any dope smuggling fees. It still cost us $40,000 for that particular crew. But, they took it into the marina with no problems whatsoever.

We left the boat at the Miami Beach marina for six or seven days and told the Colombians that we had it down in the Keys, but that it just wasn't right to unload it. There were just too many people around, we told them. So, we kept stalling and stalling.

On the seventh day after we had the boat taken to the marina, the Packer, the Big Guy and I went back to the boat and we popped it right on Miami Beach. We weren't worried because we knew we'd been there so long that no one was paying attention to us any longer. So, we loaded it into sail bags and we got all of the merchandise off.

We put it into a van, delivered it to Homestead, where we'd rented a house from the good Cubans. A couple of days later the Colombians came and picked up all the merchandise and drove it away.

With the exception of a couple of nut-tightening situations, it went off pretty much without a hitch. We did get paid for that one. Merchandise was going at $20,000 a unit. That was $6 million dollars total. We got $3 million dollars, minus what we had to pay the crew to take the boat into the Marina. We also had to pay the expenses on the house rental and we had to throw some grease around.

In the end, our expenses cost us about $100,000 while the Packer got $500,000, and Luco and I got $1.4 million each. We did pretty good on that one.

Chapter 52:

Cocaine Everywhere Lucky Shot

1986

Shortly after our nightmare with the fucking Italians and the maiden voyage to Italy with our schooner, we did a job up to Bar Harbor, Maine. That one went relatively smooth and we did get paid for it.

Then one day my friend, the Good Cuban, sent me a beep and asked if we could meet. I drove to the location and he asked me if we could do a job using our boat. I was worried that if we did a job without telling the Colombians we could get ourselves into some deep trouble because they had paid for half the boat. But as I've said, it was always *mañana, mañana, mañana* with the Colombians.

This was a business; we needed to keep the money flowing. So, I figured it might be worth the risk and we might be able to pull it off, *if* it was the right job. So I asked him to tell me more.

"Okay. Listen." he said. "We'll make it easy on you guys. We'll have you go down to Belize."

"Belize? Are the Colombians going to be there?" I asked.

"No." he responded. "This one we've got worked out with the Mexicans."

This was all I needed to hear. If we were only going to go to the Mexico-Belize border, we could do this without the Colombians finding out.

"Well, remember," I said, "everything has to be right on the measurements of the merchandise. Make sure you set up the correct presses. They need to be 2 x 6 x 8 inches, because if they fuck that up, that's going to cause a problem."

"No. No. No. No. We got our boys up there. Everything's going to be just right."

"Okay," I said. "What's the plan?"

"Take the boat over to Cozumel. At the main marina at Cozumel there's a little picnic area right adjacent to the marina. In four days, I'm going to have my guy Mario—you know Mario—come to the picnic area at 6 in the morning. He will tell you where to pick up your guide."

"A guide?" I asked, surprised.

"After you leave Cozumel you will travel down to the Mexican-Belize border. There's a river that runs into a little harbor. But you can't see it. It's very difficult. You're going to need a guide to take you down. It's best to pull in there in the afternoon around 3 p.m. on a sunny day, if that's possible."

"Why do we need to try to enter the harbor on a sunny day?" I asked.

"Because there's a little break right in the middle of the reef that you will need to go through or you'll run aground."

Well, that didn't sound that easy to me, but we agreed to go. We got the boat and we went down to Cozumel. On the fourth day at dawn I went over to the little picnic area, and there was Mario. He was an older fellow, probably 60. He didn't say much, just told me where and when to meet the guide.

When I asked him what the guy looked like, he simply said to look for the guy with one foot.

"One foot?" I said a bit surprised. "What happened to him?"

"I don't know for sure," he said, "but the story goes that his foot was bit off by a shark."

"Oh, Jesus," I said.

So, I was supposed to meet a guy with one foot at one of the little bars on the strip. I remember the cars they rented at the time. They rented these little Volkswagen convertibles. So, we had a Volkswagen convertible that I drove up to the bar. As I pulled up, out comes a guy with the one foot. He was about 55-60 years old; - Somewhere in that range.

He walked over to our car and said in Spanish, "Are you looking for a *guiar*?"

"Sure." I said and he got into the car. We took him to the boat, loaded all the gear and we got underway to Belize.

Well, we left at 9 a.m. and arrived at about 3 p.m. As we approached the harbor you could hear the surf crashing on the reef.

Our guide stood up and pointed.

"Right there," he said in Spanish. "Right there. There's the cut. There's the cut on the reef."

As we pulled closer to the reef, sure as shit there it was, a nice cut right in the middle of it. So, we went straight in. But, as soon as we passed the reef, the guide started yelling at us to go hard to the right. I looked over the bow of the boat and there was a great big mound of rocks right in front of us.

"Oh, shit!" I yelled out loud.

But, Luco turned the boat hard to the right in time and we missed the rocks. The bottom of the sea then dropped right off into this beautiful, natural harbor, with a river running into it. There was 34 to 37 feet of beautiful water and we could see right to the bottom, which was all sand. It was quite a relief to see after encountering that big mound of rocks the minute we came through the cut. That really had me worried.

We pulled in and dropped the hook. The guide told us that our contact was going to bring the merchandise out around midnight. So, we got something to eat and then went right to work preparing the boat because we only had about eight hours until they arrived.

It was about midnight when they started to bring the merchandise down. There was no moon and it was so dark that you could not see your hand in front of your face. You could hear 'em coming long before you could see them. It was so dark that even when they tied up to the boat and started to unload the merchandise you couldn't make out any details. Even today I couldn't give you a description of any of the men that brought the merchandise out to the boat.

The minute they started unloading the merchandise I went, "Oh, shit."

"What's the matter?" the Packer asked from farther back on the boat.

"The merchandise is not 2 x 6 x 8."

There were some bulging packs. There were fat ones. There were skinny ones. It was all over the board.

"Oh, Jesus Christ," I said. "What a nightmare."

We had already done this routine a couple of times, so at this point we had already popped the hatch. Of course, we had the Packer with us, and he was really experienced at this kind of thing.

The eye hook was on the crossbeam. We would attach a come-a-long wench to the eye hook and then the hatch. We would drain the water out of the compartments, and then chip the 5200 sealant away. We would use a crowbar to pop the lid of the compartment away and then we would jerk the hatch up (which weighed 350 pounds) and the come-a-long would hold the hatch up while we loaded the compartment. We had four compartments. The Packer would be on his hands and knees as he would fill the two forward hatches first and then fill the aft hatch. Then he would have to back himself out of the fourth hatch as he filled it up.

Each of these compartments could hold 75 Kilos (if it was packaged in the right dimensions of 2 x 6 x 8 inch blocks) to pack a total of 300 kilos. Once the dope was in, we had a portable welder to weld the hatch in. We also had the compound, 5200, which is a real sticky adhesive that looks like a welding bead when you run it along the edges of steel. It hardens underwater and that was the whole idea. We would allow the compartments to fill with water and the compound would harden up.

Once we were done putting the dope into the keel we would need a full day to seal the hatch, repaint the compartment, let it dry, and then get the hell out of there so that everything would be beautiful.

It didn't take the Mexicans long to unload the merchandise onto our boat and we were just starting to pack it into the compartments when the guy with one foot starts talking in Spanish really fast.

We stopped what we were doing and said, "What?"

He was speaking Spanish so fast that none of us could understand him. Well, after about five minutes or so of trying to figure out what he was trying to tell us, we learned that the Belize and Mexican Coast Guard came by every morning at 7 a.m. Now the Cubans told us we'd have all day to prepare, weld and seal the dope in with 5200, repaint the compartment, let it dry, and then get the hell out of there.

I checked the time. "Jesus Christ!" I exclaimed. "It's 1 a.m. They're going to be here in six hours."

I couldn't believe this. It was 1 in the morning and we were just getting started. Well, we went right to work packing the rest of the dope into the compartments. It took most of the night. When the compartments were full we still had another 40 kilos sitting on the deck.

"Shit!" I exclaimed in frustration.

I looked around. It was starting to get light. We needed to get the hatch sealed and get out of here. We lowered the hatch and attempted to weld it into place, but we couldn't get the welder going, it needed too much juice. We didn't try to figure it out; we set the welder aside and buttoned down the hatch with a bead of 5200. We painted the main compartment and left it open so the paint could dry and the 5200 would harden up.

When we were done I looked at the deck and saw the 40 kilos of blow with nowhere to go, and the welder. Reluctantly, we tossed the remaining kilos overboard along with the welder. We were surprised because it all floated, including the welder. So there were 40 kilos of blow floating in the harbor with the welder. I just shook my head; that was $800,000 floating in the harbor. It looked ridiculous.

But now it was approaching daylight, and we realized we had to get out of there. There was only one problem. There was a thick fog bank that came in. You couldn't see a Goddamn thing. You could see maybe 50 yards off the shore, right where the boat was. You could see the shore, no problem whatsoever. But when you looked out towards the reef you couldn't see anything. All you could hear were the waves pounding and crashing into the reef.

A bigger problem is that our one-footed guide had left with the Mexicans when they finished dropping off the dope. There were only three of us now, Bobby, Luco and me.

"Oh, man," I heard Luco say. "Now, where are those rocks? When we came in it was 3 in the afternoon, we could see the rocks."

I looked around the harbor one more time. There's that merchandise, 40 kilos floating in the bay, and the welder sitting on the bottom of the harbor. I remember thinking, "Now this is Cheech and Chong shit."

After a few seconds I just spoke what all of us were thinking, "Get out of here before the fucking Coast Guard comes. We're going to have to make a run for it through the fog bank and kind of guess."

"Alright," Luco said. "Let's get out of here."

He gave the boat some throttle and we took off, running straight up onto the rocks. We were trying to do it at the right angle, but we just couldn't see because of the fog. Luco jerked it into reverse and when we got it off the rocks we were hauling the dinghy, and we ran the painter right into the prop, stalling out the boat.

Well, luckily, the Packer dove over the side like Errol Flynn with a knife in his mouth. He swam to the back and cut the line to the dinghy out of the prop. Once he swam back around and got back onboard, we backed away from the rocks. Then the boat stalled out again.

"Jesus Christ, are you shitting me!" I shouted in frustration.

Luco was able to get it cranked. And we knew where the rocks were now because they were right below us once more. Luckily, Luco pulled us away without landing on them again.

We swung around real easy like to make it around the rocks this time. While all this was all happening, we could hear the surf crashing on the reef, but we couldn't see it.

"Where do I go?" Luco called out.

I shook my head and said, "Take a guess, right straight ahead. It was due east of the rocks."

"Ok!" He shouted back. "Hang on!"

He gave it the throttle and the boat lurched forward. I was hanging onto the railing watching for the reef. But, the reef never appeared; we ran the gap.

Just as soon as we ran the gap and got into the open ocean, the sun came out. It was beautiful. I looked back at the coast and the fog was just hovering on the reef.

We put up all the sails, and started running the engine wide open. We let the paint dry for three or four hours and then we buttoned it up and we filled everything back up with water.

Now the plan was to head back into Cozumel. Once we got to Cozumel we were going to have a girl fly over from Miami. So my job was to go to Miami, get the girl and put her on the airplane to Cozumel. The idea was that the Big Guy, the girl and the Packer were going to take the boat from Cozumel to Panama City. Now, just to make things clear, no one was going to touch this girl; this was strictly business.

They took the boat to Panama City. They brought it right into the main docks in there. Customs came down and cleared the boat. No problems whatsoever. And then they let everyone go. The girl and the Packer left the boat. The Big Guy was there alone.

I had flown into Panama City just before they arrived. The Big Guy was going to take the boat over to the marina, where it was built, and we were going to leave it overnight. Then the following night, we were going to see if anyone jumped the boat, if there were any hassles. If not, then we were going to unload it and take off.

Well, before Luco could take the boat to the marina, the customs enforcement showed up and the first thing they asked was, "Where's the crew?"

He told them that he had let the crew go. They weren't very happy; they know better than that. So enforcement agents got onboard and looked all over the boat. Of course, nothing was wrong. The only thing that bothered them was that the boat had come in from Mexico. So, no problem there—just a little ass tightening for the big guy.

Once the enforcement agents left, Luco took the boat over to the marina.

At the marina, the Good Cuban had an electrician's truck and a driver. It was beautiful. He had all the right gear; the ladders, the wire, the tools and all the shit. The name of the electric company was painted on the doors of the truck. He even had an electrician's license. I'll never forget that the cab was all full of coffee cups. When I asked the driver about it he said he had to have all the necessary tools of an electrician. He even had it down to the jeans, boots and a t-shirt with the electric company's name on it. The truck had secret compartments on the sides where all the electrical gear was stashed.

We met him at a designated place and put the 260 kilos of merchandise into the truck. We told him exactly where to go in Miami.

He drove the electrical truck back to Miami where we were waiting. We met our guy and he drove the truck away. This part went as smooth as silk.

When I talked to my friend, the Good Cuban, I said, “Hey, my friend, I only got 260 Kilos. I had to throw 40 kilos over the side. This wasn’t our fault. They didn’t pack it in 2x6x8.”
He said we could work something out.

So, even though it was the Mexicans’ fault, I had to eat some of that $800,000 loss.

Chapter 53:

Cocaine Surprise

1989

Earlier I talked about the good Cubans. They're the ones who sold all the marijuana. And I've also mentioned the bad Cubans. They're the ones who did all the smuggling. And I mean everything: marijuana, cocaine, people, guns. If you paid them they'd smuggle anything. At the time they were the best in the world. Absolutely unbelievable guys.

One morning we showed up at the Brooklyn Boy's house and the boss of the bad Cubans was there. He wanted to talk business.

"Listen," said the bad Cubans' boss. "A couple of years ago, during the Mariel boatlift, I went back and forth and brought numerous people in. In fact, a couple of cousins of mine were in prison. Fidel let 'em out and instantly, I put 'em to work."

I thought about what he had just told me and then said, "That sounds interesting, something easy and nice."

"Not really." He replied.

"What do you mean?" I asked.

"We have a situation." He continued, "They've stolen 30 kilos of blow from the Colombians and I don't want this tagged to me. Could you sell it? I just don't want it to kick back to me."

"Well, what's the quality, my brother?" I asked.

"It's top-notch," he said. "They had a good cook. It is beautiful merchandise."

"Certainly," I said, "We can sell it. No problem."

So he brought the merchandise, 30 kilos. He was right; they did have a good cook because it was fucking beautiful, just beautiful. At that time, merchandise was going for like $34,000-$35,000 a kilo at the high end. So we were ecstatic when he said, "Listen. Just dump this if you can. Dump it as quick as you can. Just give me $18,000 a kilo."

"Jesus Christ. Eighteen bucks," I said in disbelief. I just couldn't believe it.

So I instantly went to the Colombians and told them, "Hey, guys. Listen. I've got merchandise for $18,000 a kilo. I'd like to put four bucks onto this."

"Well, how'd you get it so cheap?"

I smiled and said, "Well, the Cubans—some of their Mariel brothers that they brought in here a few years ago—they stole it."

"From Colombians?"

"Well, fuck yeah. Who else?"

I wasn't worried about losing the deal. Like I've always said, this was business, just business. So, I wasn't surprised when they thought about it for a few seconds and then answered, "Well, we don't care. That's fine. How many you got?"

"I got 30 kilos and they want $18,000 apiece. Let me put $4,000 on it."

They nodded in agreement and said, "Okay. No problem whatsoever, $22,000."

What a nice payday that turned out to be. I worked with the Colombians for a couple of weeks. They asked me to hold onto it and they didn't even want to touch it. This is pretty common in the business; the bosses don't do any of the dirty work.

Well, we worked three or four kilos a days. We worked it and worked it and worked it. I mean it only took a couple of weeks. No bullshit. No stories. No dropping it in the mud puddle. We turned 30 kilos at $4,000 a pop. Hey, $120,000 in two weeks is good money.

Chapter 54:

Stealing My Cocaine Back from the DEA

1989

I still had the 44-foot schooner, custom built out of steel up in Panama City, Florida. It had four secret compartments, *caletas* in Spanish. They were underneath the fuel and water, in the keel. They each held 75 kilos. We had four of them so that we could smuggle 300 kilos at a time.

I had worked out a deal with the Colombians to get the boat loaded down in Puerto la Cruz, Venezuela. Puerto la Cruz is over towards Cumana. It's in the extreme eastern part of Venezuela, right on the coast. It's a beautiful, gorgeous place.

Well, I got the boat loaded with three sailors, a captain, first and second mate, all Key West boys, and they took the boat up to Saint Martin. There were no customs in Saint Martin so they just brought the boat in, put it on the hook, and checked in. Our destination call was Bar Harbor, Maine.

We spent a few days in Saint Martin and then traveled on to Bermuda. After a few days in Bermuda the plan was to deliver it to an island right off the coast of Bar Harbor, Maine and stash it. We had it scheduled for Memorial Day.

Everything went fine. They got the boat through Saint Martin and then up to Bermuda with no problems. However, on the way in to Bar Harbor they ran into shitty weather. Not only that, but the night before the pick-up, they got jumped by the Coast Guard on their way into Bar Harbor.

When the Coast Guard checked them out, of course, they noticed the crew were all Florida boys, but the boat was foreign flagged. To accomplish this we brought a Colombian girl over from Medellin to Caracas, Venezuela, and we provided her with a phony passport and phony papers. Then we had an attorney from the United States go down and set up an offshore corporation in Curacao with this girl listed as the representative of the corporation and the owner of the boat.

Now I'm not sure what the Coast Guard was looking for, but for some reason the boat and crew just looked weird to them and they jumped it. When they had a chance the crew contacted us and, using our radio code, wanted to know what to do.

At this time we had a bunch of boys working for us. So, before the boat entered the harbor we sent one of them down to the docks to do some recon and survey the situation.

When he came back he had one thing to report. "Jesus, the DEA's all over the place."

"The coast guard must have called them," I told the group.

We decided to play a little game with them. We knew the DEA was looking at the boat, so we had the crew take off all of the sails and put all the laundry together. Once it was all together they brought the boat in and then took the laundry off the boat and put it onto the dock. The minute they did that, the DEA jumped them.

As the DEA agents questioned the crew, it was clear that they weren't expecting to find cocaine. Suspecting weed instead, they scoured the boat, but they couldn't find the merchandise. They then told the crew they wanted to speak to the owners. Because the boat was foreign-flagged, there were no owners in the United States. So, the lead agent told the captain that the boat was confiscated until the owners showed up. And he ordered him to take the boat to West Harbor.

When we heard this it just screwed everything up. So I called my attorney and he said, "Ahh, that's bullshit. They're just fucking with the guys. There's no problem, except the boat's confiscated. Do they have a guard on it?"

I was a bit perplexed. "Exactly what does confiscated mean?"

"What it means is that they will have the captain take it over to West Harbor, drop it on the hook and the boat will not be given permission to leave until the owners show up."

"Well that's just fucking great," I said as I hung up the phone.

Luco, the Packer and I decided we needed to come up with a plan to steal our merchandise back from the DEA.

There is a little road that runs along West Harbor and near the water. We decided we could use the road. I had a brand new Ram Charger at the time and I was going to have the Big Guy drive up and down the West Harbor road with a 12-gauge shotgun and a bottle of Jack. If the police or any uniformed guys came by he was going to crash into the cop car and take a fall for drunk driving.

Meanwhile, the Packer and the captain would use the Zodiac to get out to the boat, crack open the hatch and unload the 300 kilos. They would then bring each load to the shore where I would carry it up the banks of the road and load it into my Jeep. If everything worked out it should take us but a few hours to get it all.

The following weekend gave us our best chance because it started raining. It was misty and cold, as terrible as Maine weather could go. But it was also foggy. It was so foggy and rainy you couldn't see but a few dozen feet or so.

So, we put our plan into action. Luco took my Ram Charger, the shotgun, the Jack Daniels and started driving up and down the road along the harbor. I loaded my Jeep full of camping gear and drove to the spot where I would meet the Packer and the captain when they came to shore in the Zodiac with each load.

Once they climbed onboard from the Zodiac they cracked open the hatch and started to unload the 300 kilos. They loaded the merchandise in sea bags and then into the Zodiac. Once they had had loaded the Zodiac, they brought it to the shore. Once they got to shore, the Packer dragged it all the way up over the bank to me.

I was standing there with my Jeep all full of camping supplies. Well, the Packer brought it all up by himself and I would stash it under the camping supplies. Then they would go back to the boat and get the next load. It all went off flawless. It was a crazy, hair-brained scheme, kind of Cheech and Chong-ish once again, but it still worked.

Once we had all the merchandise we headed down the road to my brother's house in Auburn, Maine.

Instead of going down I-95 we took the back roads and Route 2 all the way down through Herman, Canaan and Skowhegan. When we got down to Farmington we jumped on Route 4 and took it down to Auburn where my brother lived.

By the time we got to my brother's house it was about 3:30, 4 o'clock in the morning. My brother always left a key under the mat, so I opened the door and went in.

My brother came downstairs half-awake and said, "What's the trouble?"

"Listen, we've been working. We have 300 kilos of cocaine in the Jeep out in the yard."

My brother seemed to finally wake up and said, “You have 300 kilos of cocaine at my house with my wife and my little children here?”

“Yes.”

He shook his head and said, “Have you lost your fucking mind?”

“We need to keep it here for two days. You get 25 grand.”

“Oh,” he said, and thought about it for a few seconds before saying, “Well, let’s get that shit unloaded.”

My brother was an antique dealer so we unloaded it into the back of his shop. We managed to get everything all squared away. A couple of days later we came back, picked up the merchandise and delivered it to the Colombians in New York City at Bayside in the Queens.

Looking back, we were lucky that storm blew in when it did. Or, maybe it was just the luck of the devil.

Chapter 55:

25 With the Bitch Running Wild

1997

After almost 30 years of turning and smuggling drugs, it all came crashing down on me by 1997. I ended up losing everything: my wife, my houses, my money, everything. And a few years afterward, I ended up in prison—convicted of kidnapping and extortion. I was sentenced to five years in a Florida prison.

Everyone I knew at the time would say, "Prison? Oh, Jesus. What's going to happen? You're a good looking guy. You're going to be raped. Oh, Jesus. They're going to rape you."

Well, prison's a little different than that. A lot of men line up and engage in homosexual activity on a daily basis. They're called punks and usually a raping is done to someone who runs their mouth, someone who causes trouble. Rape is a violent act of anger. It's not somebody having some great big love affair. There are so many punks in the prison that will do any sex act for a candy bar; so there's no need to rape someone unless that person is causing trouble.

It's strange. In prison a lot of guys really aren't professional criminals. They're drunk drivers, drug addicts and that kind of criminal. You know, the drunks hit a bus full of nuns and kill a couple of them. They're regular guys. They go to work every day. They don't feel they belong in prison. They do real hard time. Me, I only had five years. I thought it was a joke most of the time. It was just a big inconvenience to me.

The term, "25 With a Bitch Running Wild," means that if you have multiple felony offenses, say more than three, they call you an habitual offender and you could end up with a sentence of 25 years. The "bitch" stands for "habitual." "Running wild" stands for not having a date. So "25 With the Bitch Running Wild" is when your paperwork comes out at the end of every month and you don't have a date because you have to do 25 years.

There was a guy I met in prison who had "25 With the Bitch Running Wild." He was a 5' 4" Puerto Rican from the Bronx. I met him while I was running the library. He was teaching English to the Spanish. He taught next door. Every time he would come into the library to get books we would kick it back and forth. He was a very nice guy.

One day I said to him, "Why don't you teach me a little Spanish?"

He chuckled and said, "The only Spanish you need to know is, '*Yo hablo Espanol pero no muy bien.*' If you can say that then you can get away with saying, '*Si,*' or '*No,*' and it sounds good."

That's the way he was. He would joke and he was just a really nice guy and we talked all the time. By the time I got out we were very good friends.

Something was on his mind one particular day and he wanted me to know about it. He said to me,

"Hey, listen. Do you know that big white cracker boy named Yaya?"

"Yeah."

"That piece of shit is fucking with me all the time."

"Well, what do you mean?" I said.

"He's disrespecting me." He said, "He's saying shit to me and he called me a spic."

Seventy-two percent of the 800-plus men in this prison were black; about 10-12 percent were Latino; and the rest were white guys like me.

"What about your boys?" I asked. "You know, isn't there anything your guys can do?"

"If I ask the boys to help me then I'm going to owe them a favor. They're going to want me to do something; have some dope brought in, a number of things. I just don't want to be beholden to anyone. I want to take care of this myself."

I was a little puzzled and asked, "Why are you telling me this?"

"I'm telling you this because if this cocksucker ends up killing me, I just want you to know."

"Well, listen, bro," I said. "You've got to deal with this. You've got to take care of this, but you have plenty of guys around you. You've got some bad motherfuckers with you. I hope you just take care of this piece of shit and straighten him out, tune him up, and tighten him up."

"No." He said calmly, "I've got to take care of it myself."

Well, about a week went by and one day I was on my rack reading. I could see him standing down in the corner with four or five Latin guys around him. That's called, "spooking," in prison. They're like lookouts. The section I was in was an open dorm, so it wasn't hard to see what other people were doing. There were 72 of us all stuck in the dorm together.

So, I can see the Puerto Rican and his friends are up to something, but I'm not quite sure what it is. Of course, in prison you don't want to stick your nose in anyone else's business, but because of my vantage point it didn't take much to see what they were doing without looking like I was nosey. I could see that they were doing something with a mixture of hair remover that all the black guys would use. It smelled really bad, but it prevented them from having to shave. They called it "Magic Shave." The black guys would rub it on their face and when they got into the shower, they would wash the hair right off.

So, my friend is making some concoction of Magic Shave mixed with baby oil. They had also brought in a couple of extra mattresses. Once he was done with the concoction he and his lookouts went over to one of the mattresses and one of the guys cut two or three big long strips of plastic off the mattress.

"Oh, shit," I muttered to myself. "What the fuck?"

He took it back to the corner. Every time that he or one of his lookouts would look my way, I would kind of turn away, but the longer they worked the more curious I became.

The Puerto Rican had of course mentioned that this big cracker, white-honkey bitch liked to pick on little guys—just a fucking asshole. And I don't like guys like that, so I was really interested in what they were doing.

Anyway, while I'm looking over, he looks up and sees me watching. He smiled and said, "You know, this cracker boy goes to the bathroom every night, just like clockwork, after the 9 o'clock count."

"Yeah, okay," I said. And I'm wondering why he's telling me this. I really, really didn't want to know any information because if something went wrong it could come back on me, so it's best to know nothing. But, he proceeded to tell me that he was making a combination of that stuff the black guys put on their face to take their hair off, baby lotion and then plastic.

He mixed this concoction in half of a soda can, so he had about six or eight ounces. Then he boiled it with a lighter.

Sure as shit, after the 9 o'clock count I looked over and I could see him working on the lighter. He brought the concoction to a boil and he wrapped it in his sock. And the minute the cracker boy went in to take his crap after the 9 o'clock count, the Puerto Rican walked right in the bathroom and drove it into the cracker boy's face.

The concoction melted his hair, his face and his eyeball. The screams were unbelievable, but that's what you get. You can't go messing with a guy just because he's 5'4", trying to humiliate and bully him. That was the way of dealing with a fucking white cracker.

Chapter 56: Christmas in Prison

Christmas 2001

In 1997, when I was arrested for kidnapping and extortion, with ties to organized crime, I thought the rap was kind of weird. I joked to myself that I belonged to a disorganized crime family, not an organized one.

When I was arrested, 36 members of an organized crime task force jumped us with machine guns after closing off South Dixie Highway. The Big Guy, Luco, and a guy from Boston that I had served in Vietnam with were arrested along with me. We were all charged with kidnapping and extortion.

They took us to FDLE headquarters, put me in a room and said, “Hey, you want to walk? All you have to do is give up the other two.” I chose not to. I can’t go into the case because I never said a word about this kidnapping.

I never talked to the police. I never talked to the judge. I never talked to anyone. We were PBL’d, which means facing life. We were taken to Fort Myers, Florida, where the crime had taken place, and they locked us up in the Lee County Jail.

I’d been in jail a few times before this. You know? Overnight. But these were some pretty serious charges, and the bond was set for $3 million. Jesus Christ! I didn’t even have $300,000. And if I had, and put it up, more than likely they would have grabbed it and revoked it. You know? Just regular cop games.

So we sat in that jail for four months. And then the attorney that was involved in the case was arrested as well. When he was arrested they presented the victim as an upstanding citizen of the community. But the Big Guy and I were just a couple of morons who just kidnapped him, like it was sort of legal. But we never said a word.

They had us all over the newspapers, in the news, all over the fucking country, making us out to look like real fools. Quite embarrassing really.

They locked us up in a segregated section. There were only white boys. There was room for 16 guys, but they had 32 of us locked up in there.

So, as I said, the bond was set at $3 million dollars. And after the attorney was arrested, he said, "This guy isn't exactly an upstanding member of society or the community." But they came at us with a deal: six years in the can, three years on paper.

When I went in front of the judge, he asked me "Jack, are you sure you want to take this plea?"

And I guess I was paranoid because all I could think was, "What the fuck? The judge, he's trying to set me up." I was worried about him vacating the plea, then coming at me and slamming me with 25.

But I held my tongue and simply answered, "No. I'm sure. I'll take the six and the three on paper." So after four or five months in jail over in Lee County, off to state prison we went. I first ended up in Marion Prison. Then, on my 51st birthday, I got sent up to Apalachee.

Apalachee is up in the Panhandle of Florida. For those who don't know, and you wouldn't unless you have served time, Apalachee is full of right-wing, redneck, fucking shitheads. I mean moronic, fucking, idiotic prison guards, some of the worst shit on the fucking planet. I don't have one

Goddamn good word to say about prison guards; they are the scummiest cocksuckers that ever walked. They bring in all the shit. They bring in all the dope. They're the scum that run the joint. Now when I say that, I hate to generalize, but I'm talking 98-99 percent of those fucks are worthless.

The Florida Panhandle is where the shit washes in from the North and even from all over the South— shitty, fucking, moronic, scumbag fucks. Every county has a prison: Santa Rosa, Washington, fucking Apalachee. Just name 'em. These are dirty fucking cocksuckers, I mean just scummy fucks. I can't say enough bad things about the prison guards up in the Panhandle.

Am I comparing Florida with the Texas boys doing time? Or California? No. That's much worse. In Florida, it's different. It's open, man dorms with 70 prisoners in each dorm. The prison is made up mostly of child-molesting scumbag fucks called "diddlers."

But most of the prisoners were not hardcore criminals really. Most of them were guys that worked straight jobs all their lives. They may have killed someone while driving drunk, or hit a bus full of nuns and killed three or four of 'em. Doing their 25 years for it. A lot of the guys were in there for shooting their wives. These were guys that didn't do crimes on a daily basis. And most of these guys didn't think they belonged in prison.

Those motherfuckers do hard time. I mean hard time. I would laugh at 'em every day. "You fucking idiots." It was just a fucking joke.

Now, of course, everybody worries about prison. "Oh. Goddamn, am I going to be grabbed and raped?" That is not the case. There are lines a half-mile long of guys that will suck a dick and who love fucking another guy or getting fucked by one. They're the punks.

Me? Well, I had belonged to that disorganized crime family and smuggled dope. Plus, FDL charged me with kidnapping and extortion. Those are honorable charges in prison. Some may say about me, "What a piece of shit this guy is." I say in response, fuck you. Fuck you. This is prison. This is talking about survival time. This is no time for the weak.

In prison if you're weak, you've got a problem. If you're a regular, straight cocksucker, and you're bad, you've got a problem. If you're six-foot-six, and you're a white cracker boy, you've got a problem. If you hate blacks, and you think you're something and can fight, you've got a problem. You would get a toothbrush in your neck within two or three fucking days.

Toothbrush means that one end is shaved down. When you do that it's just as sharp as a fucking razor. The bristles are taken out and replaced with razor blades, melted in with dental floss. It's a terrible weapon. I saw a lot of those when I was in prison.

There were also a lot of shanks going around. The heaters were taken apart and inside there were big steel rods. You could take these rods and sharpen each end. If someone knew how to use it they could drive into you. Prison was a lot of trouble. Apalachee was a lot of fucking trouble.

But the guards were all scumbag motherfuckers, all but a few. There were a few who were decent, but they were very rare. And now that I've gone through all that shit and slammed the whole Panhandle of Florida—not everybody, but certainly the guards—I'll jump to 2001, Christmas Eve.

On Christmas Eve, 2001, I had a weird feeling on my right side. And I thought, "Oh, fuck. Man, I feel like shit. Oh, damn. I think I'm having an appendicitis attack." Well, this started at 10 or 11 at night, so I didn't say anything. But as the night wore on it kept getting worse.

At about 5 o'clock in the morning I went to the guard. He was black, but this guard was one of the few good ones. He wasn't on everybody's ass. He was a good guy, and he was a sergeant.

"Sarge. Hey listen," I said, "I'm fucked up, man."

He looked at me for a few seconds and said, "Well, what's the matter?"

"I've got this pain in my right side. I think I'm having an appendicitis attack. I feel like shit."

He simply nodded slightly and said, "Okay. Well, let's get you down to medical."

I had been at Apalachee for three years, then I was transferred across the street to this little soft-ass cotton camp called River Junction. And I was at River Junction when this bad pain occurred. They didn't have a doctor or anything at River Junction, but they did have some sort of a nurse. She came in, took one look at me and said, "Well, we've got to get you over to Apalachee, where the doctor is."

So, they took me over to Apalachee to see a doctor. And, in walks this worthless little piece of shit doctor. I mean what a fuck-head. He spoke very strange English and when I asked him where he was from he said he was from India.

He walked over to where I was sitting and he pushed on the area where I said I felt the pain. He asked, "Does that hurt?"

"No it doesn't."

He just stepped back and said, "You don't have appendicitis."

"Well, what the fuck? I've got something."

He didn't say anything, just said he wanted to monitor me. That was about 7:30 or 8 in the morning. But by 7:30 or 8 that night, Christmas Day, I was fucking dying. So they transferred me up to Marianna County Hospital in Jackson County. Mariana is the county seat.

They took me into the hospital where this guy came in and said, "Hey, you have appendicitis. And we need to take them out right now."

"Okay," I said, "Go ahead. It's better than dying."

So they took me in into the operating room and took my appendix out. When I woke up my leg was handcuffed to the bottom of the bed, and my right arm was handcuffed to the side of the bed. There was a sergeant and another guard standing by the doorway. They were each armed with a 12-guage shotgun and a pistol. They weren't pointing their guns at me, but they were making it very clear that they were armed to the teeth.

I was still a bit groggy, but was able to spit out, "What the fuck are you guys doing?"

I knew both of the guards. They were both from River Junction.

The sergeant just looked at me and said, "Listen. You make a run for it, we get $50 and two weeks off."

We all started to laugh, which caused quite a bit of pain and reminded me that I had just had my appendix taken out. So we laughed. Now these two guards were good guys. Both of them were good. I have nothing bad to say about 'em.

While I was lying there recovering, the second guard leaned over and said, just loud enough for the Sargeant to hear, "When you get back to the yard, do not say anything about how nice we've been to you. Or we'll be fucking mad at you." That really broke the ice and we joked the whole day through.

After the second day, I couldn't piss. So they came in and ran a catheter up me. For those who have not had this done, Jesus, I can tell you it is not good. I did not like that. But I couldn't go to the bathroom, so they used the catheter.

They finally took the handcuffs from my hands, but kept both feet shackled. Eventually I said I had to go to the bathroom for a you-know-what. I had a catheter in me, but I had to go to the bathroom. So they helped me get out of bed and when I went into the bathroom, I was in there for like five or six minutes.

I cleaned up the best that I could and started for the door. As I was reaching for the door this male nurse jerked it open. I was carrying the pole with the catheter still in me. And the fucking nurse reached out and grabbed the tube of the catheter and jerked. That took me to my knees. The dumbass only got the catheter half-ass out of me. So he came in and finished taking the catheter out. Then he helped me get back into bed. As soon as I was in bed the guards handcuffed me again.

I spent the rest of Christmas Day just bleeding and halfway dying. At least the guards were nice and friendly. After four days I was taken back to the camp to finish out my last year in the can.

There's a Christmas story for you.

Chapter 57:

Legalize it

2014

As of 2014 it has been 45 years since I started in the dope game. Initially I started off selling pills and hash on the *USS Intrepid* in 1969. That's a long time ago. The dope business for me really took off when I moved to Miami in 1969. By 1972 I was smuggling weed out of Jamaica and Colombia and I continued to smuggle weed and cocaine until 1993. I've been out of the business for 21 years now.

I started working with the cartels in the '80s when the cocaine business was prime. They had five major bases of operation, 'offices' they called them, in the United States: Miami, Houston, Los Angeles, Chicago and New York. They had a crew of men at each one of those offices who would be in charge of the distribution of cocaine

They also had the money launderers who would pick up the money and send it back to Colombia. They were very complex organizations. Each arm of the business did not know what the other arms were doing so that if one arm got taken down, the organization wouldn't go down with it.

The first time I heard of 'the war on drugs' was in 1972 with Nixon's big campaign. Nixon ran for office partly on a promise to stop the smuggling of marijuana. Well, that didn't work out so well. That's been 42-plus years, but I think the barn door has been opened.

Dr. Sanjay Gupta, MD, the chief medical correspondent for the health, medical and wellness unit at CNN, went out to Colorado and talked to those young men who came up with the strain of marijuana called Charlotte's Web. It's also called Controlled Dangerous Substances or CDS for short. This strain of marijuana is used to help people with epilepsy. Since he aired his show, the country seems to be leaning more and more towards legalization.

My point here is they wanted to put us in prison for the rest of our lives for smuggling that weed, and they still do. But you can see that none of it works. There's nothing you can do to stop the smuggling, trading or use of marijuana, cocaine or heroin. Nothing, absolutely nothing. There's just too much money in it.

And to all you pundits out there who are saying, "Oh, no. Oh, Jesus, this is terrible" and who are worried about your kids at school and at home, you should be more worried about tobacco that kills 500,000 people a year, or alcohol, which kills some 50,000-70,000 people a year. And let's not leave out fast food—McDonald's, Arby's, Burger King. By serving that fat, greasy, shitty food to everyone, those fuckers kill more people than anything combined. It's terrible!

As I write this two states have already legalized marijuana for 'recreational purposes' (Colorado and Washington) and about 20 more have made 'medical marijuana' legal. In other words, you cannot stop this. Eventually this all will become legal just like alcohol during prohibition. That didn't work out so well. Everyone who was involved with that now looks foolish, though most of them are dead by now. But marijuana, it is becoming legal.

So am I some pontificating peckerhead? No, it's just right here in front of us. It's something that you cannot stop. So, let's make it legal. That's my point.

And the ones out there who keep pushing, "Oh man. It's bad, it's bad," it's not as bad as fast food, tobacco, and alcohol, not even close to it. So, no one should be going to jail for marijuana.

Author Biography:

Luck of the Devil is the true story of Jack Collins, a Vietnam veteran who was part of the whirlwinds of change during the late 60's and early 70's. Looking to score free drugs for himself and his friends, he started dealing blow and pills on the side. Eventually his "street wise" experience allowed him to meet some of the biggest players in the world and he became one of primary smugglers for the Colombian Cartels and a Italian Mafia Family from Rome.

www.ingramcontent.com/pod-product-compliance
Lightning Source LLC
Chambersburg PA
CBHW050107280326
41933CB00010B/1004